The Continental Affair

THE CONTINENTAL AFFAIR

The Rise and Fall of
The Continental Illinois Bank

James P. McCollom

DODD, MEAD & COMPANY
NEW YORK

Copyright © 1987 by James P. McCollom

No part of this book may be reproduced in any form
without permission in writing from the publisher.
Published by Dodd, Mead & Company, Inc.
71 Fifth Avenue, New York, New York 10003
Manufactured in the United States of America
Designed by Elizabeth Frenchman

First Edition

1 2 3 4 5 6 7 8 9 10

Library of Congress Cataloging-in-Publication Data

McCollom, James P.
  The Continental affair : the rise and fall of the Continental
Illinois Bank / James P. McCollom.
     p.   cm.
  Includes index.
  1. Continental Illinois National Bank and Trust Company of
Chicago.   2. Bank failures—Illinois—Chicago.   I. Title.
HG2613.C44C686 1987
332.1′223′097731—dc19   87-21471
ISBN 0-396-08809-0   CIP

To the men, women, and spirit of Bank B

Contents

About the Writing of The Continental Affair

T HIS BOOK WAS WRITTEN FROM A LINE OFFICER'S POINT OF VIEW. It attempts to convey both the awareness and the confusion of the bank's line officer corps during the Continental affair.

In May 1984 the destiny of the Continental Bank was taken out of its officers' hands by the press. In July 1984 it was taken over by officials of the government, just as a decade before it had been surrendered to outside experts.

In both periods the people inside the bank had to follow events the same way others followed them: by rumors. In 1984, of course, the rumors were printed and broadcast all over the world. By the end of the crisis of 1984 the chairman of the bank was as powerless as the youngest banking officer to manage or to anticipate the results.

The heart of this book – the description of the character, characters, and events of the bank through 1980 – is a memoir; the dialogue has been taken from personal experience. Ed Bottum and I arrived in Brussels at the same time, for example; I hosted the Barcelona meetings because I was the bank's representative in Spain at the time. During this period, when the corps was very close, I had the pleasure and the honor of spending a good deal of private time with Dave Kennedy, Roger Anderson, Al Miossi, and others. In Chicago my principal training period was with the old Group U, when it was headed by George Baker, and my first job assignment was with John Jones's trade finance group.

However, I chose not to use the first person in this narrative for several minor reasons and this major one: the "team" or "corps" quality of the Continental Bank, as corny as it may sound to noncorporation people, was a genuine ethos. That I was present at Brussels, Barcelona, Group U, and so forth, was incidental to the narrative; many others were there as well. That I had a writer's view and most of the other Continental people did not was insufficient reason to impose the *I* on a *we* story.

1980 was my last year with the bank. The narrative of the 1981–84 period is based on conversations with Continental Bank people and financial analysts during and after the crises and on published information: press reports, the Congressional Record of the hearings in Washington, New York Stock Exchange figures, the quarterly and annual reports of the bank, and so forth.

My talks with Continental Bank people were conversations, not interviews. There were reasons for this as well. The first was that this is not a reporter's book. In the Continental affair the press was not an impartial bystander; it was an active participant. One cannot look to the Continental people alone for the inside story. In this day of "perception is the only reality," the inside story was outside. The actions of reporters and editors were more influential than those of Roger Anderson and Dave Taylor.

The second reason was personal. Membership in the officer corps of the old Continental Bank still means too much to me to exchange it for a reporter's role. The most difficult thing about doing this book – and the sheer effort of sorting the data was difficult indeed – was telling Roger about it.

I knew in advance that he could not discuss the matter, under advice from his lawyers, because of the lingering lawsuits. But I talked with him and explained my purpose. Our cordial conversation, my visit as an old friend, trailed off. The tone changed as the matter became clear.

I had a long and enjoyable meeting with Dave Taylor, and I put it to him straight: There were questions I would like to ask him if he would answer them, mostly about things that had already appeared in the press. What I really wanted from Dave were some details on the Bahamas transition; the color of the narrative – giving bankers human touches – was a big problem in the opinions of book people.

Dave was interested. He said he might do a book himself one day. A long time after, he wrote to say that his lawyers had advised against it. That was a banker's reaction, and that was okay.

If I had been a reporter, I would have questioned him during the original meeting.

These were the only formal approaches I made. The conversations with the people of the corps were easy. Everybody wanted to talk about it; they still do talk about it every day. And everybody has an opinion, people who were involved in the daily crisis meetings, in the treasury operations, in the Japanese bank contacts, in the European bank contacts, in the Penn Square investigations. (For the record, there were about three dozen in all, short and long.)

The crisis dialogue is reconstructed from these conversations, from the known sequence of events, from the bank's statements, and from press reports. Its purpose is to move the narrative; it does not pretend to be verbatim. When someone is quoted by name, the words appear as recalled by the speaker for me, or else they are a matter of public record. None of the principals recalled conversations exactly; nobody does. But they did remember what was discussed.

The sequence of events was widely reported. In looking back at the reporting of it, by the press, one sees great differences in emphasis and some differences in interpretation but virtually no difference at all regarding what happened when. *The New York Times* and *The Wall Street Journal* carried the greatest amount of coverage. Among the magazines the detail work in *Newsweek* and *Fortune* was notable. Among individual reporters the work of Robert Bennett of the *Times* – doubtless the most knowledgeable American banking reporter, and the most faithful to the theme – and A. F. Ehrbar of *Fortune* earned particular respect among the line officers of the banking industry.

Needless to say, the work of Reuters did not.

CONTINENTAL PROFILES

ROGER ANDERSON – Thirty-eight years at Continental, he was the executive of Dave Kennedy's international plan, and the chairman 1973-1984 during the bank's last glory years. Of Chicago, Northwestern, and the wartime U. S. Navy.

GEORGE BAKER – Thirty-one years at Continental, he directed the reorganization of the bank in 1977, and became its chief credit executive. Of Chicago and Coe College, he came straight to the bank from school in 1951.

ED BOTTUM – At Continental from 1959, the bank's first manager on the European continent, he was president under Dave Taylor in the awful three months of 1984. Of small-town Indiana, Purdue, the 1950s Navy, and Harvard Business School.

GENE CROISANT – At Continental from 1954 as a schoolboy and from 1961 full-time. An early master of data processing and a trusted lieutenant under six chairmen, he was head of personnel during the "survivor" period. Of Chicago, Loyola and the 1950s Army.

ED CUMMINGS – Thirty-six years at Continental, he headed the internal investigation of the Penn Square fiasco. Of Chicago, Yale, and the wartime Navy. The son of Walter Cummings.

TILDEN CUMMINGS – Forty-one years at Continental, he was president of the bank under both Kennedy and Graham. No relation to Walter Cummings, whom he preceded to 231 South LaSalle by two years. Of Chicago, Princeton, and Harvard Business School (1932).

WALTER CUMMINGS – Twenty-five years at Continental, he retired as chairman in his eightieth year, in 1959. The executive of Franklin Roosevelt's bank-stabilization program in 1933 and the chairman of the Continental from January 1934, he and the building at 231 South LaSalle were the symbols of conservative banking. Of rural Illinois, Northwestern, Loyola, and DePaul.

DON GRAHAM – Twenty-five years at Continental, the originator of its energy lending division, principal executive under Kennedy and his successor as chairman, he retired in 1973. Of Pittsburgh and Northwestern.

CHUCK HALL – Twenty-six years at Continental, he was a model executive whom many expected to become chairman of the bank prior to the events of the mid 1970s. He resigned in 1980. Of small-town Kansas, the University of Kansas, and the 1950s Navy.

GENE HOLLAND – Thirty-six years at Continental, he headed the oil and gas division (Group U) and was the ranking executive for commercial banking prior to the McKinsey reorganization. Of Lincoln, Nebraska, Princeton, and the wartime Navy.

JOHN JONES – Twenty-three years at Continental, he created the bank's trade finance group under Kennedy and Anderson and typified the American "over-achiever" in international business. He was made head of metro banking after the 1977 restructure. He left the bank in 1980. Of Omaha, Nebraska, and Carleton College.

DAVE KENNEDY – Twenty-one years at Continental, as chairman from 1959–1969, he led the bank into the modern age. Celebrated as a visionary, Kennedy introduced the "four-universe" concept that inspired the bank's logo, and made the bank first in Chicago and fifth among U.S. banks internationally. Of small-town Utah, Mormon missionary work in Europe, Weber State, George Washington.

GAIL MELICK – Thirty years at Continental, he was the bank's chief operations executive during the 1970s and early 1980s. The key thinker behind much of the high-technology applied by the modern bank, Melick was considered George Baker's only rival for the chairmanship. Of Carleton College and the University of Chicago.

DON MILLER – Twenty-six years at Continental, the bank's principal treasury officer and then vice-chairman, he was a member of the Corporate Office with Anderson and John Perkins. He was widely respected in the bank as a symbol of the quiet professional, the team player. Of small-town Illinois, and UCLA.

AL MIOSSI – Thirty-four years at Continental, he was one of the triumvirate, with Kennedy and Anderson, who guided the bank's international expansion. Moved aside by the 1977 restructure, he was called upon to meet with the European banks during the 1984 crisis. Of small-town California, the wartime Army, Stanford, and Thunderbird (graduate international management).

JOHN PERKINS – Thirty-eight years at Continental, he became president of the bank when Anderson was named chairman. As president of the American Bankers Association, he was nationally the best-known of the Continental bankers. Of Chicago, Northwestern, and the wartime Navy.

DAVE TAYLOR – Twenty-nine years at Continental, he inherited the chairman's job on the eve of the 1984 disaster. He was the prototype of the Continental loyalist-professional (see Part Three, the "Profiles"). Of small-town Michigan, the Continental Bank (his father worked there sixty years), Denison College, the 1950s Navy, and Northwestern Business School.

The Continental Affair

BOOK

ONE

Continental Bank loans to Argentina were $390 million, to Chile $67 million, to Venezuela $415 million, at the end of 1983.
　　　　　　　　　—THE WALL STREET JOURNAL, EARLY 1984

. . . Credits related to the Oklahoma bank [were] about $1 billion . . .
　　　　　　　　　—THE WALL STREET JOURNAL, LATE 1982

Don't talk to me about no millions of dollars. I don't understand that. Talk to me about the fifty-five dollars a day we're paying for that summer cabin. That's what I understand.
—ROCKFORD'S FATHER, IN AN EPISODE OF THE ROCKFORD FILES

PART

ONE

*The
Disaster
Movie*

ONE

S OMETHING SCARY WAS HAPPENING IN CHICAGO.
It was May 1984. A short report on one of news wires had sent a jolt through the international media. Suddenly there were reports of a looming disaster that could affect millions of Americans' lives.

The Continental Illinois Bank, the biggest bank between the American coasts, seemed to have gone out of control and to be in a crash dive.

During the second week in May rumors of a financial disaster began to run through Wall Street trading rooms. There was an item in *The Wall Street Journal.* By the third week the stories had come off the gray financial pages and were pouring in living color into the living rooms of middle America.

Dan Rather was giving daily updates on the Continental crisis on CBS News. By the end of the week it was his lead item.

One after another, bankers and economists, men with dark suits and dark expressions, were being brought before the television cameras to comment for the American public. They were saying things on national television that financial people usually never even said aloud.

The word *bankruptcy* was pronounced. The word *insolvency.*

Insolvency – failure – of one of the biggest banks in the country. But the media exaggerated; drama had become its business. People were wary.

But then on camera came the most respected of economists, Alan Greenspan, commenting for reporters. "If a rumor is credible," he said, "even if it's not true, people will react to it."

Which meant that this rumor was credible. This was Alan Greenspan talking.

Day by day in May 1984, as the suspense grew, Americans were beginning to get the idea that the rumor was true. If the Continental Bank of Chicago crashed, indeed was going to crash, then everyone in the country could be hurt.

"One hundred other American banks could go under if the Continental goes."

"The entire financial system of the United States could collapse."

These quotes were from economists, from high officials of the U.S. government, and from bankers. All over the place, bankers were saying these things.

Ordinary people worried aloud. A woman in lower Manhattan said, "Look, there are certain things that people shouldn't have to worry about. I don't want to have to worry about my money not being at the bank when I need it. I don't want to have to worry about being locked out of my apartment by a landlord when I'm away at work for the day. There are enough things to worry about in everyday life. These are things people shouldn't have to worry about."

In the distant memory of a graying generation of Americans, there was the phantom of the worst period in the nation's history: the Great Depression. There were breadlines in those memories, homeless families, grapes of wrath.

But now, because this disaster was on television, because it was in people's living rooms, it was like watching a disaster movie. The entire financial system of the United States was going to collapse before your eyes—in your living room.

You had once watched the Vietnam war, which had produced its own kind of American depression. People now understood war because of television; it showed them the effects, the explosions, the wounded, and the dead. But they could not understand what was happening in Chicago.

What did the commentators really mean? The entire financial system could collapse because of one bank?

This was a *big* bank. This was the seventh biggest bank in America.

How big was that?

It was a bigness that no ordinary person could comprehend.

The Continental Illinois Bank was bigger than the combined total of all of the American banks that failed during the Depression. Ten thou-

sand individual banks. If you added all the deposits of all of them together, you had a bank one-quarter the size of the Continental Illinois
Bank in 1984.

The size of the bank was beyond understanding, but the reason for
its problems wasn't. Most Americans watching the crisis unfold in May
1984 could have told you why the big Chicago bank was in trouble.

It was because of their foreign loans.

Everybody had read about them. The big banks in New York and
Chicago had been taking U.S. money and lending it in places like Brazil
and Mexico and countries you never heard of, while ordinary Americans
had to pay 15 percent for a mortgage loan – if they could get one.

Everybody knew about the foreign loans. And anyone with common
sense could have told these big-city bankers that they were going to get
in trouble. Everybody *knew* that's where the problem was.

But that wasn't where the problem was.

The Continental Bank was America's bank – the most American of
the big American banks. It was the leader in loans to *American* commerce and industry, not to foreigners. If you looked at the total loans
to the struggling Latin American countries, you'd see Continental with
fewer loans than any other bank in its class.

The role model of American banking – the Morgan Guaranty of New
York – had almost twice as much in loans to Argentina, Mexico, Brazil,
and Venezuela as did the Continental. Nobody was worried about the
Morgan.

Continental's problem was not the money it had lent to foreigners.

It was the money it had borrowed from foreigners.

The most American of American banks had fewer deposits from its
own community than it did from foreigners.

Less money was deposited in it by Chicago than by Tokyo. Less money
was deposited by Americans than by Asians and Europeans.

More than half of all deposits were from foreigners. The Continental
Bank owed foreigners $17 billion.

And the rumor was that the foreigners were taking their money out
of the bank.

The big banks of Japan and Germany and Switzerland were taking
their money out of Chicago. Billions of dollars.

That's what the problem was.

But in mid-May 1984 nobody wanted to hear such details. It was not
credible that the biggest bank in Chicago owed that much money to
foreigners. What was credible was that they'd lent a bunch of money
to banana republics and that now they were getting what was coming
to them.

7

The American experience with national financial disaster had happened during the 1930s, during the days of radio. People had had to live it in order to see it.

But this was 1984. America had a President who was a movie star and who spoke to the nation in movie images. Americans could stay at home and watch their financial system explode on television.

This was the biggest financial crisis since the Depression. It could be bigger than the Depression.

It was on television every day.

It was a disaster movie.

Earthquake!

Meteor!

If the Continental Bank crashed, a lot of people could be hurt.

But what an explosion it would make!

TWO

O N MAY 7, DAVE AND KIT TAYLOR LEFT FOR A CRUISE IN THE BAHAMAS.

Early May is the grace period just between the end of the long winter in places like Chicago and Toronto and the beginning of the heavy heat in the Bahamas. It seemed as if most of the tourists were from Canada and the American Midwest.

Dave would have enjoyed vacationing on Lake Michigan as much as in the Bahamas. It was Kit who had insisted on a Bahamas cruise. She thought he needed distance – place distance, people distance; she wanted Dave out of Chicago for a while. He had not had a real vacation in two years. The first four months of 1984 had been tough enough to earn him ten vacations.

Like so many men who had come of age in Eisenhower America, Dave Taylor's manner and looks made him seem much younger than he was. He was just about the same weight now that he had been as a senior at Denison College or as a lieutenant (junior grade) in the U.S. Navy in the 1950s. There was some gray in his hair, but it was still mainly black. People were surprised to learn that he was fifty-four.

Dave was a born midwesterner. He would not have wanted to live somewhere else. But it was nice to be away from the Midwest just about now. He had a quick humor and loved to meet new people, but he hadn't been able to exercise his humor for a while.

Here you could meet people and talk about things that had nothing to do with what you talked about all the time at home.

"Does Chicago really exist?" you could ask, looking out at the Caribbean horizon, at the unbounded skies.

When you met someone on vacation, the usual question is, "What do you do?"

"Oh, I'm a banker."

"Oh."

If you are a banker, you don't expect much enthusiasm when you say so. People aren't thrilled about being seated next to you at a dinner party. It's the "bean-counter" image – not very interesting. Bankers are one step away from accountants.

But on the other hand, if the two people meeting each other on a vacation had been American Indians, the question, instead of "What do you do?" might have been, "What is your tribe?"

Dave Taylor's tribe was the Continental Illinois. Just as Eisenhower was a professional soldier only for the U.S. Army, Taylor was a banker only for the Continental. He wouldn't have joined someone else's army. This made him rare nowadays. It was the norm, particularly among business school graduates ("the hired gunslingers of the 80s," writers were calling them), to move from one army to another. But Taylor was a Continental man first, and a banker second.

This attitude was not unusual at the Continental, which had been both praised and criticized for the loyalty of its people for years. When the Continental was on top in the industry, finance analysts said the ésprit de corps was its secret formula to success. When the Continental had problems, some writers said it was a handicap, particularly for Dave Taylor.

Taylor's was a special loyalty. He had been part of the Bank since he was a small child. He had been inside the imposing building at 231 South LaSalle Street in Chicago before he had been in a kindergarten room. His father had taken him there when he was four years old. Frank Taylor had worked for the Continental Bank from the time he was fifteen until he retired at seventy-five. Frank Taylor was the classic American business success story. He had started at the bottom and worked his way to the top, as the head of a department. Dave Taylor started higher, and he finished higher.

"He let me push the big door to the vault closed," Dave talking about his dad, had told reporters some weeks before his vacation. "I'll never forget it. It's silly stuff, but there are just some things you never forget."

Some of the reporters picked up on that remark. Maybe his sentimental attachment to the Continental would handicap him, would hamper him from doing a good job. But other reporters had let it pass. To them, Taylor was a "no-nonsense executive," the man who had saved the Continental Bank once already. In the language of the sports pages so popular in American business, Dave Taylor was the best athlete available in the draft. He was the best man in the bank.

At fifty-four, Taylor was the chairman – the chief – of the Continental Illinois. But the job had not come to him because of his long attachment to the Continental. He was chairman as a result of a battlefield promotion.

Two years before, the world had found itself with an oil glut and the Continental Illinois, incredibly, out of nowhere, had been hit with losses on loans to oil drillers in Texas and Oklahoma. A small bank in Oklahoma had had to be closed by the U.S. government. The name of the Penn Square Bank, which had had a ten-year lifetime in an Oklahoma City shopping mall, was to remain a notorious symbol in the financial press.

Because of Penn Square, the Continental had lost money during the second quarter of 1982. But relative to the Continental's size, it had been a manageable loss, and the bank went on to make a profit for the whole year, 1982, and again for 1983.

But the embarrassment had been enormous. Financial analysts, the sports writers of banking, had not left the Continental alone. As copy in the business press, it had been irresistible. A few short years before, Continental Illinois had been selected as one of the five best-managed *corporations* – not just banks – in the United States by the prestigious *Dun's Review*. Other journalists had written that competing American banks considered Continental "the most feared bank in the country."

The problem was in being called "the best." It would have been all right to be the richest; that can be measured, and it resists argument. But "the best" is something else. People contest that. There are few satisfactions as great as seeing a "favorite" fall. People liked the joke about Henry Kissinger, "the smartest man in the world," jumping out of the plane in the hippie's knapsack. People liked it when the Dallas Cowboys lost out in the playoffs. And Bobby Knight, the Indiana basketball coach, could tell you that there are a lot of people in other countries who like it when Americans lose at anything.

When the Continental Bank took a loss in the second quarter of 1982, financial analysts would not leave it alone. The "what else is wrong?" questions kept coming, without rest, through 1982 and again through 1983.

Where money is concerned, all it takes is for the question to be raised, to be said aloud. A mere suggestion of risk is enough to make people start covering themselves, whether a true risk is there or not. The thought is, If it gets to the press, somebody must know something.

With the questions raised, with public perception now the issue, the leaders of the Continental Illinois were forced, one by one, to leave. Even after the removal of the officers who had lent the money to the Penn Square Bank, the pressure did not stop.

George Baker, the man whose lending genius had made Continental the single most important source of funds for American commerce and industry, was forced to resign. Investigators found he had no blame, but that didn't matter.

John Perkins, the president of the Continental and the president, too, of the American Bankers Association, was asked to take early retirement. He had had no association with oil lending at all.

Don Miller, the vice chairman of the bank, was also retired early.

And finally, in late February 1984, the celebrated chairman of the Continental Illinois, Roger E. Anderson, was forced to step down from his job.

To the drums of the analysts, to the howls of the press, the finest banker Chicago had produced was forced out. Roger Anderson had guided the Continental for eleven years and had made it the single greatest motor for American business growth, for jobs, for the inner workings of the city of Chicago.

Roger Anderson was forced out, and a new management team was elected: Dave Taylor and Ed Bottum.

11

They were pure midwesterners – Continental men through and through.

The sports metaphor was used again: they had been sent in "to make a goal-line stand." Continental had been on the defense since the Oklahoma problem. The new team had to hold, take the ball back, and go on the offense.

Dave Taylor was the chairman, the funding genius of the bank, the man whose knowledge of money markets had stabilized the bank after Penn Square.

Ed Bottum was the president, an Indianan, a full-blooded member of the Continental tribe, a veteran of lending, trusts, planning, international – and everything else.

"Banking is a business of people," Dave Taylor had said when he took the job. "And Continental has people who will see the company through its problems out of sheer pride, unbelievably hard work, and overwhelming talent."

During the crucial month of March 1984 they had done just that. With one day to go before the close of the first quarter, with an above-all commitment to meet the shareholder dividend payment of $20 million, they showed how much financial power the Continental Illinois could produce.

It was a victory.

The new management unloaded the Continental's charge-card operation to the Chemical Bank of New York for one *billion* dollars.

"A rabbit out of the hat," *Business Week* called it. It was "Continental's carefully calculated signal that the nation's seventh-largest bank was finally on the mend, its earning power undiminished."

The imprint of Taylor's style was on that one. He had negotiated under the gun – in a fifteen-day period that came right down to the day before the end of the quarter, the final deadline.

He had disposed of a business activity that was not central to the bank's wholesale banking business.

He had made the sale at a price beyond the analysts' expectations.

And he had prevented the First National Bank of Chicago from getting the business.

It was no accident that the Chemical Bank bid had been exactly one million dollars higher than that of the First, on a one-billion-dollar transaction.

"We believe it is incumbent upon us not to discuss the details of how the business was bid for or sold," Taylor said, straightfaced.

Never the First National Bank of Chicago, the archrival through decades. Anybody but the First.

After that, the question was how the "market" would react to the new Continental team. The news was good.

Three weeks into spring, the respected Batterymarch investing group – a specialist in banking stocks – announced that it had bought *two million shares* of Continental Illinois stock for its portfolio – 5.2 percent of all Continental shares.

This was a major signal, a vote of confidence by the top investment pros in the industry.

In 1984 the Continental Bank was 127 years old. Its history dated back to antebellum Chicago, to before the fortunes of Marshall Field and Cyrus McCormick.

But in all its history, never had its leaders been installed under more pressing circumstances than Dave Taylor and Ed Bottum were in 1984. Not even during the 1930s, when the legendary Walter Cummings had been sent from Washington to Chicago to take charge of the Continental.

Cummings had started out with the backing of FDR's government and a bundle of new federal programs designed just for ailing businesses.

Taylor and Bottum started out with no backing other than that of their own people. The last thing that was wanted at 231 South LaSalle Street was the support of the U.S. government. The Continental Bank – like Middle America – would handle its own problems with private enterprise, Yankee knowhow, and a bunch of other ingredients.

The Continental's 1984 annual meeting was something special. People knew there had been a new beginning. There was excitement.

It was held in the Art Institute of Chicago on April 23. One great Chicago institution was celebrating its renewal within the halls of another great Chicago institution.

The place was filled with Continental people: officers, workers, Midwestern neighbors who held shares, representatives of the big institutional shareholders, executives and leaders, and Chicago community officials.

Roger Anderson said his good-byes, passing the gavel. "As you know, we have had our own problems. . . . None of this has been easy. Nor will the months ahead be easy. David Taylor and Ed Bottum have been given a difficult and challenging job. . . . The problems that they face are not of their making. I feel strongly that they are the best possible team to turn Continental around."

Then Dave Taylor addressed the Continental shareholders. "It's now time for you to join us in accelerating Continental's recovery," he said. "I'm asking you to allow me to bring the gavel down on Penn Square.

"I ask that you go out of this meeting with a firm resolve to promote this institution. . . . If we can add 21,000 stockholders to our team of salespeople, the results could be dramatic. . . .

13

"I'm asking you to join our team."

It was a new beginning, an emotional one, for the Continental Bank. April 23 at the Art Institute was only two weeks before Dave and Kit left. Now at sea in the Bahamas, that time seemed as far away as the place. Everybody here was on vacation, out of reach. Nobody was working.

The Taylors had been on the ship little more than a day when a call came in on the ship-to-shore telephone. It was Ed Bottum.

"Dave, I hate to tell you this, but I think you'd better get back to Chicago."

THREE

A LARGE PART OF COMMERCIAL BANKING IS PROTOCOL. There are many ceremonies.

The marble, the dark wood, and the thick carpeting that decorate big banking houses and the huge columns that stand beside their entrances are no less formidable than those of courthouses and cathedrals. The style in which dark-suited bankers congregate with peers from the financial "community" is no less ritualized than it is in the State Department.

That is why Dave Taylor probably wouldn't have become chairman of the Continental Illinois in normal times.

Not that he didn't have the polish; he did. Taylor had been at the high executive level for fifteen years. He had been a U.S. Navy officer in his early twenties. He looked right. He was confident in any group.

14

But the protocol in commercial banking has mainly to do with the lending of money, with the slow, ponderous, ceremonial process of study and restudy, review and review again, with the special compenetration, the special language, of committees.

Taylor was a trader.

A trader's job is to bring money in, not to lend money out. The style, the "culture" (as business is calling it now), of traders is one of action, of getting it done, rather than of slow, labored process. Committees have the right of time, time without limit, to reach their judgments; traders have no time. In the constant action of the money markets a trader might be dealing with a half-dozen telephone calls at the same time; might have only minutes to make a decision for which he or she alone will be responsible. By contrast, in the lending divisions a committee of six will rehash a single credit proposal and probably delay action on it until the following week.

A trader cannot sit around waiting for five or six other people to make up their minds. (Of course, if they were traders, too, it wouldn't take them very long.) As a trader, you deal with the objective. You decide. You call it. (You make it your business to know all the pertinent opinions before you began work for the day.)

If the culture of the trader means self-reliance, it also means a certain intolerance for protocol. The Chicagoan Ernest Hemingway used to say that he had a "built-in shit detector." Most traders have the same device.

So with Dave Taylor it wasn't a problem of his not being aware of the kind of protocol and diplomatic phrasing – often incomprehensible, because it was expected to be – that made analysts and other bankers comfortable. It was a problem of whether his instincts would tolerate it. Would he say the appropriate thing? Or would he go directly to the point? Would he say what was on his mind?

"I encourage people who work for me to be open with me in terms of advice and suggestions. As I work for you" – he had said this to the shareholders – "I assume you will extend that same benefit to me."

In the time that followed he dealt with the analysts and the journalists.

Taylor was leery of journalists. On the other hand they liked him; that was evident. He found it easy to talk with them, to deal straight. But on the other hand he knew too much about them. They were not as interested in the truth as in a story, in filling space. They would take phrases and angle them to prove points.

They had caused the bank enough problems over the past two years. Many of them had been unnecessary problems, bullshit problems. It was

15

not easy now for Taylor to treat some of them as friends, as if nothing had happened. They had not been friends. They had trashed the bank at every opportunity, had trashed the tribe.

If a trader makes a commitment on the wire, there is definitely money behind it. The trader is responsible for it. The system functions on that certainty.

If a journalist sends a story on *his* wire, he isn't responsible for it. A journalist doesn't have to identify a source or back up the facts.

A few years before, some of the foreign exchange traders at Continental Bank in New York had done a test on Reuters, the British-based wire service that specializes in banks. For the FX (foreign exchange) traders, Reuters was the most unreliable news service of them all. They would print *anything*. And since every big bank has the Reuters financial wire in its trading room, everybody can play the rumor game.

It was during a French government crisis; Charles DeGaulle was still in power. The traders chose to make DeGaulle the subject of the rumor; and they chose a rumor about which New York traders could have no inside knowledge. The question was whether or not he would step down. He had withdrawn from public view; no one knew exactly where he was.

One of the New York traders selected the name of a town on the southern coast of France and told a German trader in Frankfurt that this town was where DeGaulle was staying. Two days later, the item came over the Reuters wire. An FX trader in New York had told an FX trader in Frankfurt where the French president was; that was all it had taken.

If a rumor is credible, people will react to it whether it's true or not.

FOUR

*T*HE CALL THAT STARTED THE RUMORS ABOUT THE CONTINENTAL BANK ON TUESDAY, MAY 8, 1984, CAME FROM REUTERS. And the call was answered by a trader.

The Reuters reporter asked to speak to the chairman of the bank but was told that Mr. Taylor had left Chicago the day before on vacation.

Mr. Bottum, the president of the Bank, was there, as were Mr. McKnew, the chief financial officer, and Mr. Buldak, the chief press relations officer.

The call was put through to the fifth floor, the traders' floor, to Robert McKnew.

There are rumors, the Reuters reporter said, that the Continental Bank is on the verge of declaring bankruptcy. Can Mr. McKnew confirm or deny them?

"That rumor," McKnew said, "is totally preposterous."

That Tuesday morning call from Reuters was no big deal. Continental people were used to such calls by now. For two years slurs had been thrown at the bank. The losses over Penn Square – a dinky Oklahoma correspondent bank that had turned out to have the fire power of Lee Harvey Oswald – had exposed the bank to people you never had to talk

17

to before. It was as if someone in your family were hearing an emotional problem, so your whole family has to open up to psychiatrists.

The May 8 Reuters question was merely the kind of why-do-you-beat-your-wife question the Continental had been dealing with ever since Penn Square. You never knew when somebody would call in with an off-the-wall question that was based on nothing except an interest in creating a headline. Many of the reporters knew nothing at all about banking. They would try the shock method – an outlandish rumor – to see how you would react.

McKnew – in his mid-thirties the youngest senior vice president in the bank – was an example of how talent moved past ceremony on the treasury side of the bank. Pale, blond, wearing a moustache so he wouldn't look more like a kid than he did, he had been singled out by Dave Taylor two years before to be Taylor's successor in treasury.

He now ran the treasury department: corporate finance, three different foreign exchange divisions, and a funding division. By speed, volume, number of foreign and American locations, Telex machines, and television monitors – not to mention the special delicacy of the Continental situation – it was the largest and most intricate such operation in the electronic world. There were forty officers and associates in this department. It was good enough to have overcome the mighty funding problem that had arisen two years before.

McKnew, in the Continental style, still answered his own telephone. So when the Reuters reporter called his number, he took the call. "Preposterous."

It was a good thing Dave Taylor was on vacation. He had already handled his share of this nonsense.

But no big deal. Not that Tuesday, May 8, 1984. They had been doing it for two years. They could keep on doing it; some of them could. The question rankled, but McKnew brushed it off.

About an hour later, one of the traders came in with a Telex tearsheet. "You ought to look at this."

"What is it?"

The Reuters wire contained the following "information":

Rumors of the impending bankruptcy of the Continental Illinois Bank, the nation's seventh largest, circulated through the international financial community today.

Robert McKnew, senior vice president and treasurer of the Continental, reacted angrily to the rumors. He called them "totally preposterous."

The guy had actually printed it.

There had been so many reporters like that before. But none of their stories had ever been printed.

Reuters would print anything.

Before another hour went by, the Dow Jones News Service had run the same story. Telephones all over the trading room started to ring. Telephones all over the block-long, block-wide building at 231 South LaSalle Street started to ring.

In the president's office Ed Bottum took a call from the Commodities News Service: "Is it true that the Continental is being taken over by a Japanese bank?"

"No. It is not true."

Commodity News moved that story by the middle of the afternoon. The president of the Continental Bank had said that the bank was not being taken over by a Japanese bank.

By now, wire rooms throughout the financial world were alert for the next dispatch on the Continental "situation."

The new twist also came from Commodity News: "Informed sources in Chicago said that federal monetary authorities would convene a special meeting on the financial performance of the troubled Continental Illinois Bank."

Out of nowhere!

Out of nothing!

The president and the treasurer of the Continental Bank could stand face to face on that Tuesday afternoon in the executive offices of the institution they managed and echo the question:

"*Is* there a Japanese bank making a bid? Are the federal regulators planning a meeting?"

"Do *you* know?"

There was no Japanese bank. There was no federal action. The bank's first-quarter results, widely celebrated as a victory, had been public for weeks. The annual meeting and report to the shareholders had taken place to applause only two weeks before. The dividend had been paid. Taylor and Bottum had laid it all out clearly. It was the new beginning.

There was no crisis.

There *used to be* a crisis, but they had *solved* the crisis.

That didn't mean a thing after the first Reuters story hit the wires.

A rumor doesn't have to be true to be believed. It just has to be credible. In 1984 the suggestion that a big Japanese bank would buy a big American bank was credible. It had happened before. A crisis meeting by federal regulators? That too was credible; they do it all the time.

Before the end of the day the United Press International had moved the story to its economic service wire.

19

On that Tuesday in May many officers of the bank lost their entire workday. Dozens of rumors were wasted on the telephone telling customers and friends and family that everything was all right.

An entire day was lost because of the one reporter's phone call.

It seemed a terrible expense at the time.

FIVE

MAY 9 WAS A WEDNESDAY.

During the morning commute it was a relief to see that the serious financial press had not given space to the Reuters report. *The New York Times* mentioned it – in a three-inch story under its smallest headline type at the bottom of a back page in the financial section. *The Wall Street Journal* didn't acknowledge it.

The Democratic primaries in Ohio and Indiana had gone to Gary Hart. Mondale had won North Carolina and Maryland – or at least the party machine had. Some people were surprised but not impressed. Neither could beat Reagan.

Moscow was pulling out of the Los Angeles Olympics.

The Chicago weather was a little gray. Cloudy but mild. Pleasant; a good day.

By the time the doors at 231 South LaSalle opened on Wednesday, the Japanese had long since completed their workday. The Europeans were nearing the end of theirs.

While Chicago slept, the UPI story had been translated into *kanji* and had moved across the Jiji-United Press wire service in Japan.

Reuters was back on stream, too – now with its own joint-venture wire with Jiji, in Japanese – and with a twist:

Mr. McKnew had denied not "bankruptcy" but "insolvency."

In trading rooms around the world these news wires were being torn off machines and rushed into the hands of senior managers. But there were other wires in these trading rooms, too. These were business wires, direct communications between banks. On these wires, using codes, the banks transferred hundreds of millions of dollars between themselves.

Reports on foreign bank deposits arrived at the fifth-floor treasury operation from traders at key Continental branches in Tokyo, Singapore, Frankfurt, and London. The New York traders were also on the telephone, only an hour ahead of Chicago.

The reports were bad. "The sun was moving west," a Continental trader said, later, "and every place it got to, it set on us."

By the close of business that Wednesday, the Continental Bank had lost a billion dollars in deposits.

SIX

T HERE WERE PEOPLE IN THE BUILDING THAT DAY IN 1984 WHO had banked with the Continental Illinois for more than fifty years. They were lifelong Chicagoans, white-haired customers with passbooks, for whom the trip to the foot of LaSalle Street – to deposit the odd check in a savings account or perhaps to make a withdrawal –was a retirement routine.

None of them were aware that there was a problem at the bank.

If any one of them, having finished his business and gone out through the revolving door to LaSalle Street, had paused at the corner of Monroe Street to look back at the classic buildings that were the foundation of the Chicago financial district, he might have even wondered if time itself really passed at all.

The newest of them, the Board of Trade building at the base of the street, had been there since 1930. It had a art deco facade, created by the great architects Holabird and Root. Its original clock still told the correct time in Roman numerals, not digital flashes.

The oldest of them, the Rookery building, close on the left as you stand looking south, had been built by Burnham and Root in 1886. Its courtyard had been remodeled in 1905 by Frank Lloyd Wright. It now housed the Continental Bank's personal banking office.

And on either side of the first block of LaSalle stood the six great columns of the city's most powerful financial institutions.

On the west side, the Federal Reserve Bank of Chicago, designed in 1922 by Frost and Grange.

On the east side, the Continental Illinois National Bank and Trust Company of Chicago, designed in 1923 by Graham, Anderson, Probst and White and completed in 1928.

There was a near-perfect symmetry to the scene. The facing buildings varied only between the Doric style of the Federal Reserve columns and the Ionic style of the Continental columns.

The scene reflected order and permanence, unlike any other in the country. This was the foundation of Middle America. It had been for a lifetime. It was unchanged.

Standing there on May 9, 1984, one looked at time itself, stilled by the legendary architects of Chicago. It could have been 1934, the year Walter Cummings took charge of the Continental Bank. Or 1945, when V-E and V-J days were celebrated along LaSalle Street. Or 1960. Or 1970.

But on any of those other dates, our fortune would have been our own. On this date it belonged to foreign peoples ten thousand miles distant from either side of LaSalle Street.

PART

TWO

*The
American
Challenge*

SEVEN

*T*HE PHRASE *INTERNATIONAL BUSINESS* HAD AN EXCITING SOUND. More exciting than, say, just *business*.

By the late 1960s many Americans had taken a personal interest in international business, if only indirectly. In towns across the country it seemed as if everybody knew someone who had gone off to work overseas. Local kids ended up working for a big company in London or for some bank in Paris, just as before they ended up in New York or Chicago or Houston or Los Angeles.

And you could visit them there. The vacation trip abroad – the European tour – by the 1960s was familiar in the American experience. If you were from Middle America (and everybody west of the Hudson River was) and you were going to Europe for the first time, the highlight of the trip to London or Madrid or Amsterdam or Munich would turn out to be a visit with some fine American kid who had grown up in your home town.

What he was doing there, exactly, and what the American companies and banks were doing there weren't clear.

One Frenchman called it "the American Challenge."

"Fifteen years from now the world's third greatest industrial power, just after the United States and Russia, might not be Europe, but

25

American Industry in Europe. Already, in the ninth year of the Common Market, this European market is basically American in organization.''

This view was expressed in the book *Le Defi Americain,* an immediate best seller in Europe. The author was Jean-Jacques Servan-Schreiber, a French journalist and politician, a businessman, and a spiritual co-pilot of Andre Malraux. The English title was *The American Challenge.*

The internationalization of U.S. business occurred in the late 1950s and 1960s. It happened so abruptly that by the time the American Challenge was named, there was a notion that American companies had always been international.

It was far from true. A handful of companies – General Electric, International Harvester, and some others – had been running overseas operations since early in the century, but most U.S. business was domestic until the 1960s. American exports were a mere footnote – 4 percent of the gross national product at their peak. Americans earned ninety-six out of one hundred dollars at home.

The multinational corporation was a phenomenon of the 1960s. The term meant, first, a company that owned companies in several countries, and second, a company that was a citizen of each country in which it operated. The idea was merely an extension of the time-honored European principle of dual nationality. ''We may look American, but actually we're just as French as American, and just as German and . . .''

Nobody believed that.

It was the American Challenge.

The watchful Frenchman knew a foreign language when he heard one, and he knew a foreigner when he saw one, whether the foreigner came from Islam or from Indiana.

The funny thing was, most people of Middle America in 1967 would have been just about as dubious about American companies running off all over the world as were the readers of *Le Defi Americain.*

To midcentury Middle Americans, it was no mystery why General Motors and Monsanto and Philip Morris products were wanted by Europeans. Everybody in the world wanted American things if they could get them. That was no mystery at all. Camels and Lucky Strikes were more valuable than money in Europe after the war. (Who knew? They might still be.) Anyone who went to the movies knew what European cars looked like. *They'd rather have a Chevy? Big surprise. You can't even make European soap lather. And their toilet paper? Don't talk to me.*

Thousands of American families had spent time at U.S. military bases overseas, where the greatest of their privileges was the Post Exchange:

American candy, American television sets, American cigarettes, American *stuff*. Just for us, but everybody wanted it.

So there was no mystery. Nobody could make things as well as Americans could, so everybody wanted American things.

But what the American banks were doing over there was something else; that wasn't so clear. Banks didn't make anything. And if there was anything that Europeans had enough of, it was banks. They might not have money, but they had plenty of banks.

Why did we have to go over there in the first place? Haven't we done enough for those people? Let them make their own products. How else will they ever learn?

People would say that, people whose adult lives had seen scarcity and long waits for Fords and Frigidaires and Hershey bars and who still weren't sure, twenty years after the war, that the new abundance would last.

And let 'em use their own money!

Many of the people who felt this way were midwesterners, far from the coasts, where the fact of foreign trade was a fact of life. There would be no more shortages in twentieth-century America; to the contrary. The world's American quarter-century was well under way when the 1960s arrived – the global outreach of Yankee knowhow, Yankee ingenuity, and Yankee enterprise. While American idealists were sending thousands of college kids around the world as Peace Corps volunteers, American companies were starting thousands of new businesses overseas.

And the most dynamic new businesses of them all would come out of the Midwest – from Chicago, Detroit, Peoria, the Quad Cities, St. Louis. The very motor of international business would be the isolationist heartland of America.

Some folks were just a little cautious, that's all. They just wondered if it would last. Things had a way of coming back to the way they always had been. The whole international business thing could be over in a few years.

EIGHT

OF ALL THE INSTITUTIONS SWEPT UP BY THE AMERICAN CHALlenge, none fit the New York image of the old-style conservative, the isolationist, as well as the Continental Illinois Bank and Trust Company of Chicago did.

There were broader American groups that carried the banner of conservatism: Republicans. Midwesterners. Small towns. And there were thousands of midwestern communities that were as Republican in tone as the Bank. There were thousands of other commerical banks. But among single institutions, single companies, the ranking conservative entity was the Continental.

First of all, the Continental had Walter J. Cummings.

He was the chairman. He was eighty years old.

Even in the glory stories a decade or more later, long after the Continental was at the top of the first tier, journalists couldn't resist the old image. Like tourists coming to Chicago and asking about Al Capone, the journalists were never as interested in what the bank was now as in what it was supposed to be: the fulfillment of the old-style bank cliché.

"The only good loan," reporters would write, referring to the banking philosophy of Walter Cummings, "is a loan that's been repaid."

28

In 1933, during the deepest gloom of the Great Depression, Walter Cummings was head of the Federal Deposit Insurance Corporation, formed by the first Roosevelt Administration to close the barn door on the banking industry left open by the Coolidge and Hoover regulators.

During that year there were 4,004 bank suspensions, but Walter Cummings closed the door before the Continental Bank of Chicago became one of them. The Roosevelt Administration's Reconstruction Finance Corporation made a $50 million loan to the Continental. Walter Cummings came to Chicago himself with the money. He was a Roosevelt Democrat, a regulator, a defender of the line. There was no way that anybody was ever going to close this bank.

He did the job. He was a man for the times, which meant that he summed up *conservatism* to American imaginations. When the country started booming, image makers and image keepers would point to him as a figure of the past. But when it was falling apart, Walter J. Cummings and men like him were called upon to put the country back together again.

The Continental Bank shaped by Walter Cummings made lots of loans to the U.S. Government but not as many to U.S. companies. A difference of opinion with a corporation as worthy as Caterpillar kept that American giant off the books until 1969. The bank took deposits from big corporations but politely referred most individual savings accounts to the First National Bank of Chicago.

And if something like Playboy Enterprises was formed in the mid-1950s, it might take its business elsewhere, thank you. The Continental Bank was as careful in the selection of its depositers as of its borrowers. It was happy to handle the accounts of religious orders and civic organizations.

The Women's Christian Temperance Union (WCTU), based in Chicago, maintained its bank account at the Continental. The WCTU was also part owner of the property on which the building of 231 South LaSalle Street sat. The officers of the bank enjoyed excellent meals but no alcoholic beverages in their paneled dining room on the twenty-third floor.

The odd bit of foreign business – a foreign currency transfer or a letter of credit – was referred to the Continental's correspondent banks in New York City, which were more interested in such things. The foreign division of the commercial banking department, a group of four or five desks in the first-floor corner at Quincy and LaSalle, was responsible for selecting the New York correspondent. When a foreign banker visited Chicago, the foreign division was responsible for taking him to lunch in the executive dining room.

29

Walter Cummings was every conservative banker rolled up in one. His bank, deep in the isolation of Chicago, was the same thing.

From the time he got there in 1934 until the time he retired in 1959, his image remained eighty years old. He always saw that all the bank money was put into the U.S. Treasury, that no loans were made to anyone who needed them, and that everybody else in the bank was just like him.

> The bank was almost a caricature of LaSalle Street conservatism. It had shown no enthusiasm at all for lending abroad and very little for lending in the U.S. – even in Chicago. Its holdings of government bonds were actually worth twice as much as its loans. . . . It's chairman, Walter J. Cummings . . . was doing essentially for Continental what Sewell Avery had been doing for Montgomery Ward: staying liquid, resisting expansion, anticipating a depression. . . . The possibility that there would *not* be a depression was the only one for which the bank was unprepared.

This was from a mid-1960s story that *Fortune* did on the Continental. It reflected writers' general views of the bank in the America of that period.

The report was a little exaggerated, of course.

If the Continental Bank of the 1950s put more of its depositors' money into U.S. Treasury bonds than into commercial loans, it was merely doing the same thing other banks did. The prototypical bank balance sheet – the kind that would be used in college instruction manuals on banks – would have looked just about like the Continental's.

Lending money was nevertheless the highest art at the bank, and it was the function that defined the banker. It was simply done more carefully. It took much more time. It was looked on as the investment of other people's money, money that these same people had lost at other banks in the 1930s. Because it was so sensitive the officers who did it had the highest prestige in the bank. The highest accolade was "credit man."

In Walter Cummings's time as chairman, the Continental Bank developed some of the most able credit men in the industry. Their careers spanned almost as much time at the bank as the chairman's did; he had arrived when he was already fifty-five.

These were men who, in the American tradition of the great automobile and oil and electrical appliance companies, had come into the business to learn it from the bottom up. They were men like Fred Taylor, who came to the bank as a fifteen-year-old boy and worked there for sixty years. He became the head of the bond department. And they were men like Tilden Cummings (no relation to Walter), who came out of

Harvard Business School in 1932 and spent three years in the credit training program before he was allowed to recommend a loan, and nine years
at the bank before he was made an officer. There were self-made men
and college men – John Mannion and John Hoffman and Homer Burnell
and George Kernan – and they went through the same process, were
trained to thoroughness, were trained to the idea that competence meant
coverage of every detail, that detail meant time, and that there would
be no competence without the long and patient investment of time. Every
one of them paid his dues.

In the business reality of the 1930s the bank grew, slowly but steadi-
ly, under Walter Cummings. The greater part of the bank's assets was
in government bonds, but its loan portfolio – the assets at risk – was
very big.

As the Depression receded further into the past, lending became more
attractive. In 1952, the $1.3 billion in U.S. bonds, requiring no risk
analysis, earned less than the $767 million in corporate loans, under the
management of the credit men.

The greater skill, the greater intelligence, belonged to the credit men,
who could bring greater returns to the bank with a security virtually equal
to the unrisked government assets.

They were men who would tell you, "Banking is a business of people. You have to know people. You have to have the right people in the
right places in your bank."

This happened under Walter Cummings.

The young bankers who came to the Continental after the war
ended – the class of officer candidates in 1946 and 1947 – learned what
banking was under the tutelage of the seasoned Cummings credit men.

And there were carefully considered moves. There were innovations
under Walter Cummings – people innovations.

Dave Kennedy was hired from the U.S. Treasury in 1946 and took
over the bond department. In 1953 an energy lending group was created
to do new lending business with American coal and oil and gas companies under a young lawyer named Don Graham. The bank began to
develop new methods of check clearing and cash management.

The Chicago bankers also knew what the Bretton Woods agreement
was and that there was more international business on the horizon. The
members of the board were heads of the great Chicago companies –
Sears, Inland Steel, Link Belt, International Harvester, Abbott, Bethle-
hem Steel, John Deere, United Airlines, Pillsbury, U.S. Gypsum,
Zenith – and they were leading America to new markets.

But that business would come slowly. There were other priorities,
where money could be made and assets could be controlled.

The main business of the Continental Bank was Chicago, and its main competition was the city's biggest bank, the First National Bank of Chicago. Continental had once been number one. The First held the top spot in the 1950s.

For longer than most of the people at the bank had been alive, the Continental and the First had coexisted like forts on opposite sides of a gulf. There was no water in between them; just the one and one-third city blocks that separated the corner of Clark and Quincy from the corner of Clark and Monroe. A gulf.

It was a question of style. It had to do with that value but well-understood dream of the upwardly mobile: sophistication.

The relationship between the Continental and the First was pretty much like the relationship between Chicago and New York, which was pretty much like the relationship between America and Europe.

If there was anything that annoyed the city of Chicago, it was the mention of New York City. The impression was that it was the Second City complex – being number two. But it wasn't that. Chicago was number two like America was number four – in population. It wasn't being second biggest. It was an image thing.

It was the place New York had in the scheme of things, the place Chicago had. The daily imagery was full of subtle reminders of place: of who was first and who was second. By virtue of the one and two relationships, it was as if everything in each city were one and two.

The image had to do with culture. People went to *ooh* and *ahh* in Europe and New York. But the image of Chicago was a place where people worked. First-time visitors might know about its architecture, but the odds were that their only cultural question would have to do with Al Capone. And then they would go home and tell everybody that people were defensive in Chicago.

When the Europeans said, "New York is not an American city. It's an *international* city," some Manhattanites were flattered.

There was no doubt about Chicago being an American city. Chicago was *the* American City; all the others were variations. It had America's industry, America's business, and America's sports teams. By New York standards, it was a little too rough, a little too friendly. It was the perfect European image of America.

It also worked.

And the First was like that. The First faced east, toward the financial mecca, New York. The people at the First liked being told that they were not a Chicago bank, that they were a *New York* bank. They took it as a compliment. There was little hokey boosterism in the First – not enough for the managers to refuse to acknowledge that New York was the center, New York was the model.

The mannered element of nineteenth-century Moscow had looked to Paris for its manners. Some thought the Russian language was embarrassing; they learned French. Some spoke no Russian at all. Russian was unrefined; it was for the natives.

Dostoevsky spoke Russian, though. He would have banked at the Continental.

The Continental Bank faced west. It spoke American.

NINE

THE CONTINENTAL WAS A VERY CONSERVATIVE BANK.
From the outside its image – stern, glassy-eyed lenders and pale accountants with green eyeshades – did not fit the American Dream at all. From the inside, those who ran the bank were content to keep things to themselves.

In big banks doors seem to close more tightly than in others. Most Americans saw banking as local – the local bank, the local branch, the silent, highly marbled local lobby with the counter separating the people from the money, the cages with clean, faceless local tellers behind them, and local men and women with machines behind the tellers.

Most Americans never saw the big banks – the giants in New York and Chicago and San Francisco – except as tourists passing the outside of the huge buildings. As imposing as cathedrals, their architecture dominating urban American skylines as cathedrals dominated the skylines of Europe.

There was nothing inside them except muteness, mystery, and money. These banks didn't deal with people; they deal with corporations. They were wholesale banks, corporate banks.

In the 1950s and 1960s young American men expected to spend two or three years in the military. Many who went to college became members of the ROTC - or went to OCS afterward - and spent their service years as lieutenants or ensigns.

Many of these went into banking after the service; and they found that the one was much like the other.

"It's very simple," one young bank officer explained to a trainee in the mid-1960s - both had recently come out of the navy. "Banking is the most paramilitary industry you can find in civilian life. Wait till you've been here awhile. You won't believe it."

The rank system was similar. The official ranks in a bank - assistant cashiers, assistant vice presidents, vice presidents - were as distinct as officer ranks in the military. The formality with which officer selections were made, announced, and celebrated was similar in both. The yearly reviews that senior bank officers gave junior bank officers were no different from fitness reports in the military.

And an officer rank brought the same privilege: a separate dining room, wooden desks and carpeting, and paneling and drapes on the banking floors where the lending officers worked.

Banking seemed to attract the same kind of American who might make a career as a military officer. There was ambition to do well, to make a good living, but at the same time there was the knowledge that although you might never be rich, you would be very secure. You could earn enough to send your kids to good schools, to belong to a golf club, and to buy a house in Downers Grove. If you were very successful, you could buy a house in Wilmette or Winnetka or Hinsdale.

There was great responsibility. You represented - and you controlled - resources far greater than your own. There was a sense of trust - fiduciary. There was a sense of a special role in the community.

There were rituals. There were conventions.

There was a separation between the regulars and the reserves. It was defined mainly by respect for the conventions. In the navy, a regular officer prepared for years to become one, and he would remain one for a career. A reserve prepared part-time and for less time, and he would stay only as long as he had to. Each looked at the traditions, practices, and skills with a different perspective. The reserve might have greater

34

admiration for the parts of it that he found good, but he would be less willing to accept the parts he found bad.

What was important was promotion, to ascend in rank. This was the corporate bankers' greatest ambition. Promotion made up for a lot of the money that others earned in more lucrative fields.

Someone would eventually become senior vice president, president, chairman – but you did not really aim for any of these. It would happen, or it would not. There was confidence that the system would promote the best man. If you didn't get to be chairman of the bank, that was all right; you'd work for the man who did.

The ranking officer of the U.S. Navy had once said that an officer's career was a success if he made commander. If he made captain, he was very successful. If he made admiral, he was very lucky. This is the way most bank officers felt. If you made vice president over the course of your career, it was a success.

Before the 1960s, making vice president took a long time. When Tilden Cummings joined the bank in the 1930s, the training program alone was three years long. Much of it was spent in the operating and credit departments. Roger Anderson, the outstanding member of the postwar group that came in in 1946, worked eleven years before making vice president.

An officer knew that the best man must lead, and that if it were you, you would lead, and if it were someone else, you would follow. The military principle, "If you can't take orders, you can't give them," was basic. You saluted the rank. You respected the office.

The privileges of rank were symbolic. The dining room. The wooden desk. Carpeting on a broad platform. Tasteful decorations made of quality materials.

As in the navy there was a sense of belonging to something vast and important, of being part of a great purpose.

The worst thing that could happen was disgrace – an error, an indiscretion, a negligence that would move you out of line and below your peers, that would take away their esteem. In the navy this might be the loss of a ship; in banking it might be a very bad business decision, one that cost the bank money.

The important thing was approval, favorable opinion.

So both captains and bankers were sensitive to their responsibilities. The primary instinct of the banker was accountability. He had been given a trust; he was accountable for it. And in banking the accounting could be done with numbers. The books had to balance, both literally and figuratively.

Walter Cummings's bank was organized according to groups of lending officers. The metropolitan banking groups were numbered one through eight; they formed around officers who specialized in lending to certain industries. Group 3, for example, handled merchandising companies like Sears and Montgomery Ward.

The national groups were designated by letters – E, F, G, and H. Each group covered a geographic region of the United States and the companies in all industries in that region.

The main banking floor was a great open expanse. Six columns on each side matched the six outside the building. There were polished wooden desks and brass nameplates, carpeting, and draperies. Elegance. Quality.

It gave the impression not of "the best" acquired at any expense, but of natural-quality pieces, chosen with care, acquired through thrift, and maintained with diligence and good judgment.

And silence. Men in dark suits and striped ties working over stacks of thick files, the financial histories of America's grandest corporations. Analyzing. Probing. Calculating. Long into the afternoon, long past five o'clock. Documenting. Not looking for quick solutions; there are no quick solutions.

There were conference rooms for large business meetings with customers or for the weekly review meeting by a lending group.

But the essence of it was openness – the open platform, the desks placed cleanly, with ample space in between, in the pattern of the lending groups. There was nothing secret here. There was nothing to hide.

There were two odd divisions in the commercial banking department. Neither quite fit into the clean lines of the organization. They were the oil and gas division, formed in 1953, and the old foreign division.

Group U, the oil and gas boys, were specialized lenders under the geographical divisions.

The foreign division was a geographical group under the industry-group organization for Metro Chicago, a subdivision of the commercial banking department.

There was as much friendliness toward the eccentricities of the former as there was suspicion about the latter. These two odd groups represented the two extreme sides of the bank's personality. It had to do with customers. Group U's customers took one set of characteristics to the extreme. They were the midwesterners stretched to their outer limits – the southwesterner: risk takers, yes, but successful risk takers. The independent oil men were in many ways expressions of America, of what America was.

The oil business was American business wherever it was. It was invented here. The Europeans came along after it was safe; the Arabs came after we found it for them.

There was great fondness for Group U. It was a leathery group, the best professionals in the industry. They had their own straightforward style. They had loud voices, no protocol, and no sneakiness. Protocol to them was a kind of sneakiness, an effort to divert your attention from the real point of the matter, to dress it up so you couldn't recognize it.

They produced tremendous business for the bank.

The foreign division didn't do much business. Some people wondered what it did. But apparently, every bank had to have a foreign division.

The foreign division knew a lot about protocol.

The division occupied a few desks back in the corner of Quincy and LaSalle, away from the main banking activity. Its business consisted of approving and processing letters of credit for import and export sales involving Chicago companies – those that did not deal directly with the New York banks and who had big departments for such business.

The main foreign customers were banks. Several European banks had dollar accounts at the Continental, as did Mexican banks. An international trade payment could be made by debiting or crediting these accounts. Iowa and Indiana and Nebraska banks made and received payments in the same way at big business centers. Continental had more such accounts from Iowa than from Europe.

The foreign division was really a second-level version of the domestic correspondent banking division, which was a second-level division itself. All the foreign division customers were banks, and they were all a million miles away in places nobody ever went to. Their deposits didn't amount to a hill of beans. The foreign division people talked about letters of credit and foreign exchange, which nobody wanted to know about. If a foreign banker came to town, he talked about the economy of someplace like Paraguay, or the U.S. State Department, or the world soccer cup.

None of the new trainees, the bright young men of the Continental Bank's future, were assigned to the foreign division. Some of them didn't even know it existed.

It was to the foreign division that Roger Anderson was sent in 1949.

There are those who say that the main reason Roger Anderson was put in the foreign division because he was the only member of that important 1946 class of trainees who would take the job. Somebody had to make the sacrifice, but anyone with good career sense would try to get out of it. They knew that Roger, all business and all duty, would not try to get out of it. Carl Birdsell, the president of the bank then and as conservative as Walter Cummings, had to have known that.

There are others who say it was because Roger came closest to the conservative model that, for Cummings and Birdsell, was the Continental ideal. He was the most dedicated worker among all the trainees, the one who had his priorities right, the one least likely to allow the frills and affectations of foreign banking to distract him from real banking. Roger had what would later be called credibility. And that was what the foreign division, down in the first-floor corner of LaSalle and Quincy, didn't have. If there were to be any future for the foreign division, it would take someone with credibility to say so and maybe to make it happen.

Roger Anderson was from Chicago, and – as Dan Rather would say – he was *of* Chicago. He was the kind of big man who seemed even bigger – taller – than he was, maybe because he was broad as well as tall and stood so straight. Put a big man like that in a dark blue suit, and the effect is a strong one, as if the physical strength were somehow harnessed into management. Roger carried his size more easily than men as large as he, which helped the effect.

The culture of the bank demanded that junior officers call senior officers by their first names – a tall order for many of the small-town boys and recent navy ensigns who were new to the staff (and a nearly impossible order for those of the Latin culture). But if you reached the point where you could call Roger Roger, the rest of them, however gray their hair, were no problem.

Roger was born in Chicago and, except for the World War II years, had lived there all his life. He had gone to a private high school on the city's north side and had earned his college degree at Northwestern a few months after the Japanese attacked Pearl Harbor. He joined the U.S. Navy and eventually became a senior lieutenant in the the supply corps. He spent a good part of the war in the South Pacific, down in New Caledonia, not far from where James Michener and Thomas Heggen were billeted with Lt. Joe Cable and Mister Roberts.

Roger got out of the navy in 1946, returned to Chicago, and started to work in the commerical banking department of the Continental Bank. His twenty-fifth birthday was that summer, on July 29. Walter Cummings's sixty-seventh birthday was that year, his twelfth as chairman of the Continental Bank; he had twelve more to go. He was as conservative as ever, and the bank was as conservative as he was. The young men who joined the Continental in 1946 were trained at the most conservative bank in America.

For Roger Anderson the transition wasn't that great. The navy supply corps had the same disciplines that banking did: accounting, controls, budgets, statistical projections. During the four years he spent in the navy the supply corps had conducted one of history's largest exercises in commerce. Walter Cummings was as thorough in conserving the traditions of the bank as Admiral Ernest King was of naval traditions.

Perhaps most important, Roger Anderson knew what it was to be an officer. To know what being an officer was, you had to go through the military – or work in a bank. Most Americans, particularly westerners, are uncomfortable with officers, uncomfortable with being officers. Being an officer cuts you off from a lot of people. It isn't like being a school officer or a club officer.

Officers tell people what to do, approve and disapprove all the time – not a favorite pastime in America. You have to be an adult in a society where youth, hell-for-leather, and democratic disrespect for authority are the favorite images.

Roger had been an adult since he was sixteen, the year he finished high school. During high school he had been a big, popular kid, the captain – and the biggest member – of the basketball team. He left all that behind when he went to Northwestern. He went there to study business – commerce, it was called then – and that was what he did. His grades were the best. Northwestern was a ten-scale fraternity school, with Big Ten sports teams. If Roger Anderson had been a thirty-year-old war veteran with a wife and kids, he couldn't have treated the school side of school more seriously than he did at sixteen. The navy had been a natural for him; it was Duty, Doing the Right Thing.

So the bank was a natural for him. Banking was about accountability, balancing the accounts, giving a good account of yourself.

231 South LaSalle Street was not a place where people went to have fun. They went there to find the kind of man Roger was.

Roger was sent to the foreign division. After all those years of top-of-the-class grades, promotions, and doing everything right, he was sent to the corner – literally. Just because he was the only one who would go.

It may be the toughest thing he ever had to do, at least before 1982. Three years into his career at the bank, after working harder than anyone, after observing all the rules, he saw his ambitions cut before he could express them. He knew – he confided this to friends – that he would not rise high in the management of the Bank.

But you do your duty. *If you are fair with the bank, the bank will be fair with you. After this assignment is over, things may change for the better.*

He never dreamed, even in his deepest disappointment, that they would *leave him there.*

TEN

WALTER CUMMINGS, NOW ALMOST EIGHTY, retired as chairman at the 1959 meeting of Continental Bank shareholders and was succeeded by Dave Kennedy.

They didn't have much in common.

Walter Cummings was a Catholic, a Democrat, and an authoritarian whose idea of banking was to control it. He had been raised in an urban environment and had come of age before the twentieth century began. He didn't laugh a whole lot. He moved slowly, as if there were no real hurry to get to where he was going because he was already there.

Dave Kennedy was a Mormon and a Republican. He had a great curiosity about the way things work and about the varieties of personality. He had made his banking career in the bond department, in the milieu of deadline-sensitive traders.

He laughed frequently and smiled usually, and he gave you the impression of being thoroughly pleased with whatever he was doing at the moment and interested to find out more about it. He moved rapidly; he seemed to always have somewhere to go.

Dave Kennedy came out of the wide-open West, with all its space. He had grown up in rural Utah, gone to a local college, and married his boyhood sweetheart. He had worked on a ranch in his teens and at twenty went abroad to Great Britain for two years of Mormon missionary work.

The only common experience that Walter Cummings and Dave Kennedy shared was Washington. Both had worked for the Treasury Department.

But when Carl Birdsell, the president of the bank, died in 1956, Cummings chose Dave Kennedy as his successor. Walter Cummings, the oldest and most traditional American banker, had managed to keep everything in one place, under one roof, for twenty-five years. Dave Kennedy, Cummings knew, intended to take the Continental all over the world.

People at the bank said the only thing they had in common was character.

"They were the same kind of man," someone said.

ELEVEN

DURING THE 1940S AND 1950S the chairman of the Continental Bank spent his afternoons in the big office on the main banking floor of South LaSalle Street. The chairman in the 1960s spent many of them in London, Buenos Aires, and Rabat.

The favorite Dave Kennedy story was the one about the calves' eyeballs.

He had been guest of honor at an official dinner in one of the North African countries – Algeria or Tunisia or Morocco. The president of the country was hosting the dinner. There were several courses, and then the *pièce de resistance* was served with hush and flourish in a covered dish. It was one of the region's foremost delicacies, proof of the country's high esteem for the guest. Off came the cover.

It wasn't Baked Alaska.

According to the story, which was about Dave telling the story, Dave said, "I looked at them. And they looked at me."

And?

"And I thought to myself, 'The bank pays me a lot of money to do this.' So I dug in."

It was the kind of story American travelers like to share with friends at home. It didn't need any more explanation; you could easily imagine yourself in the same spot. Dave Kennedy had been a world traveler since he was twenty. He had taken stories back to Utah then, just as he took them back to Chicago now.

The Dave Kennedy experience was fascinating. Here was this fatherly – no, grandfatherly – man with all this energy, all this intellectual curiosity, as fascinated as ever by the vast differences in peoples' customs and by the vast similarities among the people themselves.

The international banking department (IBD) people told that story frequently. Most of the IBD people had found themselves in similar situations from time to time, and not just in Africa or Asia. The *angulas* – baby eels – in garlic and olive oil that were so prized by your hosts in Madrid might be a test. Even escargots, which the French consider a very haute part of their haute cuisine, could be a pretty strong challenge for someone who had come from the Midwest for the first time. The ultimate standard, though, was calves' eyeballs.

Meals were a big part of foreign business protocol. There is probably no better signal of the affection the Spaniards – the Banco Atlantico people – had for Dave Kennedy than the story of a dinner they hosted for him at the Jockey Club in Madrid. Knowing that Mormons do not drink alcohol, Pepe Ferrer arranged for the Jockey to serve grape juice – squeezed there that day, red and white separately – to the Kennedy family. And in the land of Rioja wines, all the Spaniards present drank grape juice with the Kennedys.

Dave might not have told this story back home, because the gesture of the Spaniards simply wouldn't translate as well as the calves' eyeballs. It was a purely Spanish gesture, both in its excess and in the fact that it was never mentioned. Dave would have had a hard time explaining that you show Spaniards how much you appreciate gesture like that by not acknowledging it with words.

And you got the idea, joining Dave Kennedy at the Jockey Club after the formal dinner was finished and people were sitting around and visiting, that the essence of Kennedy, the reason all these people felt at ease with him and trusted him, was that he knew that there were differences.

And he liked differences. Differences fascinated him. He thought differences were great.

Why are people different? Why do they use their mother's last name, too – and after *their father's? That just confuses people!*

Most foreigners have a hard time with differences. You came to expect it of them: Gringos. *Gallegos.*

Dave Kennedy never had that problem. He sat down with the Japanese and persuaded them to allow the Continental Bank to open branches in Tokyo and Osaka, even though the Japanese had refused anyone else such permission for a decade. He worked out partnerships in Argentina and Holland and Lebanon and Italy. He was a natural. Some people said he developed the knack as a Mormon missionary in England from 1920 to 1922. But if you know any Mormon missionaries, you might think he got it somewhere else.

In any event foreigners acted as if they didn't think he was a foreigner.

He grew up in the American West, in rural Utah – about as far from Europe as anyplace in the world, with the possible exception of Chicago.

Out West, the expression for people like Kennedy is, "He never met a stranger." It's an old expression.

The Spanish word for *stranger* is *extranjero.*

The English translation of *extranjero* is *foreigner.*

TWELVE

"*I*F WE CAN'T HANDLE INTERNATIONAL BUSINESS," DAVE KENNEDY
WOULD SAY, "it will go to New York. And once it gets there, it
will stay there."

That's where it had always gone – and stayed.

At the beginning of 1959, on the brink of the American Challenge
across the Atlantic and across the Pacific, the bank still consisted of the
one giant redoubt at 231 South LaSalle Street in Chicago. The biggest
bank in the world under one roof. All under one roof. The eighty-year-
old chairman was retiring, but everything else was the same.

Dave Kennedy was convinced that the main expansion of American
industry was going to be international. If the Continental Bank didn't
want the New York banks to do to it what Sears, Roebuck had done
to Montgomery Ward, the bank would have to go international as well.

It was more than that. If the Continental didn't take the lead, then
the importance of Chicago itself as a financial center would be diminished.

There was enough irritation on that point already.

It was the image problem.

The conservative's discomfort with change seemed to relate, more
than anything else, to *place*. The spoken rationale was risk, of course.
But place was the thing – keeping one's place. In the year that Dave Kennedy took over the bank, everything was in its place. Nothing had started

to move yet. President Eisenhower, the symbol of the moral forces of World War II, was in place. College life was in place. Blacks were in place. Women were in place. The 1950s were in place. All the images were in place.

Chicago was in place.

And that was going to be the main problem in making Continental an international bank. Walter Cummings knew where Kennedy stood; it had been Kennedy's condition for accepting the presidency that he be authorized to set policy, and Cummings had assented. But Walter Cummings was the sculptor as well as the chairman of the bank, and there were many officers who liked it the way it was.

The New York banks also liked it the way it was. From the New York perspective, Continental was a regional bank. It was going to take a long time for that to change.

In one sense *regional* referred to the customers: individuals, companies, schools, churches, and city and state treasuries. In that sense banks that dealt with customers all across the country were *national* banks, and those that had customers in other countries were *international* banks. Bank officers would travel to other states to visit national customers – usually manufacturing companies – and to other countries to visit the international customers – usually government ministries, of treasury, public works, and commerce.

But for New Yorkers *regional* referred to the bank's location. New York was the capital of American banking, and that made everywhere else a region. The common phrases, when talking of large banks, were *New York banks* and *regional banks*.

It was still another New Yorkism, out of the many that annoyed Chicagoans, and it was a problem. Both inside and outside Chicago people seemed to prefer that Chicago stay in its place, in the American midlands. The Continental was a regional bank – and an American bank.

Kennedy wanted it to be the first such American bank to go international. That's what his plan amounted to.

Traditional bankers in Middle America held two impressions about international banking.

One impression had to do with Latin Americans. If lending money to places like Peru and Brazil and Bolivia made sense to anybody, they had to be either in the State Department or on the romance language faculty at Northwestern. If the New York banks wanted to do that, fine for them.

The other impression, the main one, had to do with Europe. The Swiss. Paris. The Germans. London. Madrid. Rome.

Europe made a little more sense than Latin America as far as lending money was concerned. But the problem was, "What do we know about Europe?"

Banking was a people business. You heard that in the training program; all the old pros said it, too.

It was man to man with the customers. If you were going to bank somebody, you wanted to see them as well as their balance sheet. You also knew they wouldn't use you if they didn't like you. People do business with people they like, people they trust. It was a "relationship" business, commercial banking. A long-term business. You stuck with the company and the customers through the ups and downs of the business cycles, and they stuck with you.

We don't know any Europeans.

There was another side to it, too – the one about the people inside the bank.

"It's a people business," Bob Ruwitch used to say, "because you've got to have the right people in the right places inside the bank. You've got to be able to rely on your own people."

But that was the main problem for Dave Kennedy when he decided the Continental would have to become a great international bank in order to remain a great American bank.

There weren't any international banking people. The foreign division obviously couldn't handle a big international expansion. The main corps of Continental lending officers had been trained in American banking. One currency; one set of bank regulations, accounting rules, and tax laws; one language. If you grew up next door to somebody in Evanston, it was hard enough to communicate with him. And even if you could translate into English what a Japanese was saying to you, would you really know what he was saying to you?

Art Roberts, who had run the foreign division since the 1930s, was retiring, which meant there would be only one international banker at 231 South LaSalle Street. This was Al Miossi, who had come to Chicago because he was in love with a blonde who lived there. Al had grown up in California, had served in Italy with the Fifth Army, finished Stanford after the war, and joined the Bank of America for tours in Tokyo and Manila. He might have stayed in California the rest of his life, except that he met Blanche.

He had been in Chicago since 1953, trading Pacific seasons for Chicago winters, trading the biggest international banking organization for the smallest. The most exciting times were spent listening to Art Roberts talk about the glory days. Continental had actually had an office in Germany during the 1930s. Roberts had been there, helping people get their money out. He had been to dinners with Goering, had negotiated payments due to Chicago companies. This was as fascinating for Miossi as knowing that the United States had once made it to the soccer World Cup and had beaten England. But it was fascinating only for Miossi. Soccer didn't cut it at the Continental any more than foreign banking did.

The problem with Kennedy's expansion plan was people. To staff it he would have to go outside the Continental culture, bring in the kind of people who had not worked at the bank before.

But to do this, he would have to have more than the little foreign division down on the first floor. He would have to have the right man to run the international banking expansion.

It had to be someone who everyone – particularly the domestic bankers – in the Continental Bank knew had the right stuff.

Dave Kennedy, as Walter Cummings had done before him, chose Roger Anderson.

THIRTEEN

K ENNEDY'S FIRST MOVE WAS TO MAKE THE FOREIGN DIVISION INTO ITS OWN DEPARTMENT: the international banking department, or IBD.

In 1961 he negotiated the acquisition of the City National Bank, the neighbor bank across LaSalle Street. This made the Continental the largest bank in Chicago.

In 1962 he opened the Continental's first branch abroad – its first branch anywhere – in London. He acquired the Tokyo and Osaka branches of the Nationale Handelsbank of Holland. In 1963 he established a wholly owned international banking subsidiary in New York. By 1967 the Continental had investments in banks in Argentina, Spain, Belgium, Holland, France, Italy, and Switzerland. It had representative offices in Mexico, Venezuela, and Brazil.

In doing this, Kennedy observed the rule that the old Continental bankers had always recited to the trainees: "It is a people business; you have to have the right people in the right places."

Someone remarked that anytime an institution makes a great step forward, it is because of a nucleus of four or five leaders who just happen to be there at the same time.

One isn't enough; there is too much of a staff to deal with. And more than a small group brings bureaucracy. You need a nucleus – four or five.

At the Continental there were four. Kennedy was the motor, of course. Roger was the executive. Al Miossi was on the other side of Roger. And there was Don Graham, then vice chairman, later Kennedy's successor as chairman. He was as underrated as a chairman as Chicago is as a city.

The core management group oversaw the training of Continental Bank people for the new international role. In the meantime they solved their immediate need for experienced officers the way other American banks would a few short years later when they followed the Continental into international business: the Continental hired people from the New York banks. Citibank – then called First National City Bank – was the main source of people for most banks. Irving Trust was also a good source. So was Bank of America, and there were others. Ron Meringer and Hector del Rio came from the now-forgotten Empire Bank, a first-rate international outfit later absorbed by one of the big New York banks. Al Fern came from Chemical. Bill Termyn from Irving. Joel Smith and Bill Anderson and Chuck Davis from City.

The Japanese deal with the Dutch produced not just branches but operations staff with them; several transferred to Chicago. Leo deGrijs came to the Continental this way. Some of the British bankers hired when the London branch was opened in 1962 eventually came to Chicago: John Biella. Don Adley. Peter Shaddick, whose foreign exchange trading skills were unexcelled, was with the Bank of England itself.

Continental Bank International, the New York subsidiary, was opened by Jacques Stunzi, previously of Manufacturers Hanover. Harvey Fleetwood was there, from the Federal Reserve Bank. Joe Welch had been with Irving. Andy Grimbergen had been with another Dutch bank. The operating staff was drawn from every bank in New York that took part in the international payments system.

The foreign division was removed from its corner on the first floor to occupy, as a department, the entire sixth floor at 231 South LaSalle.

There were New Yorkers all over the place. There were Englishmen and Dutchmen. There were State Department people. There was a European group and a Latin American group and an Asian group, side by side on the carpeted expanse that fronted South LaSalle Street. And around the corner, on the Jackson Street side, there was an operations area where you could hear English spoken in every imaginable accent.

The new international banking brought a lot of people to 231 South LaSalle Street who would never have been there otherwise. It was no easy change. There were a lot of people there who just weren't Continental Bank people.

It was hard for some people to get used to it; some never did.

FOURTEEN

S ERVAN-SCHREIBER'S *THE AMERICAN CHALLENGE* OWED ITS SUCCESS TO THE FACT THAT IT CONTAINED IN ONE SLIM VOLUME ALL THE STEREOTYPICAL FRENCH FEARS ABOUT AMERICANS, the kind of Americans you found on the second floor at 231 South LaSalle. It invoked the image of big, awkward, crew-cut ex-GIs – so recently, so thankfully gotten rid of from France – now returning to Europe permanently as businessmen. They had no respect for the culture but were business wizards and had the capacity to seduce the younger generation of Europeans with irresistible American treats – if not the candy bars and chewing gum handed out by smiling corporals, then the washing machines and blue jeans and detergents produced by U.S. companies. (And ultimately, worst of all, hamburgers. There would be fast-food joints on the Champs-Élyseés!)

One Continental recruiting brochure from 1966 might have made Servan-Schreiber's hair stand on end. It was entitled "Continental Bank – A View of the Future," and it was sixteen pages long, with a pocket inside the back cover for inserts. Each insert was a "Profile" of a career. There were pictures, with background notes, of several young officers who were representative of the Continental Bank.

George Baker. Age 37. Position: Vice President, Commercial Banking. Schooling: BA Coe College. George heads the division responsible for loans to finance companies, the leasing industry, and small business investment companies. Loans made by officers within his group average $150 million per year. George joined the Management Development Program in 1951. At the age of 27 he was made an officer. At 31 he was advanced to second vice president, and at 34 he was made a full vice president in charge of this group.

Eugene Croisant. Age 29. Position: Electronics Officer, Operations Division. Schooling: BSC Loyola University. MS (Industrial Management) Loyola University. Gene Croisant is a new breed of banker. Data processing is his specialty, and he's responsible for two IBM 360 computer systems now being phased into Continental's check clearing operation (which involves close to 1 million items per day). He also oversees daily operations of the two GE 210 computer systems which handle the bank's bookkeeping. Gene started with Continental as a part-time employee in 1954 while still in high school, began full-time in 1961 after a tour of duty as an infantry lieutenant, and was elected an officer of the bank in 1964 at the age of 27.

Charles Hall. Age 37. Position: Vice President, Commercial Banking. Schooling: BS University of Kansas. Northwestern University (evening school). University of Wisconsin Graduate School of Banking. Chuck Hall handles primary relations with banks and industry in five western states. He is specially qualified in finance relating to the air frame and air transport industries. One current project: "How to Finance the Supersonic Transport Program." Currently Chuck is on the faculty of the Southwestern School of Banking, Southern Methodist University. Chuck began his career at Continental in 1955 after a tour of duty as a naval officer. Less than 3 years later, at the age of 28, he was made an officer of the bank.

50

John Jones. Age 32. Position: Vice President, International Banking. Schooling: BA Carleton College. As the officer in charge of international banking transactions for all of Continental Bank's domestic customers, John Jones is responsible for more than $100 million in credit. He is a specialist in the financial problems of domestic companies doing business abroad. Frequently, he must make on-the-spot decisions in matters concerning imports, exports, the financing of overseas subsidiaries, and the acquisition of foreign interests. John began his Continental career in 1957 and became an officer within 4 years. He is now a full vice president at 32.

Gail Melick. Age 38. Position: Vice President, Operations Division. Schooling: BA Carleton College. MBA University of Chicago. Gail Melick is responsible for the direction and control of operations for six significant areas of the bank: Loan, Loan Review, Credit, Commercial Groups, Real Estate, and Methods Research. Among his important assignments are: Management Succession, Expense Analysis and Control, and Manpower Budgeting. Gail joined the bank in 1952, became an officer in 1958 at the age of 30.

David Taylor. Age 37. Position: Vice President, Bond Department. Schooling: BA Denison University. MBA Northwestern University. As assistant department head of the Bond Department, Dave Taylor manages about $900,000,000 of Continental Bank's investments and is responsible for more than $1,000,000,000 worth of deposits and borrowings. He is also involved in the underwriting and trading of municipal and government securities. Dave joined the Continental in 1957 after a stint as a naval officer. He became an officer of the bank in 1961 at the age of 32.

The pictures showed them all to be clean cut, clear eyed, and strong jawed, with hair cut short; they were symbols of the American accession.

All these men had come out of 1950s American college classrooms, and each of them fit the all-American boy image that World War II movies had impressed on every citizen of the world who had the price of a ticket.

You were looking at the entire bomber crew from *30 Seconds Over Tokyo*. At John Wayne's Marine platoon in *The Sands of Iwo Jima*.

And in Jean-Jacques Servan-Schreiber's theory you were looking at the starting lineup for the American Challenge.

FIFTEEN

T HE PURPOSE OF THE BROCHURE WASN'T TO ALARM THE FRENCH, of course. In fact, it had nothing to do with Europeans' image of Americans. It had to do with Americans' image of bankers.

The Continental brochure, in its small way, gave the same message that *Le Defi Americain* did: *The world, our world, is changing. The clichés, the old expectations, the stereotypes have all changed.*

A VIEW OF THE FUTURE

Banking *is* an exciting business. And it needs intelligent, well-educated people to run it. . . .

Peter L. Bernstein observed: "And now we begin to look at these proverbially starchcollared, fishy-eyed businessmen from a new viewpoint. These fellows who sit so sternly in judgment on the financial habits of the entire community are actually involved in a much more exciting business than they might be willing to admit. They are, in fact, star players in the drama."

It was a tall order, to convince people that bean counters are star players. But if there was one image that was more compelling than that of the stodgy banker, an image that could change it, it was the image of the all-American. The brochure was intended to show that at least at the Continental Illinois Bank of Chicago, you had a new kind of banker, a new kind of banking.

Here was Continental's idea of the right stuff. These were Big Ten men that the Ivy colleges had only wished they could attract. Few of them had gone east, and those who did went only as far as Princeton – still west of the Hudson. You gained prestige by going east, but of a kind that didn't cut much ice around here, unless you worked at the First. But its price was too great. The values were different. The exchange was a loss.

You didn't have to go east to learn that you don't wear white socks with business suits (and later, that you don't wear polyester double-knits). You didn't want to go somewhere where they called football "American football" and told you that you paid too much attention to sports and that friendliness was, well, quaint, and where they smiled when they said *Iowa* or *Nebraska* or *Kansas*.

In the Northeast the school was more important than the man. Out here, the only thing more important than the man was the place.

In Iowa and Nebraska and Kansas there was unbounded interest in "American football" and enormous respect for athletes. Most of the men in the Continental "Profiles" were athletes. Jones had been all-state in Kansas high school basketball. He and some other Continental recruits – Gerry Bergman, Caren Reed, Roger Sherman, Dave Colburn and Hollis Rademacher – put together a team that had played winning ball in the tough and tall Chicago suburban leagues for years. They did this with only two players, Bergman and Colburn ("The Enforcer"), who were six feet tall.

These late-1950s basketball players were close friends, and their friendships would last throughout their careers. They had all arrived in Chicago in 1956 or 1957, not long out of midwestern colleges; some had already married college sweethearts, some had babies. They moved with U-Hauls into small urban apartments. Chicago was the biggest city that any of them had ever lived in, that most had ever seen. They would look, in the 1980s, as if they might still make a pretty decent basketball team.

Most of the lending groups at the Continental at this time were about the size of the basketball group. There were six officers and group men in Jones's group, for example, and that was typical. Typical, too, of the bank groups was the team closeness. People talked less about "team play" in those days than they do now because it was a natural part of the environment. Jones was close to the guys in his group; the import-export group had been formed by now, and he was heading it. And Bergman was close to his, and the others were close to theirs. At the Continental you knew the families, you knew the home towns. You all got together.

It was more or less what every one of them had been doing all his life, and it fit right in at the Continental. It wouldn't have fit so well at the First, and it didn't fit at all into the public image of what bankers and big banks were.

What it did fit was the eastern image of the Midwest – too friendly, too hokey.

But of course, that was also the European image of all Americans.

None of the new officers could remember the Depression. They had all heard it talked about, but they considered it just that – talk of the past, war stories about an event that was important only to those who had experienced it. It was the property of the old.

Men like Walter Cummings had long since retired.

Walter Cummings of the Depression, eighty years old, older by decades than even the classical old building that housed the Continental Bank, was only around in image.

Times had changed. Change had changed. The American Challenge was upon us.

So the Bank had good reason to do the recruiting brochure with all-American "Profiles."

The new officers were the new breed. They talked about the old breed with a smile.

"There've been too many changes around here," an old banker said. "I liked things better the way they used to be.

"I'd sit here at my desk.

"And people would come in and ask me for a loan.

"And I'd say no."

That was a story that the new breed at Continental told about the old breed (but carefully, carefully). Other stories, told with the same careful smile, also distanced the new breed from the old.

There he is at his big desk, still waiting for people to come in and ask him for money so he can say no. Stolid, stodgy, in a three-piece suit, dark and expensive; in black shoes, polished this morning (Oxfords; wing tips are too racy for him). Large man, stationary. His face is a frown, always a frown. Disapproving, of course, but now with all these changes taking place, befuddled as well.

He is the image of the old, the embodiment of the three-six-three rule: pay 3 percent for deposits, charge 6 percent for loans, leave the office to play golf at three o'clock.

It wasn't going to sit still for him anymore. Not the three percent deposits, not the three o'clock golf. He was supposed to be the banker of the companies that were waging the American Challenge, but if he couldn't keep up with them, he couldn't be their banker anymore.

Right behind *The American Challenge* came Alvin Toffler's *Future Shock*. It was an American book that was quoted by both IBM computer experts and parish priests.

It said, "Change."

The concept of change, of broad-scale change, of change in just about everything Americans did, was suddenly fashionable, was "smart."

This meant that conservatism – the conservatism that stood for maintaining order, doing things the same way they had "always" been done, preventing change – wasn't fashionable.

This conservatism had served the old breed well for decades. It had been unchallenged since the Great Depression. But suddenly, it was not "smart."

"I wish things were like they used to be around here."

The new breed would tell the story, but carefully, carefully.

Because it was still the same bank, the bank that Walter Cummings had made. Although he was gone, the staff that he had created was still there.

There was great respect for it.

He was the Old Man. He was the captain.

It is an American tradition to rag your old man, to ride him about the out-of-date things he is interested in. But the fact is you're kind of pleased about it. You like it. You really don't want him any other way.

Times had changed, yes. The American Challenge was afoot, and there was new business to be taken care of. The old-time banker wasn't what you needed to take care of it.

But the new breed were the same kind of Middle Americans as the old breed, just out of a different time. All the big reference points were still the same; all of them knew what Duty was.

The old image of bankers was severe. It lacked warmth and gentle understanding. The old bankers may not have been lovable, but you trusted them.

SIXTEEN

*T*HERE WERE IN-HOUSE STORIES ABOUT ROGER ANDERSON, just as there were about Dave Kennedy. People still talked about Roger's first international trip, the one to the Mexican Bankers Convention in Acapulco in the 1950s. The very senior, formal, and domestic Herman Waldeck, who was then the bank's only executive vice president, had advised him to take along a tuxedo for the receptions.

"The Mexicans are very formal. Very formal. The Latin Americans are very formal."

So he did. And he was the only one in Acapulco wearing black tie. Sweltering. Everyone else was in a guayabera shirt with open collar. One of the Mexican bankers helped him find a guayabera and loved to talk about it ever after. Years later, in his fifties, when Roger was chairman, Paco would still say, "I was the one who taught that boy about international banking."

It drove Luis Calero nuts to hear him say that – which was probably why he said it. Luis was the Continental's representative in Mexico. He was an old-line Mexican banker, very formal, the son of a Diaz minister, and several years older than Roger.

"Five minutes after I met him, I would have trusted him with my life," someone said about Roger. Not Luis; it was the wife of one of

56

the other Continental people. But Luis would have said it. Most of us would have said it.

The story Roger liked to tell on himself was about Argentina. One taxicab after another refused to take him to the address he gave them, driving off angrily, leaving him totally confused until he looked up and saw the building across the boulevard in front of him.

Roger called on banks in Argentina on that trip. He called on them in dozens of other countries as well. A banker made calls.

Commercial banking was a relationship business. You called. You got to know the people. They did business with you because they knew you.

It was the simplest and truest article of faith in this industry, commercial banking. (Investment banking, to be sure, was something else.) Banking was a personal business, a relationship business. You got to know everything there was to know about the companies you called on, about the people who ran them. There were reports on each call. There were monthly summaries of total calls made.

The rule was generally understood that calls were the measure of work. On the international side Roger made them with the enormous energy. Most of the Roger stories came out of these long trips to Europe or South America or Japan or the Middle East. Almost always, two officers travelled together. The calling officer was your top gun, your pro. Everybody wanted to be one. When you made your first trip, your first call schedule, that was your real test, your badge.

International banking was business's state department. The banks smoothed the way, verified the creditworthy, and spanned the distances and language barriers. They did this through their trusted correspondent banks in other countries. Companies in different countries did not know each other, could not trust each other; banks could. Trust took time. Time was tradition. Tradition means protocol. There was beaucoup protocol.

After you had been to a place a few times, the protocol eased a little. You got to know some of the foreign bankers better than you knew people in your own bank. Good guys. Close friends.

Most international banking – then and now – was with other banks.

SEVENTEEN

WITH THE EXCEPTION OF THE LONDON BASE, which began as a Continental branch, all of Kennedy's early bases were made through investments: the acquisition of the Dutch branches in Japan and minority investments in smaller European banks.

The thorniest part of building the overseas network was to break the news to other foreign banks. They were, after all, the principal customers of the old foreign division. A lot of them weren't going to like the idea of your coming into their territory.

In Germany and in Holland the big banks so honored tradition that they refused to call on another bank's client. This was part of the Hausbank tradition. Jean d'Arenberg, later Continental's ranking Belgian executive, likened it to a marriage. Tradition wedded a bank and a company for better and for worse. Tradition meant that you didn't flirt with someone else's spouse, much less get in bed with the spouse.

A handful of U.S. banks had maintained branches in London since the early part of the century. Morgan had one in Paris. But these were quiet and stately branches. They were there to take deposits from the rich, to give loans to the government, to stay close to the central bank, and to finance trade with America. Later, Bank of America and First National City Bank set up chains of more active branches. *Aggressive* was the American term for it, and it fit. Aggression was annoying, but it was to be expected. The Americans were what they were. What they were not was traditional bankers.

There was also the matter of place. In Europe as well as Chicago, the greater part of tradition was place.

London was easy. You didn't have to go through the protocol there. London styled itself as the world's great financial center, and it wanted all the banks that cared to come. In 1965 there were thirteen U.S. banks in London. In 1973 there were 108.

But continental Europe was tough, and Kennedy took it slow. European banking was still closed in many places, and you had to wait for an opening.

Some of the moves were held up because of this. Some people in the Continental's international department thought it would be better to stay back, to protect the bank relationships. A lot of "you'll be sorrys" came out of the international as well as the domestic floors at 231 South LaSalle. But Dave Kennedy was moving on. And Roger, with Dave on the one side and Al Miossi on the other, was moving on with him.

Go see 'em. Tell 'em nicely. We're still friends.

Dave handled a lot of the protocol personally. Roger did it, too, and Al Miossi. Once they decided that the Continental would move into a particular country, the first thing they did was to call on the correspondent banks in that country – every one of them – and tell them face to face. Nicely. Gentlemanly. Explaining why. Asking for their support, their continued business.

It was tough protocol, but it worked out okay. The more traditional the bank, the greater the chances of resentment. But even Europeans knew the times were changing.

The Continental formed a partnership with a group in Holland called the Nederland Oberzees Bank, which owned a Belgian bank, Banque Europeen d'Outre Mer. It formed another partnership with the Italian banker Michele Sindona, thereby acquiring 25 percent of the Banca Privata Financieria in Milan, which had a Rome branch and which also controlled a Swiss institution, Finabank.

The strategy of the early expansion was to gain a position in countries important to U.S. multinationals so that the Continental could effect banking support – local currency credit, operating accounts, credit evaluations, direct investment advice – for the Americans.

The Continental opened offices in Brussels, Geneva, and Milan to give local coordination to these operating investments.

"We'll be able to make a thousand calls a year," Roger said.

The international emergence of Spain was an attraction, too. Then in its second quarter-century under Franco, still decades away from entering the Common Market, the country had begun to open to foreign companies. Procter & Gamble was there, as well as Colgate, Abbott Labs, Pfizer, and almost a hundred other multinationals, both U.S. and European, by the late 1960s.

Spain had a weaker currency than the Common Market countries. It had as well a top-heavy, old-fashioned, and therefore politically powerful banking industry. It was an example of a country that limited foreign investment in banking, placing that industry in a protected-national-interest category along with military arms, public utilities, and public information.

Foreign banks could not open branches then, and their investment in existing Spanish banks was limited to 50 percent. Only Bank of America, which was in a fifty-fifty partnership with one of the large Spanish banking groups in a small commercial bank, was present among the American banks.

Roger made several trips to Spain and found a bank in Barcelona that was interested in a partnership with Continental. He made one last trip to close the deal.

This was the favorite Roger story. The owner is a Catalan high roller, long on style. After a day of business meetings in which they reach a tentative agreement, he takes Roger out to celebrate, to the Acapulco Club.

There is Roger with this guy at the Acapulco. He had gone along on protocol, drinking Scotch with the music playing.

"*A ver si te gusta esta,* Roger." Let me show you what we've got here, Roger. And the guy motions over one of the many hostesses.

Roger has this wheeler-dealer sitting across the table from him and an immensely friendly chick sitting on his knee, and he still hasn't finished his Scotch.

But he does. He finishes the Scotch. Then he excuses himself. Then he goes back to his hotel. Then he cancels the deal. Then he flies on to Paris, the next stop on his itinerary.

The Catalan can't understand what happened. He flies to Paris, too, to try to head him off. But it's too late. That was the last conversation with that bank.

There were a lot of other Roger stories that the corps enjoyed. There was one about the time he and Charlie O'Hara were sitting in a locked hotel room in Riyadh, about to enjoy a bottle of Scotch that Charlie had sneaked into the country, and there was a loud knock at the door.

Roger and Charlie rush – glasses, ice cubes and all – to flush the only bottle of Scotch in Saudi Arabia down the toilet. (The name of the bank is at stake!) Then they open the door, and it's a bellhop with a letter from a banker.

But the favorite Roger story was the one about the Acapulco. It was because the Acapulco deal didn't go through that the Continental later formed its partnership with Banco Atlantico in Spain. The Banco Atlantico people hung around church, not the Acapulco. They felt particularly comfortable with Roger. It later turned out to be the best foreign investment the Continental ever made.

In 1960 the Continental lent $100 million to U.S. companies and foreign institutions abroad. By 1965 the figure was over $500 million, out of total loans of just over $3 billion.

The IBD trade finance group, newly formed to do business with medium-size companies, had supplanted the New York banks as the primary source of export financing for the equipment-manufacturing giants of the Midwest.

That was the work of John Jones and his group – a bunch of midwestern boys who had been told they should concentrate on the small stuff because they didn't have the experience to compete with the New York banks.

EIGHTEEN

THE INTERNATIONAL EXPANSION OF THE CONTINENTAL ILLINOIS BANK was part of a huge cultural adventure for the city. The industrial imagination of Chicago and the Midwest now reached all over the world, just as Jean-Jacques Servan-Schreiber was telling his Common Market compatriots. Sears, Roebuck, International Harvester,

Abbott Laboratories, Deere, Swift – all of whose executives sat on the board of the Continental – did business on several continents. New logos and acronyms appeared atop office buildings, replacing names and companies that Americans had known for decades.

These were heady times in the Midwest.

Continental had its first acronyms: IBD for the international banking department. CBI for Continental Bank International in New York.

It also had a new symbol. In the 1967 report to shareholders the bank defined "the character and goals of the Continental Bank . . . in context with its four major geographic customer areas: metropolitan Chicago itself . . . the Midwest . . . the nation, and at last the entire free world."

It was nice stuff.

"The view then is fourfold: The city, the changing prairie, the country of builders, and nations in concert. Continental Bank's life is at the center of this complex."

The logo was an enclosing C with four green leaves inside it.

By 1968 the Continental – still prevented from branching in Illinois – was taking more than $1.5 billion in deposits from the growing Eurodollar market in London. The New York subsidiary, CBI, had developed more than $100 million in operating deposits from foreign banks. With the Bank of America and the eight major New York banks it formed the U.S. interbank system for international payments. The traders at CBI New York made the Continental's foreign exchange operation one of the three largest among all banks. The Continental had an office in every business capital in Europe and in Japan.

In fifteen years, Jean-Jacques Servan-Schreiber warned his fellow Europeans, the American Challenge would create the third largest economic force in the world. U.S. multinationals would rank above Europe, above Japan – above all but the United States itself and the Soviet Union.

Americans were that good.

Perception, even then, was the only reality. The new order of international business was symbolized not by suave agents in the James Bond movies then playing in Chicago, but by the midwestern heirs of Tom Sawyer and Huck Finn and Penrod and Nick Carraway: the faces in the Continental "Profiles."

Sometimes the perception was symbolized in unexpected ways.

One slow afternoon in Chicago one of the letter of credit clerks passed in front of Jones's group. He stopped at the desk of one of the junior officers he had trained in letters of credit and stood looking at the scene: the lending officers, the oak desks, the nameplates, the paneling.

This group, the import-export group, was on the Jackson side of the sixth floor, just around the corner from the foreign lending groups – Europe, Latin America, Asia – that occupied the entire LaSalle side of that floor. Just beyond Jones's group was the operations section of IBD – what the guys down in Metro Midwest called the funny-money department because everybody there spoke with an accent. IBD operations was staffed with European emigrés – many of them had arrived after the war – who held the clerk jobs in letters of credit and foreign loans and transfers.

The carpet actually stopped, a clean cutoff, just pass the Jones group. A partition, then a wall, had been put up to complete the separation between administration and operations. On the Jones side were paneling, fine wooden desks, carpet, and silence. On the other side were linoleum, metal desks, and noise.

Mr. Rykovich was the letter of credit clerk who was standing there.

Mr. Rykovich. There was a World War II movie for you. He had been an officer with the Yugoslav resistance, fighting the Germans in the hills. Fighting the Communists, too. That's why he wasn't in Yugoslavia anymore, running a business or maybe running the central bank. Now he was glad to be processing letters of credit in the Chicago winter, glad to have a clean place to live.

"You look just . . . right," he said to the Jones group man sitting immediately in front of him.

He was admiring the scene as if it were a piece of artwork, as if it had been arranged just for him, to confirm what he knew in his heart. He might have been an American tourist walking through the Louvre.

"Sir?"

"You have it all," Mr. Rykovich said. He looked at the man, then at the brass nameplate. "Your name. It's just right. Your looks. Just right. You and John Jones. You have it all."

It was embarrassing, of course. It might have been funny if he had spoken to Jones, but Jones's desk was far away. But it was kind of touching, too. If you had been overseas in the military, had seen the daily life of postwar Europe or Japan, you knew what the man meant.

There were thousands of once-Lithuanians, once-Latvians, once-Poles in Chicago who, sharing Mr. Rykovich's experience, might have said the same thing.

World War II was long behind but not the stories and not the images. And Cuba wasn't so far behind, and there were Cuban doctors and lawyers and teachers glad for Chicago winters who had never thought to see one. Many of the Cuban emigrés were in American banks, now that the banks were dealing abroad. Joaquin Rodriguez, doctor of laws, bank manager, father of a family, was with Continental Bank International in New York. He had once been in school with Fidel. But Fidel was still south, and Joaquin had landed in Florida, had painted houses to make a living while learning English, word by word, so he could get a clerk job. The American Dream was the only dream.

There stood Mr. Rykovich – there stood old Europe – admiring the officer corps of Middle America. He walked back to the letter of credit section. It was on the other side of the partition, where the carpeting became linoleum and the desks were metal instead of oak.

It was late in the 1960s, nearing the 1970s, and the American Challenge was upon the world. We were number one, as we were born to be.

The Continental "Profiles" was a recruiting piece that probably was meant to be reused several times: other photographs, other profiles could be inserted into the pocket inside the back cover.

But it was used only that once. There is just that one set of Continental "Profiles": Baker, Croisant, Hall, Jones, Melick, and Taylor. It is as if a strange and ironic hand had selected those pictures for a time capsule, to be opened in fifteen years – the time frame in which the American Challenge was to complete its success; to be opened in 1984.

PART

THREE

*Mother's
Day*

NINETEEN

MAY 10, 1984 – A THURSDAY.
Even with Daylight Savings Time, sunrises in the spring months are early for farmers in the Midwest. Above the fortieth parallel, where you have some of Nebraska and Illinois and all of Iowa, Wisconsin, Michigan, and Minnesota, the sun comes up well before 6 A.M. It was light in Chicago and the temperature was in the fifties when Dave Taylor emerged from his house on Wildwood Lane in Northbrook.

No Caribbean dawn here; no lazy blue waters or sleepy white one-level island towns. Here the seas were amber and the island was the water, Lake Michigan, a small indention in the flatland ocean.

Nassau and Chicago – what a contrast! There was a saying among the traders those days: "Wherever you go, that's where you are."

In a big black stretch limousine (Cadillac, American made) Dave Taylor rode into Chicago. The sun was up; the traffic along the Edens Expressway was lively already. From Northbrook to the bank is about half an hour. Once you pass the rims of Northfield and Wilmette, you drive through the more industrial area of Skokie and Lincolnwood, then go on a diagonal from the northwestern parts of the city of Chicago. These are old working areas. Worker neighborhoods. Basic. Weathered. Past that is the Loop.

North Shore commuters, after years of this daily routine, don't notice the areas anymore unless they drive themselves. Most commuters read on the way to work. Dave Taylor had a lot to read that morning.

As you come upon the Loop, the entire aspect of the place changes. Huge buildings rise above the flatness of the Midwest. The world's tallest building rises there, symbolizing both the preeminence of Chicago architects and the power of Sears, Roebuck. In a society that counts its citizens as consumers, it is only right that the tallest building belongs to the maximum retailer.

Upper Michigan Avenue. The John Hancock Building. Buildings. Architecture. London had Shakespeare, and Chicago had Frank Lloyd Wright. It was only right that the Loop should become a wondrous place of architecture, a man-made mountain range, spaced and spacious. That its Picasso should be as big as a house and outdoors, so everybody could see it.

Some of the Europeans who had come to work at the bank – the Germans, especially – often remarked that Chicago was the most beautiful city in the United States. The most underrated, they said.

It made for the best postcards: The skyline. The river. The bridges. Lincoln Park.

But then, Chicago isn't about *pretty*. By the time you get to the Loop, you find steel and glass marvels. But to get there you drive through acres of houses and factories and warehouses and depots. Chicago is the city that works. People work here. They have always worked. It is the soul-opposite of places like Nassau, the Bahamas. Chicago is tough. Chicago has big shoulders. Chicago supplied Grant's army, Pershing's army, and Eisenhower's army. Pittsburgh made more steel than Germany and Japan combined, but Chicago turned that steel into armaments.

Chicago was not about pretty, then.

But it is pretty now. It is beautiful. The architecture – pride of place. It is only natural that people want to talk about how pretty it is, that postcards show its most beautiful spots.

Things have changed. Many of the shops and plants and warehouses of Greater Chicago are worn down now, out of use. The great highways and overpasses are worn. Business – busyness – has moved on. The Loop is not only the center of beauty, it is the center of industry, because the industry of America now – you hear it everywhere – is the service industry. And that is pretty. Hotels. Entertainment. Travel agencies. Retailing. Insurance. Advertising. Banking. Kids who once might have worked in foundries or in the stockyards now work in the offices of service industries.

In Chicago the center of this is the point where LaSalle Street meets Jackson Street. There the trinity that formed the foundation of midwestern business stands shoulder to shoulder to shoulder in a three-sided rectangle; the fourth side stood open, down LaSalle Street to the rest of the world.

The limo came east on Jackson and did a left turn on to LaSalle, then let Taylor out in front of the building. The office of the chairman of the bank was on the second floor. There was a private elevator.

On Tuesday, two days before, Reuters had run the story on the bankruptcy rumor.

On Wednesday, the Japanese banks – others, too, but mainly the Japanese – had withheld a billion dollars in CD renewals.

Today was Thursday.

A day and a half had passed since the Reuters story about bankruptcy started making its rounds among the treasurers of the world's banks and corporations. A day and a half was about how long Dave and Kit Taylor had had for their Nassau vacation, before the telephone call. A day and a half wasn't much time.

But some days are longer than others.

This one, this Thursday, was going to be a long day. The run had to be assessed and controlled. The rumors had to be traced and stopped. The investment houses – the financial analysts – had to be reassured. So far the stock market hadn't reacted.

The bank's customers had to be reassured.

And the bank's people.

It was just about 6:30 A.M. in Chicago, two hours before the city's schools and businesses would be fully in motion. But for the bank Thursday had started with Tokyo's morning, not Chicago's, and that was fifteen hours ago. Tokyo's morning had started yesterday, not long after the Continental had closed.

Tokyo's business decisions for today had been made already.

So had London's. So had Frankfurt's.

Let's calm everybody down. There are nearly three thousand officers and managers in this building alone, and most of them are going to spend the day answering telephone calls from people asking them what's happening. Most of these telephone calls will come from other officers and managers. Nobody knows why this is happening. I damned sure don't know why it's happening. Nobody I've talked to knows why it's happening.

Where do we start?

69

"The deposits are still down. The Japanese haven't come back."

"Our people in Europe say the Swiss and the Germans are nervous, but they haven't made a big move. We're still waiting to hear from some of them. It's still a couple of hours before they close for the day."

"What does London say?"

"Well, there seems to be no problem with the British. It's the Germans and the Swiss they're worried about. But there's nothing hanging fire that we can't deal with."

"It's calming down."

"It looks like a two-day run to me. Jitters. First reactions."

"Two-day run?"

"Two- or three-day run."

"That's what I think. Probably. Sounds about right."

"You don't think we should send somebody over to talk to the Japanese and the Europeans? Leo? Al?"

"We could. I guess we could touch all the bases."

"We don't want to overreact."

"We don't want to appear too nervous on this. Let's don't make more of it than it is. It's probably a two-day run."

"That's what I think."

"We have to calm people down around this place."

"We've talked to the senior managers. We'll get 'em together again. They'll spread the word."

"It's slowed down. Everybody knows the rumors were bullshit. I think some of these people are feeling stupid because they reacted so fast. We've got to be careful not to overreact."

"Now, we need to monitor anything new coming over the wire. Bob has people doing that. And there's one other thing. Can we get to the bottom of where these rumors are coming from? Let's get people on this."

"If there are any new ones, any new rumors, let me know what they are right away."

McKnew had the ball for the money market and foreign exchange communications. Dave and Ed would keep in contact with the bank directors. Ed was keeping close contact with the department heads, who in turn would keep the word flowing to their own people and who would talk personally with corporate customers when necessary.

Joe Anderson, the controller, who always wore a white shirt, had as steady a hand as anyone in the bank. He was in on all the major crisis meetings, as was Dick Brennan of the legal staff.

The foreign banks were still McKnew's baby for the time being. It was still trader to trader.

If we have go sit down with the foreign banks – but it's too early to say now; it might not be the best thing to do. Al Miossi is the one to go see them. Al can hit Europe; Leo deGrijs can hit Japan. Let's wait on this.

The big stuff – the Federal Reserve, the chairmen of the New York banks – Dave was handling directly. He knew everybody. Some of them had called him before he had a chance to call them.

But these were the rational functions, the business functions. This was not where the problem had arisen. The problem was the press.

Jerry Buldak was a public relations pro. Since the Tuesday calls had surprised McKnew and Bottum, he and his people were now fielding all calls that came into the bank. This made the bank's story consistent and depersonalized it. "A spokesman" could now be quoted. Nobody was about to get through to McKnew again.

This didn't keep reporters from calling all over the bank to people they might know in the groups. Or calling around Chicago – to the First National Bank, to the Board of Trade, to the state superintendent of banks, to corporate customers, to the man on the street – to see what they thought about the situation. There was no lack of quotable material.

The men and women on Buldak's staff gave a consistent story.

But what was the story?

TWENTY

O N THE MORNING OF THURSDAY, MAY 10, while the leaders of the Continental Bank were deep in crisis-management sessions in the second-floor "war room" on LaSalle Street, few Americans were aware that there was trouble in Chicago.

They didn't know that a billion-dollar bank run had taken place the day before.

The only mention of the Continental rumor to appear in the major print media had been a three-inch item the day before near the bottom of a back business page of *The New York Times*. It was headed, in the *Times*'s smallest headline type, "Continental Bank Denies Rumors."

But the international banking community had had other sources. In less time than it takes for gossip to get around Knot's Landing, the gossip about the Continental had reached every big bank and investment house in America, Asia, and Europe.

Traders don't have to read newspapers. Wire service Telexes and electronic mail reports come directly into the trading rooms.

Newspaper and television editors select what news is fit to print or broadcast, how much to print or broadcast, and whether it was a front-page story or a filler item.

It is an approval process not all that different from a bank's. Editors are credibility people, as bankers are credit people. Reporters in the field know that.

If editors are a credit committee, if they kill some of a reporter's best stuff, they are also a back-up, a means of perspective, that keeps reporters from embarrassing themselves and the paper. There have been exceptions, of course; *Newsweek* bought the "Hitler diaries" and gave them two cover stories before finding out they were someone else's diaries. But that wasn't a credit misjudgment, it was a fraud.

In the trading rooms where Reuters and Commodity News Service and the other wires came in, all their earnings reports and news stories and have-you-heard and what-have-you-heard items intermingle. There are no editors. Not only are trading rooms not *The New York Times* as far as news selection is concerned, they aren't even *The National Enquirer*. They are beyond *The National Enquirer*.

The biggest financial news service in the world is Reuters. The company sells a general news wire of mostly European news to hundreds of newspapers and broadcast companies. But it also maintains an electronic network through which bank, bond, stock, and foreign exchange information goes instantaneously to more than fifteen thousand subscribers around the world. In 1984 it fed more than thirty thousand video terminals and almost seven thousand Telex machines in trading rooms on every continent – for stockbrokers, commercial banks, investment banks, central banks, and government treasury departments.

This is how big Reuters was and how small the international banking community was. Fifteen thousand was about the population of Knot's Landing or of Winnetka, for that matter. In towns that size rumors get around fast, as fast as they do in the banking community. But they aren't as expensive.

TWENTY-ONE

WHERE HAD THE RUMORS COME FROM?
We know that some guy from Reuters called on Tuesday morning and asked for Dave Taylor. Taylor was on vacation, so the guy called Bob McKnew. Bob McKnew answered his own telephone, so he had to talk to the guy. The guy said he wanted to confirm a rumor that the Continental Bank was thinking about filing for bankruptcy.

Maybe McKnew should have used different language. The public relations people seemed to think so. *Preposterous* was a little strong, maybe. A public relations spokesman told the press that Mr. McKnew had not been aware he was speaking on the record.

Given a little notice, McKnew might not have said "preposterous." He might have just told the reporter he was nuts. That is still a time-honored expression in the Midwest.

But McKnew had merely told him no. *Preposterous* meant "no." And then he had gone back to work.

Nobody could have expected the guy to run this slander.

That was the call. But why had the reporter made the call to begin with?

Is it conceivable that he had been sitting around his office on Tuesday morning and, just for the hell of it, had decided to see if he could get something started?

Conceivable, it is. A reporter can say he has a source that had told him this but that he can't reveal the source. It happens all the time. There have been court cases; law enforcement officials have tried to force reporters to reveal their sources, without success.

The Reuters reporter had not called any of the regulators – the comptroller, the FDIC, or the Federal Reserve – to ask the same question.

If there had been anything behind the story, he would naturally have called the regulators, since only they define if there is trouble, genuine trouble, in a bank.

Had there been a source?

A couple of things had happened over the weekend that might have triggered a rumor.

One had happened Friday morning at the Chicago Board of Trade, across the street. Traders on the floor at the financial futures market had talked about problems at the Continental. The Continental had a large open position in the market (meaning a bid for future CDs that had not yet been covered). The position had been on the monitors for a while. Traders had begun to speculate about the bank being unable to get deposits. Eric Dowen, working as a runner on the trading floor, had heard the talk. He mentioned it to his father, a Continental vice president, at dinner on Friday night. Others at the bank had heard about the rumor, too. Someone said people were talking about it at The Sign of the Trader, a bar, on Friday afternoon.

But another thing had also happened, and if there had been a source for the Reuters reporter's question, this was more likely it. This is the incident that Dave Taylor would talk about in staff meetings and that the print media would later use when it tried to make sense of the Continental panic.

Among the numerous political talk shows that come out of Washington – *Face the Nation, Meet the Press, Washington Week in Review,* and so on – was one called *The McLaughlin Group.* It consisted of five old-hand journalists who apparently knew each other very well, who disagreed on just about everything, and who had a hell of a time on the show arguing about politics and politicians and what the world was coming to.

It was carried over the local NBC station at eleven o'clock on Sunday morning, and it lasted for thirty minutes. The journalists would argue about selected topics. They would carry on about one thing for ten minutes, then carry on about something else for another ten minutes, and so on. At the end of the program each was allowed a final individual here's-what's-absolutely-going-to-happen statement without the others interrupting.

That day, Sunday, May 6, a nice morning in Chicago, the McLaughlin group was talking about the monetary policy of the Federal Reserve, a subject which affects average Americans more than they care to know. It was a big subject in 1984. The Fed, symbolized by its president, Paul Volcker, was keeping a tight-money policy at the time, and some of the McLaughlin guys thought that was good because it was holding down inflation, and some thought it was bad because it kept a lot of people and businesses from working.

Robert Novak, one of the group, thought it was terrible, the worst. And when he made his final here's-what's-absolutely-going-to-happen statement, it was this: "The only thing that's going to get Volcker to loosen up would be a bank failure – maybe something like the Continental Illinois in Chicago – or one of those South American countries failing."

The program ended.

Something like *the Continental Illinois in Chicago. One of those South American countries. One of those . . . Chicago banks.*

Cut. Program over.

(There was a small irony, although no one was in the mood for irony. Novak, though identified wholly with his Washington work, owed his column syndication to *The Chicago Sun-Times*.)

You may think nobody watches those Washington television talk shows. They do.

As soon as the program ended, people in Greater Chicago neighborhoods started calling people they knew who worked for the Continental Bank to ask if they had seen it. Tom and Marlene Dowen, in Winnetka, got six phone calls.

People at the Continental Bank were used to cheap shots by then, after the Oklahoma bank failure. If you were an American in Europe during the Vietnam war, you know the feeling. Any European within a ten-country radius was licensed to zap you, to let you know what calamity *you Americans* had caused today. This was not only socially acceptable, it was de rigueur. You gritted your teeth. That was one of the reasons that Kit Taylor had wanted to get Dave out of Chicago for a while – to get away from that kind of thing.

The Taylors had still been in the Chicago area and were getting ready for their Nassau cruise when the NBC station televised Robert Novak's bullet. The phone at their house on Wildwood Lane in Northfield started ringing.

"No, no, we haven't been watching television. We're packing. What group? No, I've never heard of them. He said *what*?"

Like everyone who worked at the Continental in 1984, Dave was used to cheap shots. You go on with life. He had promised Kit the vacation; by God, she was going to have the vacation.

If *The McLaughlin Group* was the root of the Reuters inquiry, why had the reporter waited until Tuesday to take his cheap shot?

A British diplomat in Washington could have heard the Novak remark and passed it along in a phone conversation to a colleague in London. Monday had been a public holiday in England. By the time the London colleague got to work on Tuesday, he might have forgotten the source (if it had been mentioned) but not the suggestion. *I had an interesting call from Washington over the weekend. I understand there's real trouble at that big Chicago bank. Does anyone know anything about it? I'll ask around.*

There was also a big rumor on Tuesday about the Federal Reserve Bank of Chicago. The Fed was going to send a troop of special examiners for an emergency check on the Continental's books. So that rumor went.

"Any ideas about that one?"

"None."

"How about the rumor that a Japanese bank was going to acquire the Continental?"

"Not a clue."

"Now, think. Was there some kind of contact, through IBD or through our branches in Japan, something we may have thought nothing of, that could have suggested such a thing?"

"We've checked all over. There wasn't. There couldn't have been. The Japanese wouldn't buy a bank in Illinois. It would upset their American organizations."

"What do you mean?"

"A Japanese bank that wants to open in the United States has to pick a home state. Once they have, it restricts the business they can do in other states; it's as if they were a U.S. bank then. Most of them take California as a home state; some of them take New York. The Bank of Tokyo is the only Japanese bank that bases its U.S. operation in Chicago. We would know right away if it was them."

"Well, there are a lot of Japanese banks. Don't tell me all of them already have branches in the United States."

"Most of them have. Mitsubishi is about to buy the Bank of California. They're in negotiation right now."

"Maybe *California* is pronounced *Continental* in Japanese."

The fact is that not only was the Reuters rumor false, it was stupid. Once it had been filed, the Reuters people themselves realized it was stupid. It was bad for Reuters. It's okay to be wrong: wrong still makes good copy, and the onus is still on the other guy to back up his denials. But it's not okay to be dumb.

Reuters, like the Continental Bank, is in the knowledge business. Reuters publishes its own book on the trade: *Glossary of International Economic and Financial Terms.* Reuters is an authority. You can't be an authority if you do dumb things, if you reveal your ignorance.

Banks do not file for bankruptcy. Reuters should have known that. *The New York Times* picked up on it at once.

"Bankers in New York said it was not possible for a bank to file for bankruptcy, saying that if a bank were deeply in trouble it would be handled by bank regulators."

It had to have been embarrassing for the Reuters reporter. He had a boss, too. He had missed the point, had not done his homework.

But Reuters had covered itself. In a stroke that a banker might not appreciate but that a media person would, Reuters simply filed a new story saying that McKnew had not denied *bankruptcy* but rather had denied *insolvency*. This was the version that hit the Jiji service in Japan.

Besides, nobody was looking at Reuters. Traders, trying to figure out how to deal with the "news," forgot the original source. They were looking at the Continental Bank.

TWENTY-TWO

NOON ON THURSDAY, MAY 10.

Corporate banking occupied the second, fourth, seventh, and tenth floors. You could stand at the LaSalle Street end of any one of these floors and see lending officers at work all the way to Clark Street.

On the block-long, carpeted corporate banking floors, the oak and mahogany desks were arranged in lending groups. Each group of desks was arranged in strict pattern. The division head had the desk closest to the draped windows, with their wrought-iron grillwork; the most junior associate had the desk farthest from them.

Some worked over papers, with thick credit files stacked on their desks. Many - more than usual - were in quiet conversations on their telephones. The scene was much the same as it was on any day. The sound of corporate banking was still silence, even in May 1984.

On the fifth floor, the sound of banking wasn't silence. Voices shouted there. There was the muted but noticeable noise of machinery. On the fifth floor the sound was rapid communication.

Treasury - and therefore trading - was on the fifth floor. Bob McKnew spent all his time there, except when he was down in the second-floor conference room.

On the fifth floor traders bought and sold government and money market paper, municipal bonds, and foreign exchange. A new group was dealing in "financial futures," the latest innovation in money. A Chicago invention, its physical location was across the street at the Board of Trade. Some people from the bank's treasury were not physically in the room: they were in New York, London, Hong Kong, and Sinapore, in touch by telephone, Telex, and electronic mail. Computer monitors on every trader's desk were glowing green with crisis information.

The wire-service Telexes were there, too. Reuters. Commodity News Service. Others.

The fifth floor was as advanced an instant-communication complex as one would find in any electronically mature part of the world. People who checked the wires and monitors from time to time on a normal workday were watching them constantly now. Three crisis areas were being followed through this equipment.

First, and most important, the foreign bank deposits. The Continental's traders in Japan, Europe, and Chicago were in direct contact – now personal contact – with the money traders at the big foreign banks.

Throughout the 1980s these foreign banks, together with big U.S. investment funds, had kept more than eight billion dollars in overnight money – one-day deposits – with the Continental Bank and more than twice that much in short-term money.

The day before, a billion dollars had disappeared from these sources. The Japanese banks that had always renewed their deposits automatically made a conscious decision to withdraw them.

Were other foreign banks renewing – or withdrawing?

The second electronically followable crises area was the rumors. These would come first over the financial news service wires. Continental Bank people would see them at the same time that the rest of the banking world saw them.

The third was the stock market. The stock of the Continental Bank had not been affected by the rumors on Wednesday. It had closed at $13.25 on Wednesday.

The stock price would be affected by the large investment funds. If the shareholders were sophisticated enough to dismiss the rumors, the stock would hold. Batterymarch, it was observed, was holding fast to its large position.

At noon on May 10, the foreign bank deposit situation seemed to have stabilized. Word was that the Japanese move had been due to jittery young traders whose banks' procedures allowed them to renew or remove daily deposits automatically with the major money center banks without notification to senior executives. They had pulled back a billion dollars yesterday. Now, at noon on Thursday, with London – the last real hurdle – closing, it looked as if nothing so big would happen in Europe. The Japanese might come back in tomorrow.

The second crisis area, the news services, was less reassuring. They moved no money of their own, but they had caused the Japanese movement yesterday. Nobody knew what would come out of them next. Normally it wouldn't matter. Today it did.

There were new items all day long. The foreign banks had calmed down; the wire services hadn't. They weren't going to let this go.

As for the third area, the stock market: at noon Thursday, the New York Stock Exchange reported that the most heavily traded stock on the market was that of the Continental Illinois. The stock, which had been worth $13.25 a share yesterday, was already down to $11.75 today.

The shareholders of the Continental Bank had just lost $60 million.

TWENTY-THREE

*T*HE BIG PROBLEM WAS THE MEDIA; the big question was how to respond to the media. The bank had told the press from the beginning that the rumors were false. Did you then ignore them and wait for the thing to blow over?

"A spokesman for Continental said Mr. McKnew did not realize he was speaking on the record when he responded to the [Reuters] reporter's question."

That sentence was in the three-inch item in Wednesday's *New York Times*. The public relations people were now in charge of statements. Their wisdom was to tone things down.

Normally the rule in business is to say nothing. Quarterly reports and annual reports – the numbers – are published, and they say all that the majority of shareholders want to know. Once a year at the annual meeting, corporation chairmen go through the ritual of responding to nuisance questions about their dealings with South Africa or Chile or other countries whose policies offend the American public's sensibilities. But these questions usually come from people who buy ten shares for the privilege of asking them. Management has language to dispose of them easily.

The ruling precept was, "Never complain, never explain." It is attributed to Henry Ford. Few business managers would disagree with it.

The best way to avoid overreaction is not to react at all. But that response was no longer available to the Continental Bank.

Holding back and rising above the situation would be possible only if the run were a two- (or at most a three-) day affair. The length of the run depended partly on the foreign bankers, but it depended even more on the press.

Journalists and bankers are of opposite trusts. One is pledged to disclosure; the other is pledged to confidentiality. No news is good news for a banker, but it is hardly that for a reporter. Bad news at the Continental Bank was the best news that financial writers, whose work is normally confined to the least dramatic section of the newspaper, had had in years.

But in a curious way the foundations of journalism and banking are alike. They are both dedicated to granting and withholding credit; credibility in journalism can be said to be the same thing as credit in banking. Both have authority to approve. In American tradition the final authority is public opinion, but the public is an authority only when called upon. Banks and newspapers are standing authorities.

The McLaughlin Group on that quiet Chicago Sunday was analogous to a credit committee meeting.

But it wasn't a closed-door credit committee meeting; it was a talk show on television. When Novak, who had the last word, said *Continental Bank* and *failure* in the same sentence, it was authority speaking – even if the only people watching were several dozen Japanese lobbyists in Washington, the staff of the British Embassy, and a few suburban residents of Chicago.

The press is a credit committee, but – unlike a bank – its mistakes, its bad credits, don't show up on its balance sheet. They show up on somebody else's balance sheet – in this case, the Continental Bank's balance sheet.

Thursday afternoon.

The wire service report on top of Dave Taylor's stack – the latest one – was a Japanese news story from Washington.

It said that the Comptroller of the Currency of the United States, the examining authority for American national banks, had contacted some large Japanese financial groups – the Mitsubishi Bank and Nomura Securities – to ask them to assist the Continental Bank.

In the second-floor conference room overlooking LaSalle Street, the heirs to the management of the Continental Bank, a dozen men who had spent most of their adult lives at the Continental in this building, looked at each other.

Only the comptroller of the currency could tell them if this last one were true.

It was not.

By Thursday afternoon the list of fictions was sickeningly long.

A rumor of bankruptcy – not only ludicrous, but technically impossible. Invented.

A rumor of insolvency – equally ludicrous, invented to cover the ignorance about bankruptcy and banking.

A rumor of takeover by a Japanese bank – totally baseless. Invented.

A rumor of Federal Reserve Bank meetings to plan emergency action – totally baseless. Invented.

A rumor that the banking authorities of the U.S. government had asked for private Japanese aid for one of the largest American banks – beyond ludicrous. Invented.

Before the day had ended there was one more rumor. A reporter for *The New York Times* filed these sentences in a story for the next day's editions.

> There were reports that the Board of Trade Clearing Corporation had pulled a large account out of Continental. William F. O'Connor, chairman of the clearing organization, which has no direct connection with the Chicago Board of Trade, did not deny the rumor but said the corporation would continue to work with Continental.

Now the rumor was that Chicagoans were losing faith: people we grew up with, people we talk to every day, traders, the neighbors next door at LaSalle and Jackson.

This was the first rumor that was true.

It wasn't the Japanese; it was the neighbors across the street. Chicago's Board of Trade Clearing Corporation had withdrawn its forty-five million dollars from the Continental Illinois Bank.

TWENTY-FOUR

NOW IT BECAME LIKE A WAR MOVIE. A U.S. Navy submarine goes into Tokyo Bay and attacks. It breaks out through the nets. Then it is trapped by Japanese destroyers. Depth charges explode all around, each one closer than the one before, jolting the trapped crew. There is fear in the eyes of the sailors but also resolution. No change of course, no effort to escape, seems to work. The attacking destroyers pound closer and closer – jolting, rattling, pounding, shocking.

This was a 1943 movie called *Destination Tokyo*. Cary Grant played the captain. John Garfield was in there with him. Alan Hale was there. If Ronald Reagan had been aboard, he might have had the Garfield role.

Few American males born in the 1930s – the grade school and high school kids of the World War II period – didn't see that and dozens of other war movies of the time.

As the depth charges explode, some of the kids crouch down on the floor and are watching through the opening between the seats. Some cover their eyes and watch through their fingers. They are trapped inside the sub with Cary Grant and his crew, fifty fathoms under water and no way to fight back. How long can they hold on? Is there any way out?

And then the captain, his eyes blazing, says, approximately, "We've taken enough of this. Let's go after them. If we're going to go down, let's go down fighting."

He takes the sub up, raises the periscope, and blasts the hell out of the Japanese destroyers with unfailing torpedoes. He takes the crew safely home.

American culture. You might not have read *Les Miserables* or *The Inferno,* but *Destination Tokyo* was definitely part of your personal unconscious. *You fight back.*

On Thursday afternoon Dave Taylor brought Continental and its crew off sea bottom, upped periscope, and launched the torpedoes.

On Friday morning the news of the battle was no longer confined to bank trading rooms. *The Wall Street Journal* had it. Newspapers across America printed AP and UPI items about it. *The New York Times* carried a business-page item with a three-column large-type headline.

CONTINENTAL FIGHTING RUMORS

In a highly unusual move, the Comptroller of the Currency issued a statement yesterday denying "rumors" that the Continental Illinois Bank and Trust Company, the nation's eighth-largest banking organization, was in serious financial trouble.

The statement from the Comptroller, C. Todd Conover, also denied Japanese news wire reports that the Comptroller had asked Japanese or other banks or securities firms to assist Continental. . . .

Not for a decade had the Comptroller's Office felt impelled to issue such a statement on behalf of a particular bank, it said in response to a question.

The comptroller of the currency is part of the Treasury Department. The function of the office is to examine nationally chartered banks to make sure they are sound and to detect trouble before it happens. There are other agencies who send examiners into banks as well. The Federal Deposit Insurance Corporation sends them. The Federal Reserve sends them. State governments send bank examiners to state-chartered banks.

The call to the comptroller was a tough one.

No private bank ever wants to call on the U.S. government for support, either moral or financial. There are any number of reasons for this. Government regulation as it stood was excessive, and the entire banking industry wanted to reduce it. The Washington bureaucrats liked it, though. It gave them more to do.

You run the risk, when you ask bank regulators over for coffee, so to speak, that they will stay for dinner, stay for the weekend, stay for the summer – that you might never get them out.

But Dave Taylor had no choice but to make the call.

If he were to make direct contact with the chairmen of the other Japanese banks, to assure them that the comptroller wasn't cutting a deal with Mitsubishi Bank or Nomura, he had to know it was true. Only the comptroller knew. He had to call him.

In 1984 the comptroller – who is appointed to office – was C. Todd Conover. Except for those members of the staff who dealt with Washington, few Continental people knew the name. Conover had been a California management consultant before he went to Washington. He had been dealing with banks for a few years.

When Dave Taylor called Conover on Thursday afternoon, he read him the text of the Japanese UPI story.

"Is it true?"

"No. Not at all. It's preposterous."

Taylor had not called to ask for support. He called to clarify the rumor.

There is another reason you don't want government involvement. A statement of support from the government implies that you really need support. It had been ten years since the comptroller had issued an all's-well statement on behalf of a bank. Many people remembered which bank that was. It was the Franklin National Bank of New York, the biggest bank failure in American history.

But once you're on the telephone, you start discussing the whole situation. One thing leads to another.

Conover agreed with the Continental Bank people. He was disgusted by the false rumors, too. He agreed that something had to be done.

"This was an unusual enough case that I chose to violate the policy," said Conover. "I decided to do something that was unprecedented. I issued this press release."

Dave Taylor issued one of his own.

Because of the seriousness of the rumors, we are concerned that these stories were not thoroughly checked before they were issued and that more care and caution was not exercised. A responsible investigation would have proved that the rumors were completely unfounded and not worthy of serious news consideration.

The rumors . . . had no basis in fact and should never have been fueled by irresponsible wire-service reports. . . .

We are vigorously examining the origin of these rumors, as well as their distribution by some of the media, and are seriously considering possible legal action. . . .

We have denied these reports, and we appreciate the reassuring statement from the Comptroller of the Currency and the support of our customers and funders, particularly the major domestic money center banks.

The New York Times called it "a vehement denunciation." *Newsweek* called it "a stinging rebuttal."

TWENTY-FIVE

CONTINENTAL HAS PEOPLE WHO WILL SEE THE COMPANY THROUGH.
A little more than two weeks before, on April 23, at just about this time of day, Dave Taylor had spoken to the shareholders for the first time as chairman.

He had talked about the team, the people. About hard work, overwhelming talent, and sheer pride.

Dave Taylor hadn't known these were clichés. They were earnest words for him; the adjectives were pressed like two-hundred-pound weights. He was an earnest man. He believed what he was saying.

To Taylor, banking was a people business. People would see the bank through.

There were eight executive vice presidents, thirty-five senior vice presidents, and two-thousand officers – in all more than thirteen-thousand people at the Continental Bank whom Taylor could call on and whom he had to reassure.

In the twentieth-floor officers' dining area, there was coffee service in the morning, then later luncheon service, cafeteria style. Until the early 1970s all officers had lunched in the elegant officer's dining room on twenty-two. Now they went to twenty. You reserved on twenty-two when you were with a customer or a visitor, or when there was a special group occasion.

A lot of the bank's work was done over coffee on twenty; it was the main circulation spot for officers of all ranks. This was where the inside word got around. This was where rumors were discussed – never more seriously than in May 1984.

From the day of his return to Chicago, Dave Taylor made a point to have coffee there, to greet and be greeted by the troubled officer corps of the bank. He ate his meals there among the officers.

In the troubled air of the coffee room, filled with rumors, it was ironic to recall that the bank had once been so staid that it did not permit coffee breaks for the officers. When Tillie Cummings was president, he had issued an official memo on this. Everybody went out for coffee, of course. But everyone took pains not to leave the building if Tillie happened to be down on the first floor near the revolving doors. They did this out of respect for Tillie.

That week, there were a lot of nervous people walking around the Continental Bank, so Taylor made it a point to keep himself visible.

Contrary to the public image, the people working for American banks are not all cut from the same cloth. When the first rumors broke, some bought them – "I knew it was going to happen. I knew at once it was all over" – and others dismissed them.

Some took the embarrassment personally. And there were those whose first concern was their career.

"I must not be living right," a reporter quoted one Continental officer as saying. "When I graduated from Northwestern, I turned down a job at First Chicago because of all the trouble they were in. I never imagined conservative Continental would end up in a much bigger mess."

Conservative Continental. Nobody really talked like that, except to be quoted.

The line officers, those who dealt with the customers, went to work as always. They walked past the same six great Ionic columns, through the same doors, to the same desks, with the same people, on the same enormous expanse of marble and carpet that was the main banking floor of the Bank. Those line officers simply dismissed the crisis and got on with their work in the unchanged quiet and decorum that, day after day, year after year, confirmed the Now, Then, and Afterward.

"Would the bank go under?"

"Nah. That never even occurred to me," one would say. "It was a mess, sure. People were on the phone with you all day, like the papers said. But we had had so much of that since Penn Square. It never crossed my mind that the bank would go under."

But there were also skeptics, or realists, depending on what you wanted to call them.

"Some of the stuff that was being said was just unbelievable," a senior officer remembered. "You would think to yourself, these guys are hypnotizing themselves."

"When Dave talked, you believed him. You believed eighty percent," a senior vice president said. "That was high. I'd watch him while one of the others was talking, going through this rah-rah, everything-is-going-to-be-fine routine, smiling, cheering – there were times they actually cheered – and Dave was serious, frowning sometimes."

"Have you ever watched an actor," said one of the participants, "who has played the same role so many times that he no longer knows he is acting? After a while, that was the impression I had of the meetings."

Everything is going to be all right.

"It's no big problem," one of the top executives said at an early meeting. "The underwriters tell us they can cover anything. Right, Joe? What do you say about it, Joe?"

And Joe, thrusting his arm upward, would say, "Buy the stock!"

Afterward, one of the division heads said, "I honestly believe some of them didn't think that anything was wrong. It was like Roger after Penn Square."

They actually cheered. They applauded, too.

It was a matter of style.

TWENTY-SIX

ON FRIDAY, MAY 11, THE BANKING WORLD GOT THE OFFICIAL STATEMENTS, the truth, not only from the Continental Bank but from the U.S. government as well.

There were major stories in *The Wall Street Journal, The New York Times,* and newspapers around the country. The *Journal* headlined the drop in the stock price but allowed that most traders agreed that "the hectic trading was based on rumors . . . rather than on any fresh assessment of . . . loan problems." Headlines in other newspapers concerned the rumors themselves. The *Times* carried photographs of the building at 231 South LaSalle and of C. Todd Conover.

The serious press agreed that the rumors were fictions.

There were no more frantic calls from reporters. Everything was out in the open now.

The stock price climbed on Friday.

Around the bank the word was that the crisis, as management had predicted, was a two-day run.

The senior managements of the Japanese banks were reassured, and they were resuming their normal activity with the Continental.

But as it turned out, it wasn't the senior managements who needed reassurance. They weren't the ones who had panicked. In the Japanese system the junior traders are empowered to roll over or replace money market CDs, however big they are, as long as they are one- or two-day maturities. It had been the least experienced Japanese bankers who had cut and run. They were too young to know that banks that big don't fail.

The building at 231 South LaSalle Street stood as formidable as always.

The big second-floor chairman's office on the corner of LaSalle and Jackson had remained unchanged since the days of Walter Cummings. Dave Kennedy had bought the oak paneling and some of the furniture in England from the remains of a baronial manor he had visited as a Mormon missionary. But the paneling's effect was to give an even more "traditional" effect to the office.

It was no small feat. The chairman's office was a marvel of bank design. It was fun to watch the faces of visiting European bankers when they came to Chicago and to the Continental for the first time. "*This is a bank,*" they would say.

When Roger passed the gavel to Dave Taylor in April 1984, the office stood essentially as Kennedy had left it. The chairman's office had an air of timelessness, as if its history were an enormous certificate of deposit, a guarantee that even fate itself could not challenge. No wonder Roger Anderson, seated in this office, had been unable to foresee serious trouble in 1982.

Even now, in May 1984, when the office was a crisis center and people were coming in and out sixteen hours a day, the old spirits were still there. In quiet moments you could look around at the woodwork and think, *This can't be happening. Not in this place.*

TWENTY-SEVEN

AL MIOSSI RETURNED TO CHICAGO FROM NEW YORK ON FRIDAY NIGHT. He took a cab from O'Hare to Wilmette and was home in time for dinner.

It had been a ceremonial trip to New York. For three years now Al's title had been director of international affairs, a ceremonial job. But he also carried the executive vice president title, and among bankers in Europe and Japan he was still by far the best known of Continental's bankers. He had been doing the work more than thirty years. Only one American banker, the estimable G. A. Costanzo of Citibank, might have logged more international travel miles than Al Miossi.

In two weeks, he was to go abroad again, to Europe. There was to be a special reception at the Luxembourg Golf Club in appreciation of the Luxembourg banks who funded the Continental Bank, S.A., in Belgium. There would be a series of calls in Brussels; then he would go on to London, where the main event would be an official dinner at Blenheim Castle, Churchill's ancestral home.

The managers at the bank's once-great New York subsidiary, Continental Bank International, liked to get Al out to the Northeast whenever it could. His customer visits commanded reception at the senior level. There had been a couple of formal dinners in New York restaurants that week. Then he had made calls at some of the New York banks.

91

It was while visiting the offices of Chemical Bank that he learned of the crisis in Chicago. The Chemical banker hadn't called it a crisis, though.

"It's an absurdity," he said. "I thought you would have heard about it by now, but I guess I'm not surprised you haven't. It's the typical over-reaction by the press. You fellows have nothing to worry about, but I know you must be getting fed up with this kind of thing."

The corporate office in Chicago had not called to inform him. But then, why would they? It had been some time since he had been active in senior line management.

By the time he left New York on Friday, everybody on the two bank floors of the Continental Illinois Center building knew about the crisis. When customers weren't telephoning them, they were telephoning Chicago.

Back in Wilmette at dinner on Friday night, Al filled Blanche in on the details. He wasn't worried about it. After thirty-odd years of dealing with crises, Al Miossi was hard to unsettle.

On Saturday morning he looked for news in *The New York Times*. (IBD people customarily look to the *Times;* CBD people to the *Journal.*) There was one small item.

CONTINENTAL RALLY

The stock of the Continental Illinois Corporation rallied yesterday, following a sharp decline Thursday on rumors about the bank's financial situation. The stock closed at $13.375, up from $12. In Chicago, William C. Harris, the Illinois Commissioner of Banks and Trust Companies, said: "Financial institutions doing business with Continental Bank should rest assured Continental will continue to satisfactorily serve its institutional and public depositors." And David G. Taylor, chairman and chief executive officer of Continental, said, "We are beginning to see a gradual improvement in market perceptions as rumors about the bank are being put to rest and calm is being restored."

It looked like a quiet weekend.

Ed Bottum called during midmorning. "Al, we need for you to go to Europe."

"I'm going to Europe next week. I sent you a copy of the schedule."

"We need for you to go right away. Today."

"Today?"

"Tomorrow, then. You've got to be there by the opening of business on Monday morning."

"Where, then?"

"Germany and Switzerland. It doesn't matter which one first."

On that quiet Saturday morning Ed Bottum, Dave Taylor, Bob McKnew, and others were moving anxiously between the second and fifth floors of the Continental Bank building.

The day before, Friday, with the rumors stifled, the stock market bidding up the price of Continental shares, and the Japanese banks calming down, the Continental Bank had suffered the largest bank run in history.

It was the Europeans this time.

In the twenty-four hours following the Reuters rumor story the bank had lost a billion dollars.

In the twenty-four hours following the statement by the comptroller of the currency the bank had lost more than twice that.

Nothing like this had ever happened before.

Nothing close to it.

By Friday afternoon, the bank had lost $3.6 billion in deposits. $3,600,000,000.

TWENTY-EIGHT

MOTHER'S DAY WEEKEND 1984, CAPITALIZED IN THE CONTINENTAL'S HISTORY, was a glorious couple of days for the American banking industry. Yes, there was self-interest among the other banks, as the press said there was, and yes, some of them dragged their heels, and yes, maybe the ignoble "herd" or "sheep" instinct so closely associated with bankers was the real impulse for the noble outcome. But much was at stake for America that weekend, and the banks came through in glorious style.

In a showdown you go to your strongest player, so Dave Taylor went to Morgan. J.P. Morgan had personally stopped the financial panic of 1907; now the name of the head of the Morgan bank was Lewis Preston.

In 1907 J.P. Morgan had shut himself up in his office and played a game of solitaire before deciding to support the stock market, but Preston didn't hesitate even that long. Before the end of the Mother's Day weekend, Dave Taylor in Chicago and Lewis Preston in New York had persuaded the most important U.S. banks to close ranks in a common cause.

They would end the Continental scare, and they would do so with a show of cooperative financial power such as had never been seen before.

Maybe the Continental run was finished that Friday, and maybe it wasn't. Maybe the move on the Continental was a threat to the American banking system – and maybe it wasn't.

But by God, we're not going to sit around waiting to see.

And by God, we'll take care of it ourselves.

"We wanted," Ed Bottum said afterward, "a private solution."

The government would be only too willing to step in and take charge of things.

Some of the bankers were reluctant to join in, but not after they were reminded of that.

Morgan Guaranty Trust was America's class bank.

Morgan was the standard for commercial banks, just as Harvard was the standard for colleges. People argued about it, of course. There were expert polls that ranked Stanford over Harvard. That didn't change anything. The highest affirmative for Stanford was not the poll but to be called "the Harvard of the West," just as Duke did not object to being called "the Harvard of the South" and the Bank of Montreal did not resent being known as "the Morgan of Canada."

In its industry Morgan was Harvard; the largest nine others in its industry made up the Ivy League of commercial banking. The analogy was imperfect. You might call Chase Manhattan the Yale of commercial banks, but Citibank was more like MIT. First Chicago affected the eastern style and would be flattered to be thought of as Princeton West, but the Continental Illinois was pure Chicago and would not have taken an Ivy League connection as a compliment.

It was stretching it to attach *Ivy League* to anything in California. But the Bank of America was the biggest in the world for many years and was obviously in the league. Of course, the only money center cities named individually in Federal Reserve statistics were New York and Chicago. Los Angeles and San Francisco were "all others."

This was, nevertheless, the league, as it was at the start of the 1980s, before the banking turmoils of that decade began.

Bank of America
Citicorp
Chase Manhattan
Manufacturers Hanover
Morgan Guaranty Trust
Continental Illinois
First Interstate
Bankers Trust
First Chicago

While these nine spots were always firm, the tenth changed often, usually between First Interstate and Security Pacific. Mellon Bank, Wells Fargo, Irving Trust, and Marine Midland were at one time all among the top ten.

Although the league consisted of rivals, it functions as a whole in the massive movement of monies. This was what the money market was. Banks, in and out of which huge but unpredictable sums of money flowed each day, were the largest depositors in and the largest borrowers from other banks. The system was like a gigantic ice-cube tray. The water from the filled-up spaces flowed over into the others.

The interbank system rested on the time-set assurance that one member was as good as another. It was understood and in some instances formalized. The brokers who bought and sold the CDs of the big banks in the secondary market allowed each other to substitute any Top Ten CD for another at the same rate. If you ordered a Morgan, you would take a Chemical. It was the same. You would take a Continental. What it was – a CD – was money. Some people thought it was a receipt.

Legends might have come out of that Mother's Day weekend – timeless video-replays for the core of the Continental corps that labored through it.

Even the coldest blood in the building knew what was at stake now and therefore the importance of the effort of that Saturday and Sunday.

Even the least imaginative might have pondered the fact that for the third time in less than two years the same man, Taylor, was being called upon to save the bank. Taylor who had entered there before any of them, who had entered there – at the age of four – *before Walter Cummings*. Not boards of directors but events – the unprojectable, the irrational, the market – had pushed him time after time into this role.

95

Legends. On Sunday and Mother's Day weekend the telephone lines to California became so filled with late well-wishers ("Is everybody's mother in California?" "No. Everybody's in California. The mothers are here.") that there was absolutely no way to get through to the Los Angeles and San Francisco banks. Not even Bill Weiss, a Continental director who ran a phone company, could arrange a line.

Hurried travel arrangements were made to get Miossi to Europe and deGrijs to Japan. Calls were made to the Continental offices in these places to prepare the way.

For long hours in treasury McKnew and the traders went over the funding position, went over alternatives and scenarios of every kind for what might happen in the week ahead.

Dick Brennan, with the other lawyers, fit together documentation that would have taken a corporate law firm weeks.

And some were just there on Mother's Day, part of the corps, keeping themselves ready and available. The list of names itself, the corps, would have made a nice legend.

And never a dour face. Great good humor throughout. Some nice cracks. The American sense of humor. It was the thing the Europeans least understood about us.

"It was kind of like a pledge dinner," Dave said later. In New York and Illinois and California and Texas, banker by banker, one would say, "Tell me how much you need" like at a pledge dinner, and another would turn red in the face (even on the telephone, red) and wish he could change the subject and then take hours to decide.

But all came in.

And on the late afternoon of Sunday, May 13 – Mother's Day – Dave Taylor concluded the last telephone call to California and the last call to Lewis Preston in New York, to go over the final list, the final amounts.

"The deal is done. They're all in."

"What's the total?"

"Four and a half billion."

The Continental affair had produced another first, another all-time grossly exaggerated record. It had created $4.5 billion dollars on a Sunday afternoon, more than twice the entire capital of the Continental Bank.

And it had been a private solution.

Electronic mail operators on the fifth floor stood by to send the announcement (reviewed and reviewed again by the chairman, the president, the legal counsel, the public relations staff, and the treasurer) to the Japanese and the Europeans.

The announcement would tell them that sixteen of the nation's leading banks, with the knowledge of the Federal Reserve System, had joined together to make a $4.5 billion line of credit available to the Continental Bank.

Morgan Guaranty was the leader of this group. It included Citibank, the Bank of America, Chase Manhattan Bank, Manufacturers Hanover, Chemical Bank, Bankers Trust, the First National Bank of Chicago, First Interstate, Security Pacific, Crocker National Bank, Irving Trust, Wells Fargo Bank, First National Bank of Boston, Texas Commerce Bank, and Mellon Bank.

The statement left nothing out.

> Because of the interruption in our normal funding operations caused by the spread of rumors last week, we exercised our ability to borrow from the Federal Reserve Bank, as is customary in cases where temporary liquidity imbalance may occur. We have eligible collateral at the Federal Reserve Bank of Chicago that is available to support additional advances several times greater than the current level of borrowing. We of course have no intention of doing so, nor do we anticipate that need, but it is important that you understand that this very substantial backup funding is available.

Mother's Day was over.

Tokyo was fifteen hours ahead of Chicago, so they were about ready to open for business about now, Leo deGrijs was there to call on all the key players. Al Miossi had left for Germany. Frankfurt was about eight hours from opening for business.

"Jerry Buldak will send the press release out in the morning, so you can expect to see it on television tomorrow. I guess the *Journal* . . . well, obviously the *Journal* won't print it till Tuesday morning."

And the core group of the Continental officers, those who had spent the Mother's Day weekend there, broke into applause.

Very midwestern. Rah-rah-team stuff. Very American.

PART

FOUR

To
Europe

TWENTY-NINE

THE U.S. EDITION OF *THE AMERICAN CHALLENGE* CAME OUT IN 1968, Dave Kennedy's last year with the Continental Bank. He became secretary of the treasury in the first Nixon Administration.

In Kennedy's ten years as chairman the Continental Bank had tripled its size and doubled its staff. It had become the top bank in Chicago –the biggest, the most profitable, and the most widespread.

And the bank had made the American Challenge. It had added the fourth universe, the world, in the Continental "C" that enclosed Chicago, the Midwest, and North America. The state of Illinois still would permit its banks no branches, but the Continental had created a network of banking units in foreign countries. There were six full-service branches, seven representative offices, and twenty foreign affiliates. The international staff numbered seven hundred, one of the largest in the country.

Kennedy, the bank's true visionary, the one who took Chicago to the world, was greatly honored by his staff when he left. His successor printed a special report to the shareholders – "A Decade of Growth and a Management Transition" – that was a tribute to Dave Kennedy the individual. It was in the bank style. If banking was a people business, Dave Kennedy was the right person in the right place at the right time.

Kennedy was succeeded by his vice chairman, Don Graham, who had created the oil and gas lending group in the early 1950s. Don continued his work.

Don was made chairman, Tilden Cummings was made president, and two younger men were given the title vice chairman. The understanding was that they would be the leaders of the Continental Bank in the future.

Both were from the noted 1946 class of recruits, the World War II naval officers who symbolized the best of America. One was John Perkins, from the bond department. The other was Roger Anderson.

It had taken almost twenty years, but Roger finally got out of the international department. That assignment hadn't ruined his career after all.

Al Miossi got the job as head of IBD.

THIRTY

I N AMERICAN BUSINESS'S INTERNATIONAL EXPANSION OF THE 1960s, there was always the underlying question of how far to go. Yes, the economies of the world were more interdependent than ever before. Yes, the Europeans and the Japanese were becoming more competitive each year. Yes, the American Challenge had brought great profit to the Fortune 500.

But how long would this last? How long would it be before the conditions that had created the phenomenon would turn against it?

In the Continental Bank some thought the expansion had gone far enough and that with Dave Kennedy gone the bank would pull back and resume its emphasis on the things it had always done. Don Graham, Kennedy's successor, had no international experience and presumably no international interest. His companion at the top, Tilden Cummings, the bank's president, was a confirmed and outspoken skeptic about the bank's role in international business.

But Don Graham ultimately out-Kennedyed Kennedy. The international role of the Continental – and its reputation – kept on growing, along with the American Challenge.

THIRTY-ONE

THE BANK MADE BRUSSELS ITS MAIN LOCATION ON THE EUROPEAN CONTINENT. It hadn't been planned that way.

The Continental's early strategy had been to make selective investments in different countries but to let the Europeans run their own banks. They could do it better than we could.

This gave the Continental's operations a local-national identity during the dicey period of the American Challenge. It won them a great deal of goodwill from existing managements – whose opinions of the situation were thus validated – and made available more local currency financing to U.S. firms than a branch could have; since interbank markets were limited for foreign banks or did not exist at all.

The willingness to trust the other fellow to do things right was very much a Kennedy gesture, and a midwestern one. It wasn't typical of either European or New York banks.

Only after the Dutch partners cut a separate deal that affiliated them with Morgan Guaranty did Continental send its first bank manager to Continental Europe to actually run a bank.

The Continental owned part of the Dutch bank, and the Dutch bank and Continental each owned half of a Belgian bank. So a trade was made: our Dutch shares for their Belgian shares. The Continental would take a hundred percent of the Belgian bank.

It hadn't been planned that way.

There was a standard rap on Americans in Europe. We didn't know the languages. We didn't know the customs. We didn't know the culture. We didn't even know one country from another.

True, it was a little shocking for Belgians and Finns visiting the United States to find that nobody here had heard of their countries.

There was a Belgian kid at the bank in the late 1960s who told about spending a summer in Lubbock, Texas. "Nobody knew what Belgium was," he said. "Nobody. I found two people who said that they had even heard of Belgium. One thought it was a town in Denmark. Another thought it was somewhere beyond the iron curtain."

Maybe if he had said Brussels. A lot of Americans knew about Brussels sprouts – hated them – and many would have recognized the name of the Belgian capital, which by the late 1960s was the kind-of capital of Europe. The European Common Market had put its headquarters there. There were three U.S. ambassadors in Brussels: one to the country, one to the Common Market, and one to NATO.

Brussels was also the European headquarters for U.S. multinational corporations. Some of them had tried Geneva or Paris for a while. Brussels was better, they found.

That's where Ed Bottum was sent in 1968: to Brussels.

THIRTY-TWO

ORE THAN ANYTHING ELSE THE DOUBTS ABOUT INTERNA-
TIONAL BUSINESS SEEMED TO BE RELATED TO CULTURAL
IMAGES; they were never quite eased. Don Graham, who was
born in Pittsburgh, educated in Chicago, and lived in Wilmette, was a
quick, personable, good-humored man who was perceived as being at
home in the University Club of Chicago but not at the Mexican bankers'
convention.

It was hard to change the long-standing image of bankers with only
a recruiting brochure depicting all-American boys, and it was harder still
to convince Europeans that the same all-American boys were up to entering the sophisticated world of international finance. International business still called for suave types, for James Bond moving easily and ar-
rogantly through the casino. It was reluctant to admit Tom Sawyer.

It was reluctant, too, to admit that French, once the language of
diplomacy, was no longer the language of international affairs. English
was that language – specifically, American English.

What you see is what you get. The American Challenge was being
run by midwesterners, in their own style. The results were evident, but
the image didn't fit.

With all the unlikely Americans being sent to Europe, the assignment
of Edward S. Bottum to manage La Banque European d'Outre Mer was
exceptional.

In the upper levels of international banking, such a thing could have
happened in 1968 only at the Continental.

Some of the international people were upset about it.

"Why do they do this? Here's a nice guy with no knowledge whatsoever of European banking. No interest. He's been through six weeks of Berlitz and speaks three words of French. They say he's a credit man, but who has he been calling on? Correspondent banks in Iowa. Ninety percent Rotary Club public relations.

"We have to compete with Citibank and Chase and Bank of America people who have been in the field for years. How can we do it if we have to spend all our time explaining what it all means?

"You'll spend 90 percent of your time educating him, and then he'll go back and call on Iowa banks again. So he can tell them about exports."

Some of the international people were upset. For a couple of years they had been laying the groundwork to open the way for a Chicago bank that most Europeans had known even less of than Americans know of Finland. Now they send some guy out of Group E.

"Why do they keep doing this? What do they think they have to prove? The Chicago people just aren't comfortable being an international bank."

Well, maybe not. Maybe it was taking a while.

But when you looked at the new symbol of the Continental Bank – those four parts, those four universes – you were reminded that two out of the four were Middle America, three of the four were America, and all of the four were basic banking.

And if the Continental Bank was to retain the character that made it different from the other big banks, all four of those universes were going to have to get along with each other.

That was the American way.

We just don't aspire, friends, to be a European bank. Or a New York bank, thank you. We like what we are.

Ed Bottum was core bank, One of Us. If Ed Bottum went into international banking, that meant it was really okay. It was safe. The bank wouldn't ask someone like Ed to do something that would cost him his place in Chicago if it didn't turn out well. And if international in fact turned out to be a winner, then you were covered both ways.

And besides, this guy was an unbelievable candidate. Earnest. Right. Correct. Straight ahead. Businesslike. He had paid his dues. He took it all with the maximum seriousness. He was also a true Continental Bank man in the sense that the bank came first, his career second, and the industry third.

He went over there to make this Belgian bank comprehensible to the Continental organization.

106

THIRTY-THREE

I T WAS ALWAYS THERE, the divide between the international side
and the domestic side. Always that difference. Roger Anderson
wouldn't have been comfortable with the word *ideology*. It wasn't
a business word. But that's what the difference was: ideology. Just as
it was between Chicago and New York, between America and Europe,
between Us and Them.

Every few years the need to establish "credibility" between international and domestic would come up. You had to do it with people, with
exposure. Ed Bottum was far from the first "real" Continental man who
had been drafted into international.

That was how Roger Anderson had ended up there, only he had been
Walter Cummings's idea of a real banker, enough to give credibility to
the unfortunate foreign division. Next to the Roger of 1949, Ed looked
like James Bond.

After Roger, Wayne Allen, an Iowa farm boy out of Coe College
and Group E, had gone over to London to head the first real overseas
branch of the Continental. And after Wayne there had been Gerry
Keeley – a Chicago boy, Fighting Irish, Group F for Michigan and Wisconsin and Minnesota. Keeley definitely hadn't wanted to go; both his
and Pat's families lived in Chicago. But Homer Burnell told him that
when Mother Bank called, you had to answer. So he did. He was run-

ning the London branch now that Wayne had been brought back to Chicago as head of Asia-Africa.

It was always there, that divide.

The problem was, once credible people were sent to IBD to give IBD credibility, they weren't credible anymore themselves. They were on the other side now. They weren't real credit men.

You couldn't know if they had changed or not. You didn't see them enough anymore.

These guys over in Europe and Venezuela and Brazil – what were they doing? You couldn't get a straight answer out of them.

"I have to live with these people," they would tell you, and it was damned hard getting anything done right.

You had to ask yourself, Are they working for us or for them?

So then a few years later some other people would be sent over for credibility, as if that were a new idea.

THIRTY-FOUR

*B*ANKING IS A PEOPLE BUSINESS, and the key to it is having the right people in the right places. That was the part of it that seemed to trouble Roger the most. How could we open offices in all these places now if we aren't sure of the people? It wasn't that he was against expansion; he just wasn't sure the bank was ready.

There was no way to analyze it. On one side he had Al Miossi, who was ready to send untried people out to run offices just because of some instinct or other. On the other side he had Dave Kennedy, who was only too happy to let him do it. *We have to go when the opportunity presents itself,* they said. There was no way to slow it down, but no way to analyze it, either, to really prepare.

And it was too late now, because they'd already moved. They were everywhere.

Roger felt all right about Ed Bottum going to Belgium. He was out of the commercial department. There was a bank to run. It was a right situation.

The word around the IBD was that Ed was the last of Dave Kennedy's personal selections. Kennedy was the visionary who had held the whole culture together. But actually Dave had had a little help on this one. Ed was John Jones's idea. Jones, who was still running the trade finance group, wasn't a visionary. He just had a very clear sight of things. And he was the one man in the bank that Roger trusted the most then. That's how Ed went over.

Whoever did it, they picked a winner. No Indiana banker ever did a better job than Ed did in Brussels.

THIRTY-FIVE

SOME WOULD LOOK BACK ON THAT PERIOD AS THE GOLDEN AGE, a time of innocence. You didn't know that you weren't supposed to be able to do what you were doing so well. But then, those were the adjectives the Europeans had for Americans: *Innocentes. Naifs.*

Before many days went by, Ed had everybody in the Brussels bank on an open-door policy. In Chicago everything was open. People didn't use offices too much – there were open platforms with desks in groups, no secrets. But in Europe there were offices, and all the doors on the second floor, the management floor, were closed. It was custom. That was a custom he changed.

"You want everybody to be able to walk right in and see you," he explained. "You don't want any barriers."

In just about the same time he had everybody on a first-name basis – at least when he was around.

Jean. Franz. Hubert. (U-bare). Jacques. André.

"Franz, where did Jacques go? We didn't finish."

"Who?"

"Jacques."

Confusion, still, some weeks afterward. They really didn't know the first names.

"Ah, you mean Monsieur Philippe."

"Right. Jacques."

Before long, he had a training program set up. A calling program. A credit section. Memos everywhere.

There was a bank newspaper before it was over, in English, with group shots of the employees.

Head shots of the winners of a promotion for bringing in the most retail customers. Ask your friends to bank with us. Nobody had ever seen such a thing. They all asked their friends to bank with Banque European d'Outre Mer.

Which was about to become Continental Bank, S.A.

A name change. Not too debatable. Among the many things the Americans brought the bank was a better name.

Now the name could be the same in Flemish Antwerp as in Walloon Brussels. Continental Bank, N. V. Continental Bank, S.A.

And to think that not that long ago there were those in Chicago who thought that First National of Chicago had the better name. But not in international banking. Not at all.

Continental Bank, S.A., had the best foreign exchange trader in Europe, Herman Veltman. A rollicking trader who was seldom wrong, he dazzled the analysts. It also had the best business development officer in the world, Albert Read. British Commando of World War II. Raised in Belgium. Three native languages. That's what you get by being raised in Belgium.

It was a golden age. Albert Read and Neil Franzen were opening business everywhere. They were surprised to see us, but not for long. They never asked twice, "And what are you doing here?" And Eddie was managing the bank.

Caterpillar came in via Belgium. The Continental Bank hadn't had a relationship with Caterpillar since Walter Cummings cut somebody off in the 1930s.

CBSA – the new acronymn now – brought them in. Ralston Purina. Monsanto. IT&T. Esso. Allen Harrison was there with Esso. You could learn more about banking from Esso than from any bank.

Ed was always learning. That was a code. You can learn a lot there. It was a Continental Bank code, but particularly with Ed. He might have been a teacher if he hadn't gone into the navy and then to Harvard Business School. His father was on the agriculture school faculty at Purdue.

Professor Bottum.

Earl Butz was on the faculty at Purdue, too. And there was another professor whose name was Outhouse.

Bottum, Butz, and Outhouse. Famous in Purdue lore.

The Belgians – on a first-name basis – called him Monsieur Derrière. He liked it a lot. He was used to kidding, and it rolled off him like water off a duck's back. He was early bald, but that was a help in this job. It gave him more seriousness. You can't get away from the American movie image, but Europeans credited baldness as a sign of serious banking.

There were the cultural adjustments, too. At a bank party he went to the bathroom and thirty seconds later one of the female clerks – a blond, loud farm girl – came in and almost sat down beside him.

"Do you know what just happened to me?" he said to another American in the safety of the outer room, pale and wide-eyed. This was a business school problem for you.

"It's not the men's room, that's why."

"It's not the men's room? You mean it's the ladies' room?"

"No. It's just the WC. Everybody uses it."

"Why didn't you tell me, for Christ's sake?"

"I didn't know. I just found out. I'm glad it was you, though, instead of me."

Then there were the cool moments, the sophisticated stuff, blending into the European mode. The formal dinners at the elegant restaurants in downtown Brussels – La Cygne, on the Grand Place, in particular.

111

In its great restaurants, Brussels was unexcelled even by Paris. What the people here lacked in exuberance they made up in cuisine. Every second doorway was a restaurant. When they weren't eating, they were planning their next meal. And the wines. And the receptions.

THIRTY-SIX

THE CONTINENTAL OPENED IN AMSTERDAM, IN FRANKFURT, AND IN PARIS. Neil Franzen, the first rep in Belgium, was sent over to manage the Paris branch and open it amid the student riots of 1968. Back and forth to Brussels on the TEE during that period. "Maybe I should have stayed here," he would say. Great eyewitness stories of wreckage, though.

The bank had a manager inside the Banca Private in Milan now, and the partnership in Spain was producing incredible results. Forty percent of all the multinationals in the country were on the books of Banco Atlantico, which could move money from Madrid to Barcelona in one day; the big Spanish banks were still taking fifteen.

In Spain a Basque named Jesus Laucirica ran the main branch in Madrid. He had put together his own right-stuff crew, and people marveled at them. We had Jesus in the south and Albert Read in the north. American bank reps in Madrid dropped by for casual visits to see if we could give them any ideas.

The open doors were all across the Continent. The treasurers over from the States remarked the contrast.

"You guys sure have a different way of doing business over here," the man from Maremont said. "I went over to the Chase office and had to wait for thirty minutes in the outside lounge."

"They have to do that. If the guy let you come right in, you might think he wasn't busy with important things. So you might think he was less important. He's very important."

"This place changes Americans."

"Well, I know the Chase rep, and he's a European. But some of the Americans change. It's the European way. You can't answer your own telephone, for example."

"Do you people answer your own telephone?"

"Oh, yeah. We answer our own telephone."

THIRTY-SEVEN

IT WAS A GREAT PERIOD. You were fortunate to have been born an American in the twentieth century, even if you did have to defend the country more. People gave you problems about Vietnam – your face and your accent were the American flag, and you were accountable; it seemed as if Vietnam made possible the voicing of a lot of old complaints about Americans.

A lot of American kids over in Europe for the first time had a hard time with that. They had thought everybody loved us, but they were hearing terrible things. There were marches and the worst kind of language on placards. It was confusing for them.

And as the man from Maremont said, some Americans changed. A lot of them did. There were Instant Europeans – Europoids – all over the place. People originally from Akron and Lexington themselves blanched at the sight of American tourists on the Rue Montaigne. ("Mon Dieu, Pierre, have you ever seen such a thing?") Their accents suddenly changed, becoming less animated and more worldly. ("We've seen it all haven't we, Pierre?") They were careful to avoid the restaurants and hotels where Americans were known to go.

But if you had read de Tocqueville on the other hand or *The Innocents Abroad, Dodsworth,* or *Tender is the Night,* on the other – all by midwestern writers – then you knew it was just more of the same old stuff. Europeans thought Americans were all right except for those few traits, the traits that were different from the Europeans'. And of course, Americans felt that Europeans were all right by the opposite standards.

It was a rough time for track record people, for those who believed they knew the place of things and the role of people. Things weren't staying in their place. People weren't sticking to their roles.

Some of the IBD people had thought Ed wasn't right for the Brussels job because he had too much Indiana in him. And a lot of traditionalists in Continental Europe and Continental Bank thought that the bank had no business leaving the American Midwest.

It had to do with place.

THIRTY-EIGHT

T HE AMERICAN CHALLENGE WAS A LONG CAMPAIGN.
For those who saw it through with the Continental Bank, there was a feeling of triumph afterward.

A formal dinner to open the European meetings was held in March 1972 on the top floor of the new Banco Atlantico building on the Avenida del Generalisimo, Number 407, in Barcelona.

The tallest building in Barcelona then was twenty-two stories high, and this was it. There was a sweeping view of the city from three sides of the great dining room.

The Barcelona meetings had the air of a victory celebration. More than a successful game, it had been a successful climb. The Continental was at the top of the hill. No more boosterism was needed. It was sinking in on everyone there that the expedition had arrived, the explorer corps.

Images die hard. This was for real.

Don Graham was ebullient. He and his wife, Jo, were at the center table in middle of the room. Michele Sindona, hearty and not quite boisterous, was there, as were Prince Jean d'Arenberg from Brussels, Casimiro and Lola Molins of Banco Atlantico, and Al Miossi.

Gail Melick, the bank's great operations mind, joined the European scene for the first time. Hearty and expansive, he sat at the same table with Antonio Gil of Banco Atlantico. He gave Antonio the damnedest English exercise he could ever want to have. Dave Taylor, the wizard

115

of the Chicago treasury operation, was ever more involved in the European markets; he sat at another table. Ed Bottum was there, over from Chicago, where he was the head of the European group. Gerry Keeley, the smiling Irishman who had authored much of what was happening, was there from Chicago, too, never looking better. Joel Smith, now running the New York subsidiary, had flown in from Asia; he had been acupunctured along the way and was able to stand up straight. Wayne Allen, who had gone to London to work at the new merchant bank, Continental Bank Limited, was there. So were Tom Dowen, in charge of the new European headquarters in London, and Roger Sherman, who had followed Ed to Brussels.

The Banco Atlantico people shared tables all over the room. There were also people from the Banca Privata in Milan, from Continental Bank, S.A., in Brussels, and from Conill Bank, A.G., in Vienna.

And there were people from the branches: from London, Amsterdam, Frankfurt, Munich, Athens, and Paris – everywhere.

It was where everything was happening. It was the symbol of what had happened.

Much of it was due to the Spaniards, for sure. They do these things so well; they go far beyond what anyone else would do. An unexpected kinship had formed between the two groups. Maybe it was the similar destinies of Barcelona and Chicago; each was the prime motor in its country, and both were held down by convention. Maybe it was also the shared sense of humor and the shared openness that the French called naiveté in both of them.

There were four days of meetings and celebrations. The guys from Chicago found a man named Mr. Baseball – Amadeo Bisbal of Banco Atlantico; he never figured out what they were laughing about. There were meals and heavy conversations and great good humor in the Barrio Chino and at every top-floor restaurant in the city; all reservations were made in the name of Manuel Fernandez of the Madrid office. Half of them were rethought and canceled. He felt he could never go back to Barcelona.

Don Graham was exuberant, caught up in it all, with his arm around the shoulders of Jesus Laucirica, he said, "This is our little guy in Madrid. Our little guy. What a tremendous little guy!" Jesus had half the multinationals in the country on his books. He didn't know what to make of this, but what the hell. These were nice American boys. Sindona there was smooth and rich. He could have bought the room. He was trying to convince Don to buy another 24 percent of Banca Privata.

And Wayne Allen. Wayne was as talky as ever. He couldn't get the attention of the senior officers, so he buttonholed any of the field managers he could isolate in the bar of the Metropole Hotel to tell them that things were not right with the bank's new merchant banking venture in London.

"We've got to do something. Nobody will listen to me."

Wayne's was the only negative voice in those meetings, even in the side sessions in the hotels and restaurants. There was too much to celebrate.

Neither of the men the Spaniards most wanted to see were there that night. Dave Kennedy was now Nixon's roving ambassador for trade. Roger was back in Chicago, running the commercial banking department.

But they both appeared in Spain shortly afterward, in the short and strangely prophetic April 1972. Dave was in Madrid at the end of the week; the Continental people who had gone there from Barcelona saw him. Roger came through Barcelona a few weeks later.

Roger spoke to a roomful of Catalan industrialists.

"Roger," said Guillermo Banares afterward – he pronounced it *Royer,* "is perhaps more the figure of a banker that Europeans identify with."

He meant it to be circumspect. Guillermo was a gentleman.

But they couldn't help wanting Roger to be chairman of the bank. He was the model. If 231 South LaSalle Street was what a bank looked like, Roger Anderson was what a banker looked like.

The Barcelona dinner, the twenty-second floor, the view across the Mediterranean night, the city lights below, the harbor to the South, the famous mountains, Montjuich and El Tibidao, in the near distance—something about the night, the expanse of the view, evokes a nostalgia that the daytime sessions—blended in with a thousand other business scenes—cannot. The event in memory seems ideal. It did at the time. The conditions, the view, the company of the people there—it was a great occasion. The Continental people felt good about it, at home in it, even those who were in Europe for the first time and still wary about being thought foolish. The Banco Atlantico people were emotional.

It was a great family reunion. This was a midwestern bank. We could call it family.

No one can remember what the outstandings were on that date, or what the deposit figures were, but all who were there remember the scene. It was a peak in the folklore. For Don Graham it was an exhilaration beyond any other. It swept him up and swept him away.

In fifteen years, wrote Jean-Jacques Servan-Schreiber in his famous book, American companies in Europe would be the third largest economic force in the world. But it didn't happen. The American Challenge was coming to an end.

PART

FIVE

*Meet
the
Press*

THIRTY-NINE

*I*N MAY 1984 AL MIOSSI WAS THE LAST OF THE VETERAN INTERNATIONAL BANKERS AT THE CONTINENTAL. He been calling on foreign banks for thirty-five years. His was the only name that the Europeans would recognize for sure.

Al first went to Europe forty years ago, in 1944, when he and some friends of his had been under fire in the U.S. Army's entry into Italy. He had gone to Stanford after the war, then to the Thunderbird foreign business school in Arizona. He was sent to Tokyo and then to Manila by the Bank of America afterward.

Growing up in California with the Pacific on one side and Bank of America everywhere else, it was natural to develop an interest in international banking. Al also had a couple of natural advantages for the trade. He was born looking like a banker; slim, pale, serious, and, some said, wearing a three-piece suit – and he had the perfect international banker's name. *Miossi* sounded Italian, so it was a good introduction in all the Latin countries, but its origin was Swiss, which took care of the rest of Europe. Add to that the Japanese tendency to read it *Mioshi*, and you had the perfect international banking name.

It was perhaps least effective in Chicago, where love had delivered him in 1953. He had left the Bank of America, left California, and moved permanently to the winter zone in order to marry Blanche Methe.

121

To look at Al – the image of the banker, the alderman, the principal – you wouldn't think he would do such a thing but he did. He was, as the old bankers used to say, a people person. His primary emotion was loyalty, and he elicited loyalty. His primary loyalties at the Continental Bank were to Dave Kennedy and Roger Anderson.

In the early days of the Continental's international business, the calls on foreign banks were made by these three men: Dave Kennedy, Roger Anderson, and Al Miossi.

There was high protocol when you called on foreign banks.

Imposing waiting rooms and high-vaulted ceilings. Buildings as old as Europe. Cathedrals. Stone. The Bank of England. El Banco de España. The Bundesbank. Hallways. Silence.

Each city had its financial district, and since the cities were all very old, since everything had been in place for so long, it was as if the financial district itself were a foundation. You called on all the banks. In Lisbon you could walk across the street from one to the other on the Rua de Oro. They were all together. So much wealth, so much substance, all in one place.

Among the ruling society of Europe, commerce had something of an odor. For them rank was with the institutions and the traditional professions: the law, the Church, medicine, the university, the military. Only there did you get titles to precede your name: Doctor. Professor. Counsellor. Colonel. In Spain the career axiom for young hidalgos was *"O la iglesia, o la marina o la casa real."* The Church, the navy, or the royal house.

Higher purpose. Above lucre.

Knowledge. Service.

The other thing the professions had in common was that they were all housed in magnificent physical structures. Forts and hospitals, halls of justice, great columned and domed buildings, magnificent in stone and concrete and marble. They were halls of congress, of knowledge, of great works.

Maybe this was how, from the middle nineteenth century, bankers edged into the circle of the professions. Bank buildings were cathedrals. They had the biggest, widest columns – Doric, Ionic, and Corinthian – in town. They were symbols of a greater purpose. And bankers didn't directly engage in commerce, in the dirty work. They just banked commerce and managed its financial resources – the clean and silent work.

The attire of banking was more formal than that of commerce. If not robes or cassocks or dark blue uniforms, then dark blue suits with shined black shoes and dark, striped ties.

For American bankers in the 1950s and 1960s, there was a need for particular discretion in the bank cells. It was not so much that Europeans considered Americans new to international banking; Europeans considered Americans new to everything. It was that we had much more money.

In 1964 at the middle point of the Continental Bank's international expansion period, only 110 banks in the world had more than a billion dollars in deposits. More than a third of them were American banks.

Of the fifteen largest banks in the world, eight were American. Bank of America, Chase Manhattan, First National City (later Citibank), and Manufacturers Hanover were first through fourth, in that order. Chemical was seventh, Morgan ninth, Continental thirteenth, Security–First National (later Security Pacific) fifteenth.

The largest bank in the world, Bank of America, had $14 billion in deposits in 1964.

Such dominance called for special discretion.

As he flew to Frankfurt in May 1984, Al Miossi didn't have to worry about European bankers feeling overwhelmed by the size of American banks.

In 1984 only three American banks – Bank of America, Citibank, and Chase Manhattan – were among the world's top thirty in deposits. The largest of them was fourth. The top three banks in the world, five of the first ten, fourteen of the first thirty, were Japanese. French, British, and German banks were the largest in Europe.

The Continental Bank, which had been thirteenth largest in the world in 1964, was now fifty-sixth. And it was dropping fast.

FORTY

AL MIOSSI STARTED THE WEEK IN FRANKFURT BECAUSE ALBERT SONNTAG, the Continental's manager in Germany, had been able to get appointments and the Swiss manager hadn't. Al called on old friends at the big three German commercial banks – Deutschbank, Commerzbank, and Dresdner Bank. Then he paid an official call on the Bundesbank. The German central bank had no deposits with the Continental, but protocol, not to mention its influence with the private banks, demanded the call.

The Germans had received the wires, yes. They were formal and cordial, with one exception, veteran international bankers whose friendships went back decades.

They were also rather embarrassed by the purpose of the meeting. They weren't comfortable. What had happened was unpleasant, difficult to talk about, as if adultery had been committed and had to be aired.

Yes, the wire had been received. The support agreement of the American banks was impressive. *Yes. We are studying the texts. I have them here.*

"By the way, you know, do you, that the wire was addressed to our chairman?"

"Yes. It is signed by our chairman."

"Your chairman is Mr. . . . Taylor?"

"Yes."

"And Mr. Roger Anderson?"

"Mr. Anderson is retired."

"Yes. The wire is addressed to our chairman. He must consult with the members of the board, of course."

A visit at one of the German banks was more delicate than the others. There were new people in charge. This was the bank that was known as "never having made a mistake." If you have never made a mistake, you are not easy when others make them.

"Now, the position of Mr. Taylor is – ?"

"He is the chairman of our bank."

"None of our managers seems to be familiar with the name."

"Mr. Taylor became chairman in February."

"And Mr. Conover?"

"Mr. Conover . . . Mr. Conover is the comptroller of the currency."

"He is with the Federal Reserve?"

"No. His office is in the Treasury Department."

"Mr. Regan is the treasury minister."

"Yes. The comptroller is a separate office – the examining authority."

"He does not control the currency? The money supply?"

"No."

"The message was somewhat unusual."

"Yes, it was. We'd all like to calm things down as much as possible. The rumors were totally mistaken from the beginning."

In many of these meetings there were long pauses in the conversations.

The Frankfurt banker had brought a file, a thick file, with him. It is customary in banking to keep detailed files on all corporate customers and on correspondent banks. Reports of each visit – call reports or note sheets – are written for these files.

"Mr. Miossi, I think I should remind you that less than two years ago your bank came to see us here and lectured us quite severely about our loans to Poland."

"I'm aware of that visit, sir."

"It was, as I recall" – he thumbed through the file pages – "a Mr. deGrijs of your bank."

"I believe it was."

"Mr. deGrijs is Dutch, I believe."

"Originally Dutch. He is American."

"I understand he visited all the German banks. He was quite severe about our lack of judgment in lending to Poland. I understand that your bank reduced some credit lines to the German banking industry on this account."

"That I cannot say."

"Mr. Miossi, I must point out to you that our bank had fewer loans to Poland than your bank had to the state of Oklahoma."

FORTY-ONE

IN CHICAGO THE MONDAY MORNING AFTER MOTHER'S DAY WEEKEND WAS QUIET.

There was only a single item in the press, a small story in *The Wall Street Journal:* CONTINENTAL ILLINOIS STOCK GAINS AS RUMORS APPEAR TO DIE DOWN.

> Most of the rumors were far-fetched, but Continental issued a statement late Thursday denying them and said it was investigating their origin.

It was essentially the item *The New York Times* had carried on Saturday. The *Journal* doesn't publish on Saturday.

No press releases about the Mother's Day deal could be circulated until this morning. It would appear on the Monday evening television news. *The New York Times* and *The Wall Street Journal* would print it in the Tuesday morning editions.

There was a tired crew at 231 South LaSalle on Monday morning.

Wires had been sent to the foreign banks; the statement had been released to the press. The show was on the road. There was nothing to do now except wait for the reviews.

Or as they say in business, to see what the market says.

The stock went up on Monday. Before the Reuters story the week before, it was trading at $13.25. Then it had dropped to $12. Now it was back up to $13.625.

FORTY-TWO

*I*N AMERICAN BUSINESS THE WORD FOR "PROVIDENCE" IS THE MARKET. *The Market* is the business word for "history," too. It evokes what Adam Smith called "the invisible hand," what Luke Skywalker called "The Force," what Norman Mailer called "the bitch-goddess." For the businessman, for the trader, all these things were *the market*.

In the market on May 14, 1984, it was only the paper numbers that were large. The people numbers were not large. And it was the people numbers that mattered that day. It was not as if it were October 29, 1929, and tens of thousands of citizens panicked the stock market, or winter of 1933, when tens of thousands of others lined up for blocks during real bank runs, waiting to claim money that they thought, because they weren't bankers, was there, but that wasn't there.

There were perhaps two hundred international money market banks in all. Of those, fifty were important. Of those, maybe twenty were crucial.

A bank in this group, on an ordinary day, could have a half a billion dollars on deposit at the Continental Bank.

One bank. $500,000,000.

No bank would lend that much money to a single company. There are legal limits as to how much a bank can lend one company, even General Motors or Exxon or Sony. In the United States that limit was 10 percent of your capital. So in 1984 the Continental could lend about $175 million to one company. Morgan could lend $250 million. Citibank $480 million. To one.

But companies aren't banks. They are not part of the banking system, in which the electronic flow of money has more to do with balancing the books than with formal lending. Banks don't *lend* each other money; these funds are not shown in a "loan" category. They are called deposits, or placements, or borrowed funds. It would have taken a full credit approval process and a Grade 21 – the highest – lender for Sears, Roebuck to get a $50 million loan from the Continental Bank. By contrast, a junior money market trader at the Mitsubishi Bank could do a one-day, $50 million bank rollover without even asking – or telling – a senior officer about it.

It was true, as Nelson Bunker Hunt lamented, that "a billion dollars isn't what it used to be." But it was also true that "all the money in the world" was a lot more money than it had ever been before. One reason there was so much more of it was that it was electronic; it moved faster and constantly. Where it moved the most – back and forth, in and out, hour to hour – was in the largest banks. Where it once moved most of all – more than $8 billion a day had been normal for some years – was in the Continental Bank.

This condition of modern life was almost beyond the grasp both of its participants and of its spectators. An average person wouldn't try grasping it because the numbers were so far beyond him. Bankers wouldn't try, because it worked. If a system worked, you never questioned it.

The 1929 stock market was a million irrational speculators, most of them uncertain why they were there. The market was irrational; the result was panic. There were twenty, maybe twenty-five highly rational banks who were key for the Continental. You can't reason with a panicked throng. You can reason with a couple dozen international bankers.

John Maynard Keynes might have disagreed; it was still *the market*.

Keynes thought the market was like the contests that English newspapers carried in the 1930s and 1940s. There would be pictures of a hundred pretty women; to win the contest you had to pick out the six most beautiful – the six that the general public would vote most beautiful.

"Each competitor has to pick . . . not those faces which he himself finds prettiest . . . but those which he thinks likeliest to catch the fancy

128

of the other competitors . . . all of whom are looking at the problem from the same point of view.''

From which Keynes concluded, ''We have reached the third degree where we devote our intelligences to anticipating what average opinion expects the average opinion to be. And there are some, I believe, who practice the fourth, fifth and higher degree.''

So now the question wasn't only what Deutschbank's foreign department head was going to think but also what he thought his chairman's reaction would be. The chairman would be anticipating the board's reaction.

Commerzbank would be wondering what Deutschbank's reaction would be. The German banks would be wondering how the Swiss would react, and the Swiss would be trying to second-guess the Japanese. And on and on.

Al Miossi was in Europe now. He could field the questions and clear them up. He spoke these people's language.

FORTY-THREE

THE IMPORTANT NEWSPAPERS IN AMERICA ARE THE MORNING PAPERS: *The Wall Street Journal, The New York Times, USA Today,* the big-city papers, and hundreds of smaller dailies around the country.

Scooped by television again, they could not print the Mother's Day story until Tuesday. They would make up for the time loss with detail and meaningful interpretation.

The message of the press release, bearing the bank's full faith and credit, was that the problem – created by rumors that had never had basis – had been solved. The bank had the backing of the industry. Everything was more than covered.

But the credit committee wasn't inside the bank now. The credit committee was outside. The credit committee was now the press.

The Wall Street Journal ran a three-column headline on page three.

CONTINENTAL ILLINOIS GETS RESCUE PACKAGE OF $4.5 BILLION IN RECORD BAILOUT ATTEMPT

The New York Times ran a one-column headline at the top of page one.

$4.5 BILLION CREDIT FOR CHICAGO BANK SET BY 16 OTHERS

Read down the columns. They tell that some of the banks allowed that they were in only because the Fed had told them it would back the Continental.

Read about how a bank failure – *failure* – that big could undermine foreign banks and could cause failures all over the world.

Read that the best option was "to hang on, like a rubbery-legged heavyweight fighter, hoping that rumors don't run wild again anytime soon and that no new unexpected big hits come along." (The *Journal*.)

Read that selling the bank would be difficult. That federal regulators could liquidate the bank.

But this was not what we said. *These things weren't in the press release.*

Television, the medium you saw most, filmed economists and stock analysts who commented on the press's comments, explained them, expanded upon them, and thereby confirmed their own authority.

Their *own* credibility.

And the foreign press, whose imagination was larger with distance, carried the news of an American disaster in larger headlines yet.

In Mexico City the report was that the big Chicago bank had closed its doors.

FORTY-FOUR

*I*F YOU WERE HERMANN BAUER and you ran the international department of the Bayerische Hypoteken and Wechsel Bank of Munich – Hypobank – you had a big problem on May 14, 1986.

You knew the Chicago boys better than anyone in your bank knew them. You had known them for years. Hypobank had gone to Spain because of Continental, had joined the investment in a Spanish bank. People spoke of the three cities – Chicago, Barcelona, Munich – as each being its country's second city, each its country's true industrial heart. When Hypobank opened its branch in New York, it had gone to Continental for guidance.

Things were changing all the time. Their people, our people.

A week ago, when the rumors had first broken, you had called Al Miossi at once. Miossi had told you there were no grounds for the rumors. You had passed the assurance in your bank. With your own assurance.

You knew that the Continental Bank could not go under.

But . . .

All the rumors, going on and on. The repeated assurances. So many Telexes, one after another. Could they all mean nothing?

A statement by a U.S. government official, the comptroller of the currency, Conover. Read it:

A number of recent rumors concerning Continental Illinois National Bank and Trust Company have caused some concern in the financial markets. . . . The Comptroller's Office is not aware of any significant changes in the bank's operations, as reflected in its published financial statements, that would serve as a basis for these rumors.

Even if such a statement had been written by a government lawyer, the comptroller had signed it. He was saying that his office has read the bank's published financial statements. So have we. We could sign such a statement.

The statement was as unreassuring and as noncommittal as the old credit reports that the British banks provided. They consisted of three sentences of basic information, enough to inform you that the company you had asked about did in fact exist. But there was nothing in the report about the company's credit standing. And as if even the basic information were saying too much, the reports had always concluded with the phrase *without responsibility* typed at the bottom.

The comptroller might as well have added *without responsibility*.

There was also the matter of lending to the Latin American countries. The Germans were concerned. We must keep explaining to our own people. And they remind us – our own people do – of the reprimand the Continental people saw fit to give the Germans about lending to Poland. There is still resentment there.

There is the matter of U.S. government help to a big bank.

If it came to a critical point, would the American taxpayers themselves consent if the government wished to bail out one of their big-city banks?

There was the inexplicable excess in Oklahoma two years ago. That was unimpardonable by any terms. Could such a thing repeat itself? No one has explained it as yet.

These are our friends. We are willing to stay with them.

But will anyone else? Can such a recommendation be made to our chairman?

The standby, back-up, safety net, whatever they call it. Why was it necessary? A greater vote of confidence would have been to continue as before. These banks operate in the money market. They could have placed those funds without the formality, without the "show" of support.

It was strained. Unconvincing.

There were reports that some of the U.S. banks in the support group were reluctant, that they had been coerced into joining, that they were not convinced.

And these were U.S. banks for a U.S. problem. Some of the supporting banks themselves were under review. Was their show of support a diversion from their own problems?

The Federal Reserve: they are not clearly committed, either.

There is the suspicion that the U.S. banks have a special call on the collateral at the Federal Reserve. Is this a safety net or an arrangement that subordinates foreign deposits to American deposits?

How can I assure my chairman?

The only other time the comptroller had issued such a statement had been when? What bank was involved?

The Franklin National.

The Franklin National was the biggest bank failure in American history. It was as big as the Herstatt in Germany.

Would the U.S. banks have rescued the Herstatt?

What will the large German banks do?

And if the German banks respond, what will the Swiss do? Will they leave the Germans to hold the bag?

If you were Hermann Bauer, like other foreign department bankers in Europe, you found you had a lot more questions than you could answer.

And your chairman wanted answers, because he had just heard the latest rumor.

The Bundesbank – the German central bank – had pulled its deposits out of the Continental Illinois Bank of Chicago.

This report was printed in international newspapers.

This report was a fiction.

The Bundesbank hadn't had any deposits at Continental to pull out.

The press would correct it later.

FORTY-FIVE

ROM FRANKFURT, Miossi went to Zurich. There were Swissbank Corporation and Credit Suisse and Union Bank of Switzerland. He also went to visit the Bank of International Settlements, a large placer of funds with the Continental.

The Swiss were formal and cordial. They were old friends. If Al Miossi hadn't been an American banker, he might well have been a Swiss banker.

But by the time Miossi got to Switzerland, the bankers there had had time to read the press reports as well as the cable from Taylor, and they were waiting for him. There were questions.

It is well and good that the American banks have provided the "safety net" financing for your bank, they said. *But from what we read, these same American banks would appear to have assurances from the Federal Reserve. The Swiss banks have been given no assurances.*

We are, of course, studying the matter.

Telephone contact with Chicago was constant. There were calls from Ed and from Bob McKnew. When he finished the visits to the Swiss bankers, Miossi telephoned Chicago to review his impressions, one by one, of each bank.

What was happening was that the Germans were not responding as a bloc; nor were the Swiss. There were big differences among the individual banks.

This meant that they wouldn't, as a group, cut and run.

The people at the Union Bank of Switzerland left no doubt about that. "Look, you don't have to come see me. You don't have to keep calling me. You know what we're doing. Go see the others." Throughout the crisis they stood fast. ("They did a fantastic job. A fantastic job!")

But if all Swiss weren't going to act the same and if all Germans weren't going to act the same, it meant something else, too.

It meant they would not be persuaded as a group to stay. The friendship of Germany and the United States could not be a basis of appeal. The Continental Bank was not the United States, and Deutschbank was not Deutschland.

Some of them might pull out.

And they were all so damned *big*.

After Zurich, Miossi went on to Brussels. There he picked up the schedule that had been made before the crisis. A reception at the Luxembourg Golf Club went on as planned. Calls were added in Brussels – to the central bank and to the big private banks – to discuss the crisis and answer their questions. He went on to London, carrying on with the formal schedule. But at the first formal dinner, he was handed a note to call Chicago.

It was Ed Bottum.

"Al, where are you?"

"As a matter of fact, I'm at Blenheim Castle."

"What the hell are you doing at Blenheim Castle?"

"You've got my schedule."

"Al, we need somebody to go to Canada."

FORTY-SIX

*I*N THE EXECUTIVE OFFICES IN CHICAGO any momentary lull in the hectic atmosphere would be filled with a call to Europe to update the news of local opinion. The bank had managers in branches in every Common Market country. Their local communication was constant.

The British were hanging in. NatWest and Midland were tremendous. Barclays and Lloyds could be counted on.

The French were more difficult. The banking system was nationalized there; the bankers were government employees.

The Dutch were also difficult.

And so were the key banking systems, Germany and Switzerland.

But several things became apparent in the German and Swiss meetings that left the Continental officers uneasy about them.

Few, if any, of the European bankers had heard of Dave Taylor. None had heard of C. Todd Conover.

They had a long memory of the calls about the Germans' business in Poland, back in the days when Continental was the bank that had never made a mistake.

But what made people in Chicago most uneasy was that the Europeans seemed unimpressed by the $4.5 billion support line put together by the U.S. banks.

Rather than being reassured about the Continental, some European bankers now seemed to be concerned about the other U.S. banks.

"We had been expecting trouble in one of the big American banks. We did not expect, however, that it would be you."

More than one of them had said that. In one way it was like an accusation. ("We thought you were okay, but you turned out to be the weak spot.") As if the Continental's crisis were an act of personal affront to European judgment, a deliberate violation of club rules.

For weeks Europeans had generally anticipated trouble in U.S. banking. The specific basis was their pessimism about the heavy and unrepayable loans that U.S. banks had made in Latin America.

At the end of April Argentina was obligated to make interest payments. Many bankers, Americans as well as Europeans, doubted that the Argentines could do so. If they failed to pay, American banks would be forced by accounting laws to take huge losses. The bank that the European banks were watching, the one they expected to take the big hit, was Manufacturers Hanover of New York.

It was as if the European banks as a whole all of a sudden became aware of just how much money they had invested in North America. The rumors from Chicago had sent lending managers to their computing machines to update and print out the amounts they had lent – their exposure – to the Continental Bank.

But banks deal in terms of "country exposure" as well, and as the Continental total was printed, so was the total for North America.

Said an American bank executive, "They were stunned when they put it all together. How *much* they had with us. They began to take a look at everything. The chairmen began to take a look at their total U.S. exposure."

The outside directors were asking for explanations now. They were not day-to-day bankers. They were businessmen, and in Germany some of them were union people. They had read about the crisis in their newspapers, which were picking up the worst parts of the wire service stories coming out of the United States.

A Frankfurter on his way to work read that a big American bank had got itself in trouble and that all the American banks were also in trouble because they hadn't recognized their problems with Argentina and the others. The Frankfurter had to be relieved that German banks were not involved, that it was a problem for the Americans.

Then the Frankfurter finds out it's a problem for Germans, too, because they have hundreds of millions of dollars on deposit in this one shivering Chicago Bank. And they have billions of dollars in U.S. banks as a whole.

This makes it his personal problem, because he's on the board of directors of Commerzbank and he's enjoyed a lot of prestige with his neighbors because of that. But now his neighbors, who are reading the papers, are going to think that he was the one who lent all that German money to the Chicago bank.

And not one of them was going to believe that he didn't know anything about it, that it had been done by someone else in the bank and they didn't tell him. The board had to know everything. Otherwise, why was it there?

The scenario of the default of South American debt to the U.S. banks, so well reasoned and anticipated by European experts, did not materialize. At the end of March the Argentines made their interest payment.

A Continental officer said afterward, "The gun was already loaded. So it shot us."

FORTY-SEVEN

D AVE TAYLOR HAD SAID PUBLICLY THAT THE BANK MIGHT TAKE LEGAL ACTION ABOUT THE RUMORS.

That part of Dave Taylor's reaction ("We're investigating the source of the rumors; we may take legal action:) was handled rather kindly by the financial press.

Emotion, even business emotion, is human interest material. The bank reacted with "deep anger" about the rumors. It was a human touch. The reporters were sensitive to this. They could have made wry comments about it.

They could have pointed out that banks didn't sue the press for reporting rumors of problems. There is the First Amendment. If the stiff men in the paneled offices didn't know this, other Americans did, they could have said. But the reporters let it go. They didn't snipe.

Whom did the Continental Bank think to sue? Novak? Reuters?

Actually, Reuters is a corporation, too, a large corporation. People tend to forget that when thinking of the press as the guardian of the public trust.

On Wednesday, May 16, a week after it had printed the first small notice of the Reuters rumor, *The New York Times* carried two stories about the Continental crisis.

One was a news story.

CONTINENTAL BANK USES CREDIT LINE

The Continental Illinois National Bank and Trust Company of Chicago said yesterday that it had borrowed yesterday and Monday against its $4.5 billion emergency credit line from 16 leading American banks.

It was not known, however, whether the line of credit, which was intended to bolster confidence in Continental, had succeeded in stopping the run on the nation's eighth-largest bank.

Alongside this was a feature story, MAN ON THE SPOT AT TROUBLED BANK, about Dave Taylor.

And directly beneath these two crisis pieces, ironically, was a story about a new stock offering by Reuters, the British financial information and news service.

Reuters was expected to raise as much as $373 million for itself and its owners in an unusual transatlantic stock sale in June. Up to 28 percent of the share of Reuters holdings P.L.C. would go on sale in London and New York.

Reuters P.L.C. was worth about a billion and a half dollars.

Business people would call it a cash cow. The First Amendment made it a sacred cow.

While Reuters was making money, the Continental Bank was losing money.

The Continental Bank wasn't worth nearly as much as Reuters on Thursday, May 17, 1984.

The price of a Continental share was as low as ten dollars. You could have bought everybody's shares – those of the Illinois farmer Rel Small, those of Batterymarch, those of the Texas Teachers Retirement Fund, everybody else's – for just about what people were going to pay for one quarter of Reuters shares. *But don't buy them. They're going to get lower, much lower.*

FORTY-EIGHT

*I*T ABSOLUTELY AMAZES ME," an investment banker in New York later said. "These guys were downtown Chicago bankers. How solid can you get?

"It was as if they were sitting on a railroad track, and one of them said, 'The train is coming.' And the other one said, 'It sure is.' 'It's getting closer.' 'Sure is.' And they sat there on the track, watching it come."

They didn't sit there on the track watching the train come. They got off the track. There was another track and another train. And another. Anyplace they moved, there was a train coming.

And so it was that the disaster movie, which a congressman would call *The Continental Affair,* was released to general audiences on six continents on Tuesday, May 15, 1984.

On Monday, before the bank story had been developed by the major financial press, trading had actually increased the price of Continental stock by a quarter, to $13.625. It was higher than it had been before the first Reuters story.

On Tuesday it dropped almost a dollar. On Wednesday, another dollar; on Thursday, another. Thursday saw the sale of 2,659,500 shares, number one in the market that day, the all-time volume for the Continental Bank. It would be down below ten dollars by the following week.

What had begun as a private affair, as scandalous gossip, but gossip within the world community of bankers, was now open to the general public. It was off the financial pages and on the front pages. It left the venue of unknown business writers and commanded that of Dan Rather and Tom Brokaw and Peter Jennings.

It commanded camera crews, who planned shots of the great columns on LaSalle Street. Anchorpeople held war-zone interviews with the generals of the financial world.

"If a rumor is credible – if it's *credible* – whether it's true or not, people will react to it."

People were reacting to it, all kinds of people in all kinds of places.

Rose Potock, a banking associate on a working visit to the Continental's office in Mexico City, found that the Banco de Comercio office there would not honor a Continental check.

Prince Jean d'Arenberg, away from Brussels on a visit to Switzerland, telephoned Chicago frantically to report the kinds of headlines that were appearing in the Geneva newspapers.

An Asian division officer in Indonesia called to report that the Continental was the biggest headline on the front pages.

"It's funny," Pat Poulakos said later. "It was almost as if he were proud of it. We had made the front page. We were known all over Indonesia."

And all over Chicago.

A woman in Winnetka, writing out a $1,200 check to pay her landscaping service, watched the supervisor hand it back to her. "This is no good, lady. This bank's out of business."

Then the bankers of America, whose banks were small in the global scheme but not small in their communities, who had not been party to the excitement of the Reuters rumors, responded to the aftermath of the rumors. If they didn't watch the six o'clock news themselves, their neighbors did.

Twenty-six hundred of these banks had deposits at the Continental Bank in Chicago.

Bob Holland was in the Central West division. He was taking calls from the Iowa banks. He was the first to know when the Bankers Trust of Des Moines cleaned out its account at the Continental: $4 million.

Bankers Trust of Des Moines – one of the Continental's oldest friends.

"It was irritating. I'm not saying we weren't bothered. What do you do? You can ask him not to withdraw the funds, but you can't tell him not to. It was lousy, sure. But we weren't worried about the bank."

The rumors were false, so there was nothing to fear.

Holland thought so at the time. Europeans would call this naive, a typical American attitude.

The Europeans were right this time. It was a disaster movie.

FORTY-NINE

O N THURSDAY AFTERNOON, MAY 17, 1984, Dave Taylor presided over a press conference in the paneled twenty-third-floor auditorium of the Continental Bank building at 231 South LaSalle Street. The place was filled.

Camera crews from CBS, NBC, ABC, and WGN of Chicago were positioned in the auditorium when Dave Taylor took the podium. *The Wall Street Journal, The New York Times, USA Today, Newsweek, Time, Fortune, The Chicago Tribune* and *Sun-Times, US News & World Report,* the wire services – the list went on. No one was missing.

Little more than five years before, in these same surroundings, the bank had hosted the country's top security analysts for a presentation that analyzed and celebrated the remarkable success of the Continental Bank. The bank had been selected one of the five best-managed corporations in America.

There had been more than eighty stock analysts there on that day in November 1977. There were many more reporters there today on May 17, 1984. This was the biggest press conference ever held in the Continental Bank.

Dave Taylor went to the podium. He wore a dark suit, a pale tie, and half glasses. His manner was stiff. He was careful with his sentences, looking away from the crowd and up at the wood paneling of the auditorium to find some of them. His eyes were sunken that day. He looked tired. Reporters were taking notes on how he looked and talked.

There were twenty microphones in front of him.

This was his announcement.

A group of twenty-eight American banks, together with the United States Government – the Federal Deposit Insurance Corporation – has agreed to provide assistance to the Continental Bank.

The assistance will total $7.5 billion.

It will be extended until a permanent solution to the Bank's recent problem is found, or until a buyer for the Bank is found.

The 28 private banks will provide a line of credit of $5.5 billion. They will also lend the Continental $500 million as capital.

The FDIC will lend the Continental $1.5 billion as capital.

Finally, the Federal Reserve System has committed to meet any extraordinary liquidity requirements. All depositors of the Continental Bank will be covered.

"There was some question as to whether we were headed for greater difficulty. I thought it prudent to take this action at this time. It's very important that we move quickly, to avoid uncertainty.

"This bank is not insolvent," Taylor said. "It's not about to fail. It just needs a little more time."

Some at the press conference that day didn't understand how this big support package was so much different from the one a few days before. There were twenty-eight banks involved now instead of sixteen. There was $7.5 billion instead of $4.5 billion. And if $4.5 billion hadn't solved the problem, why would $7.5 billion solve it?

The difference, of course, was the U.S. government.

The American banking industry had been unable to deal with the problem alone. They needed the government – at least for a while.

Questions were asked.

"Is this the largest assistance package ever put together by the federal government?"

"Yes."

"Is it permanent government support?"

"No. This is bridging to get one of the world's major financial institutions through a temporary problem."

"Is a merger inevitable?"

"It is not inevitable. But it is a real possibility. I need to know more about how the aid package is received before saying whether a merger is Continental's only option.''

"Do you blame the rumors for all the problems?"

A pause. Taylor searches the paneling.

"We are . . . deeply angry. They were . . . a real uppercut. One that really caught us good. We have investigated the source. We may yet take legal action.

"But we had some serious earnings problems. We had a higher degree of vulnerability to rumors.''

"Did the Penn Square incident lead to the need for the bailout?"

"I would say – you bet.''

It was the Continental's biggest press conference. It was the last one Dave would preside over.

"When you're a banker,'' he said, "life seems unfair.''

But he smiled when he said it. He knew that most people don't think life is unfair for bankers.

BOOK

TWO

sophism . . . (n.) 1. A plausible but fallacious argument. 2. Any deceptive or fallacious argumentation. [. . . from Greek, acquired skill, clever device, from sophizesthai, *to play subtle tricks.]*

sophist . . . (n.) 1. . . . a. A member of a pre-Socratic school of philosophy in ancient Greece . . . b. Any of a class of later Greek teachers of rhetoric and philosophy who came to be disparaged for their oversubtle, self-serving reasoning. 2. A scholar or thinker, especially one skillful in devious argumentation. [Latin sophistes, *from Greek, expert, deviser.]*

sophisticate . . . (v.). . . 1. To cause to become less natural or simple; especially to make less naive; make worldly wise. 2. To corrupt or pervert; adulterate. 3. To make more complex or inclusive; refine.

sopor . . . (n.) An abnormally deep sleep; stupor.

—THE AMERICAN HERITAGE DICTIONARY, NEW COLLEGE EDITION, PAGE 1232.

PART

SIX

McKinsey
Cometh

ONE

D AVE TAYLOR, one of the original Continental "Profiles,"
knew what the image of bankers was.

The image of bankers has never been appealing, whether clerk
or mogul. The latter, in Frank Capra movies, was usually portrayed by
Edward Arnold. He was frowning, impatient, severely groomed, heavy,
and dressed in a dark suit and tie and a white shirt.

This stereotype is almost always seated behind a formidable desk in
a paneled office. He is stationary, yet full of energy, power, that focuses
like a laser on the person across the desk. In Capra movies the person
across the desk is John Doe or Mr. Smith or Mr. Deeds or George Bailey,
the average Joe for whose naive talents the banker has devised a business purpose. Gary Cooper played this role sometimes; more often James
Stewart had it. Mr. Smith sits alone on his side of the desk. Edward Arnold might be surrounded by several silent men – a committee – as
humorless and dark-suited as himself.

The most extreme version of Capra's bankers was played by Lionel
Barrymore in *It's a Wonderful Life,* the 1949 movie that has become
a Christmas perennial on television. The banker, Henry Potter, is so
greedy in this movie that he wants nothing less than to take over the
entire town of Bedford Falls, New York, and make it serve his business
purposes. When the Depression hits, he just about achieves his aim. The

panicked populace sells out to him cheap. Only one man stands in his way, James Stewart this time, playing George Bailey. The movie is about George's life, how he wanted only to travel the world and create things, but was stuck in the community of Bedford Falls all his life. With George there Bedford Falls retains its name and character. Without George it becomes Pottersville, which is much like Forty-Second Street in the 1970s and 1980s.

But there is a twist.

George Bailey is a banker, too.

He runs the Bailey Building and Loan; his father started it, and he is stuck with it. He makes loans to average people to buy decent homes and run decent businesses. He has faith in them, and they in him.

The two extremes of the banker are George Bailey and Henry Potter. They always struggle with one another.

TWO

THE BANK AT 231 SOUTH LASALLE STREET was a fortress made of stone and marble and oak and steel that guarded in silence and security one of the world's great aggregates of hard currency and valuables and guaranteed securities. The Bank – the character of the entity – was even more of a fortress than the building that symbolized it. The building was less than sixty years old. The bank was more than 125 years old.

But the tottering Continental Bank of 1984 was not the same bank as before. It was something else. Somewhere, at some point in time, the character of the bank had changed.

It probably started in the winter of 1972, in the early months of the year. In Washington the Nixon Administration was starting its last year. The President would run for reelection. His opponent would be George McGovern.

Dave Kennedy was still an official in the government. He had made the same change in Washington that he had made in Chicago. He had left treasury and was now the roving ambassador for trade. He was trying to position America, rather than the bank, for the coming changes in world commerce.

One of his European trips coincided with the bank management meetings in Barcelona in April. He was in Madrid. Several of his old Continental staff were stopping there after Barcelona, and there was a warm round of visits with the Kennedys – Lenore was with him. He wanted to know the news from Chicago, the impressions of the meetings in Barcelona. There were broad laughs at some of the anecdotes.

It was ironic that among all the Continental people gathered in Barcelona, the person that the Spaniards most wanted to see – Roger Anderson – wasn't there. Since Dave Kennedy had gone he was the only one who, for the Europeans, truly embodied the Bank.

Roger was in Chicago. He was the chief credit officer of the bank, the head of commercial lending, both domestic and international. He had been Dave Kennedy's personal choice for the job.

When Dave Kennedy had left the bank in 1969, he took care of the leadership continuity for the eighteen years to follow. Don Graham, fifty-five at the time, would cover the next ten years; and Don Graham's successor was standing by.

The future chairman would be either Roger Anderson or John Perkins. Both had been made executive vice presidents and members of the board when Don Graham became chairman. The line management of the bank had been divided between them – Roger got the lending side, John the funding side. It would be one or the other. No surprises.

So people had years to discuss the candidacies of Roger and John, to analyze and predict what the selection would be. It was standard entertainment, always a topic of conversation.

Big corporations thrive on people rumors. The external anonymity seems to create an exaggerated sense of the identities within, personalities and idiosyncrasies. In a big bank the work of numbers – impersonal, exact, and predictable – seems to heighten the need to personalize the people who do such work.

The analysts of finance were as serious about figuring people as they were about spreadsheets. It was as inconsistent as high school popularity, but it was as serious as science.

Some people thought John had the quickest mind in the bank, but others thought it didn't run deep enough. He didn't go into the details as much as he might have. And he was a bond department man – not ideal. What you need to run a commercial bank is a credit man.

Roger was a credit man; he had been running the commercial banking department for four years. But if John wasn't thorough enough on details, Roger was too thorough.

Some said Perkins was the smartest guy in the bank, maybe the smartest in the country. Others said he couldn't remember names. Still others said he knew the names of every customer of the trust department. He had better contacts in Chicago, had more charm, moved better in social circles, and made a better speech than Roger.

No, he was too intellectual, and he didn't remember people the second time he met them. He didn't make good public appearances.

Roger was a credit man, the best in the bank.

No, Roger wasn't a real credit man. He had been pulled out of the commercial bank after a few years and had been in international ever since.

Credit to foreign companies was more difficult; it made you a better credit man. No, it wasn't the same. It wasn't credit at all.

John was a bond man and didn't know the commercial department. Roger was a lender and understood it. On the other hand John had stayed in Chicago, knew Chicago business. Roger had his mind overseas.

In any event Roger Anderson and John Perkins were the only candidates. One would be made chairman, the other president. Which became which was not of huge consequence. They were both Continental men of the essential style: both had come in under Walter Cummings and had won the special regard of Dave Kennedy. Both had come out of the World War II navy to join the bank in 1946. John had joined Dave Kennedy in the bond department; Roger had been Dave's selection for international. It was a gentlemanly succession. Each man wanted the top job; each placed the bank above his own career; each was willing to accept the second job if the bank wanted it that way.

The fact that so many of the key officers of the bank had been in Barcelona seemed to seal the success of the great international expansion that the Old Man had started. There in Madrid he obviously felt good about it. It was family talk. He was as warm as ever. He remembered all the names.

152

He remembered John Jones and the boys on the trade finance staff. He spoke fondly about Roger.

He had already heard the stories from Chicago that Roger was carrying the whole bank home with him in his briefcase – two briefcases – every night, that it was hard to get any work through him.

This was the one concern that Dave Kennedy had about Roger. Everyone knew it. Dave had told him that to run the bank, you had to be able to delegate. You couldn't do all the work yourself, even if you could do it better.

It was a rare visit with the Kennedys in Madrid.

Time was deceptive. It was hard to believe the Old Man had been gone from the bank for three years. It was harder to believe that Roger had been gone from international for the same amount of time. He had worked there for almost twenty years.

THREE

THERE ARE THOSE WHO SAY that the first yellow bricks on the road to the disaster of 1984 were laid over South LaSalle Street during this same season in 1972. It would help this story if a particular event had taken place during the same week as the Barcelona meetings, but it didn't. It had happened earlier, either in January or in February. The event is part of the folklore of the Continental Bank, but no one seems to recall the exact date.

The event was a meeting between Roger Anderson and George Baker, a senior vice president who was then heading the Continental's oil and gas group. It was a closed-door meeting; it took place in Roger's office on the LaSalle Street side of the second floor.

More changes would occur at the Continental Bank because of that meeting than because of any other in its history. There wasn't a person in the bank who wouldn't be affected by it.

The meeting came about because of a promotion list.

Just before Christmas 1971, Al Miossi had received a telephone call at home from George Baker.

"Have you heard anything from the bank?"

"I'm on vacation. I haven't heard from the bank. Why? Is something happening?"

"Well, I heard something, and I just wanted to find out if you had."

Miossi heard from the bank the next day; he got a call from Don Graham's office. He was wanted at the bank the following day.

"You know I'm on vacation."

"Come."

There is no area in which banking is more like the military than in the promotion list. It is the highest ceremony. It is more important than money.

Perhaps it derives from the old concept of professionals as learned, as above personal enrichment, as trustees of the public well-being. Since professionals can't explicitly aim for wealth, they have to aim for something. They aim for titles: the promotion list. You wanted to be colonel, vice president, or bishop.

Whatever it is about, the promotion list is the source of hope, disappointment, gratitude, anger, envy, and admiration for every officer and secretary in the bank.

That December there was a major promotion list, and that was why Al Miossi and several others were asked to take a break from their Christmas vacations and come to the bank.

Nine officers were given the exalted – and particularly exalted in the Continental Bank – title of executive vice president.

It was a title that only one man, Herman Waldeck, had held in the Walter Cummings bank of the 1940s and 1950s. Only Roger Anderson and John Perkins had held it since then.

In the Continental Bank community this was the *Gone With the Wind* of management casting. Nine executive vice presidents in the most understated bank in the country.

Charles R. Hall. Donald C. Miller. Eugene Holland, Jr. Robert C. Suhr. Alfred F. Miossi. Gail M. Melick. Ray F. Myers. Edward M. Cummings. John C. Colman.

George Baker hadn't made the cut.

That omission made a big impression down on the main banking floor among the national and metro lending groups. Gossip is a community affair. It's only as good as its nuances. Only the people who lived there were sensitive to George's ambition. He had really wanted the title. He had wanted it more than anybody. The local folks saw that Chuck Hall had become the chairman of the future. The distant future, of course – after Roger or John Perkins. But thinking in terms of continuity, the long haul, the full career, it was Hall who was being groomed.

The pictures of the nine were printed in the new annual report, emphasizing to the importance of the list. In the "Year in Review" part, the lead item was "Management." The lead story of the year. The annual report had never printed photographs of officers other than those who were also directors.

It was more of a final selection than a promotion list. There were no more doubts about the way banking was moving. Anyone who was still expecting another Great Depression had retired by now. Those who had expected the expansion – international, the holding company, retail banking – to fall flat on its face now knew that wasn't going to happen. America had reached the moon, and American business was close behind. It wasn't just a promotion list. This was the Mercury program. These were leaders for the 1970s and 1980s, the symbols of the Continental Bank's values.

George hadn't made it.

It was a big bank, and there were departments where nobody noticed the omission. But down in commercial banking, where George had his staunchest supporters and his driest detractors, there was much to gossip about; there were rich nuances. If George hadn't cared about it, it wouldn't have been rumored about. *What's he going to do? He must be mad as hell. Has anybody seen him?* And that he had lost out to Chuck Hall! Those two guys were so different from one another, they could have been of different races – different species: the quick, flip, impatient, business-oriented Baker and the buttoned-down, moderate, highly presentable Hall. *Has anybody talked to George? He must be mad as hell.*

The promotion list was announced in December. The annual report with the full treatment – the pictures, the spread – was mailed on January 18.

At about this time was the meeting between Roger and George.

Soon afterward, in a special promotion announcement George Baker was made an executive vice president, to share the management of the metro department with Gene Holland. The cold weather had not yet ended before the special announcement memo was circulated through the bank.

This had not happened before.

Nothing was more formal, more locked in convention than officer promotions. Such an alteration required the assent of the board of directors as well as that of the chairman. The Continental Bank was no more likely to bypass its fundamental procedures than the U.S. Navy was. It was not done.

But it was done in 1972.

The rare event revved up the rumor mill on the main banking floor, where many of the officers were still trying to figure Roger Anderson.

The simplest explanation was that George had threatened to quit and that Roger had felt he was too important to let go. This enlarged his reputation in the lending groups, and his close friends, who seemed to know something, didn't discourage that perception; it enlarged their own reputations by association.

But anybody who bought the story that the little guy had faced the big guy down didn't know the big guy.

In Roger's code the bank was both a cause and a team: the cause was above the individual's interest, and no one player was indispensable to the team.

Roger had never succumbed to a threat from anyone. Folklore had recorded the story of an IBD star who came to him and said he had an offer from another bank. Roger told him, "I'll give you thirty seconds to decide." The idea that Roger would back down on this matter just wasn't credible.

And George himself would not have personalized a complaint or made a request for a special privilege, let alone issued a threat to someone whose basic convictions about team play and bank purpose were as strong as Roger's. He would not have done that anymore than he would have run headfirst into a stone wall or tried to sell liberalism to a Chicago Republican. The first rule of the bank calling officer was to know the customer, to know his business, and George was as good a calling officer as the Continental Bank had.

FOUR

*I*F ROGER HAD LISTENED TO A SPECIAL REQUEST, the request would have had to appeal to team play and bank purpose. If the right man were doing the talking, there was a fair argument to be made.

Roger Anderson and George Baker had so little in common in terms of personal style that it was hard to imagine them in the same room together. No doubt there were greater contrasts: Eisenhower and Joe McCarthy, for example, or Connie Mack and George Steinbrenner. But maybe not; maybe not even these contrasted more.

In Roger's code, the gentleman preceded the banker. In George's code, protocol could cost you business.

Roger was patient, formal, and courteous. George was droll, quick, usually well ahead of a speaker, waiting to get on with it. Roger had a hearty laugh; George's was sharp.

Roger took great pains to prepare for the customs and manners of the foreign peoples with whom he had dealt. All the customs that were of concern to George he had mastered before he got out of college.

In business negotiations Roger had a straight-ahead manner; fair dealt with fair until the other party showed somehow that he would not deal fair, in which case there was no negotiation. George was more artful, and the art of it was what he enjoyed most.

Roger was a big guy – six two, heavy and getting heavier until he deliberately lost weight in the image-conscious 1970s. George was on the short and wiry side. Roger dwarfed him.

In college Roger had avoided all campus activities and had absorbed himself in business studies, receiving straight As from Northwestern in 1942. George had been deeply involved in student groups, had been a big man on campus at Coe College in Iowa, one of the Midwest's excellent small colleges. He was accustomed to being at the center of influence in groups – of both students and adults – before he was out of his teens.

Roger graduated Northwestern in 1942 and went directly into the World War II navy. Everybody was fighting the Germans and Japanese in 1942. When George finished Coe in 1951, not everybody was fighting the North Koreans. He went directly to work at the Continental Bank.

Roger's formal associations outside the bank were with the Chicago Committee (he was chairman), the Chicago Council on Foreign Relations (vice chairman), and the like. George took part in the Joint Civic Committee on Elections and the City of Greater Chicago Election Laws Committee.

There was no close personal relationship between the two men. George, now forty-two, had joined the Bank in 1951, when Roger was already in the foreign division. He had spent twenty years in domestic lending and all but the past three in the metro Chicago groups. They had not worked together until Roger was put in charge of commercial banking, which hadn't been long before. (Someone recalled George asking at the time, "Tell me what this Anderson is like.")

On the other hand, the absence of a personal friendship might have worked in George's favor. Roger had a ship captain's tendency to separate personal feelings from command decisions. He tended to overcompensate to make sure of this separation.

They had some things in common.

They were both Chicago boys, lifelong except for Roger's years in the navy and George's years in college in Iowa.

The only jobs either of them had had in their adult lives had been at the Continental Illinois Bank.

What they had in common was place.

Pride of place.

FIVE

*I*N CHICAGO THE ISSUE OF PLACE HAD ALWAYS BEEN SENSITIVE. American banking was being "internationalized," the press was fond of saying; the economies of the world are interrelated.

New York, styling itself an international city, the biggest port in America with a tradition of foreign business, easily directed itself to Europe. Even so, conflicts between the international and domestic sides of New York banks had been a big internal problem.

The issue of the great midwestern bank's new international personality, then, was much larger.

The world was a big playing field. It was hard to see the sideline markers. No matter how many countries you were in, or how many units you had in them, most of your people were in one place. If you were the original bank of Chicago, your main business – your mainstream – is still Chicago.

And your main competition, the team you had to beat, was still the one down the street.

Perhaps this had been forgotten at Continental by some people during the Kennedy period.

But it hadn't been forgotten at the First Chicago.

The First had started constructing its immense First Chicago Plaza in 1965 and had completed it in 1969. Before the mid-1970s the First had moved its entire staff into the sixty-story steel and glass structure that covered the block between Clark and Dearborn, Monroe and Madison.

The building was an immediate landmark in the center of the Loop, and it contributed to the First's image as the most important bank in the city.

Besides the building, the chairman of the First Chicago, Gaylord Freeman, was a Chicago statesman of commanding public presence. During the 1960s the Continental executed its formidable overseas expansion to Japan, Europe, the Middle East and Latin America and booked more international business than all the other banks in the Seventh Federal Reserve District combined. But Gaylord Freeman's public presence was sufficient – with but one important branch in London and a series of articles in *The Chicago Tribune* – to make the First Chicago the standard of international banking in the eyes of the Chicago public.

During his years at the First Chicago Gaylord Freeman had assured future management of the First by recruiting a generation of young bankers that had the finest credentials that a midwestern bank had ever seen. While the Continental was hiring Jones and Bergman and Taylor and Hall out of Big Ten schools and the small private colleges of the Midwest, the First went to Harvard for MBAs, getting the jump on even the New York banks.

By the early 1970s Gaylord Freeman had developed four mature, proven bank executives from this 1950s class; any one of them would have been capable of assuming the chairmanship. Their names – Robert Wilmouth, Robert Abboud, Richard Thomas, and Chauncey Schmid – were well known in the Chicago financial community, as was the issue of their future.

In 1972 Gaylord Freeman was among the most prominent public speakers in Chicago. The chairman of the Continental, Don Graham, was much less sought after by the city's media and business associations.

But the First Chicago was still the second bank of Chicago.

A decade had passed since the Continental took over the top spot among Chicago's banks; and the First had been unable to overtake it. The First had gone full throttle trying to do so: in the early years of the 1970s, impelled by Freeman's highly titled management and his army of young MBAs, the First more than doubled its assets.

But it couldn't catch up.

The First came close. At times it was only a couple hundred million behind in year-end balance sheets. One quarterly report actually showed them ahead. But they couldn't close the gap.

160

Everybody knew they were trying to do so. And that they had put together much talent and much science.

The senior management of the First met every Friday morning and reviewed the week's results. The source was the Call Reports of the Federal Reserve.

"Anytime we had excelled the Continental in any category, there was a feeling of elation," one First Chicago officer said. "People would cheer, applaud."

Asset growth was the main thing – loans. No matter how small the difference, it was a victory.

"Two things were important," a First Chicago vice president recalled. "The first thing was to be the most important bank in Chicago. The second was to remain in the top ten of American banks.

"Under no circumstance would it be acceptable to fall out of the top ten."

Results were monitored constantly. The information available from the financial industry was infinite. Corporate strategists analyzed it. Strategic planning departments were bigger now, along with the computers.

Every Friday there were the meetings and new expectations. There were cheers but no groans.

Deputy chairman, executive vice presidents, senior vice presidents were there – the American business elite. Thirty guys in business suits, every Friday morning, with billions of dollars to manage, cheered like mad.

This was the real ballgame. The home game. Chicago.

Everyone at the Continental Bank knew what was happening at the First. They were coming on, always coming on. They were aiming for the future.

Consider the argument: What message did the Continental's 1972 promotion list give to the bank?

It was a picture of the past.

The three credit men on the list – Holland, Suhr, and Cummings – were of the same age group as Roger Anderson himself, as was Don Miller, a treasury man. Myers was the corporate counsel. Miossi was purely international.

Of the younger men on the list, Hall had been out of commercial lending for years, running administrative services. Melick ran operations.

John Colman had been hired from outside the corporation, mainly to oversee the new merchant banking operation in London, Continental Illinois Limited.

So two of them – Cummings and Colman – were basically running real estate operations. Colman was an international type, hired to run some oddball operation this bank knew nothing about. In London.

Hall had been at the European meetings last year. Melick and his people were going over this year. The chairman spent half his time in Europe – or so it seemed to the people around the bank.

So the image this list gave of the Continental Illinois Bank – the bank that had complex new demands, according to the press release – was one of old-time bankers, staff people, and international types.

And the message to the people at the core bank – Metropolitan Chicago commercial banking – was that what they were doing wasn't important and that to get ahead in this bank they'd do better to transfer to international.

Which might have been all right except that commerical banking still produced – as it always had – most of the income and most of the ideas.

How could we attract bright young people – the best business school graduates – to commercial banking if the message was that the way to get ahead was to go to the international side?

Is that the United Nations flag out in front of this building, or is it the red white and blue?

We may be winning the battle of Paris and Madrid and Osaka, but maybe we ought to look out the window. Are we winning the battle of Chicago? While we are putting up six-story offices in Brussels, the First National Bank of Chicago is building a sixty-story skyscraper in the middle of the Loop.

Roger would have thought about this. Much of what had been done in international had been done in spite of him, not because of him. The entire expansion had been done with a haste that was not in rhythm with Roger's approach to business. Had it been up to him, he would have gone international more slowly. He would have made sure that the bank had the right people to put in those places. He would have made sure of the places themselves.

It had not been thoroughly planned, thoroughly analyzed. Dave Kennedy had wanted to do it that way. Dave had always gone along with the recommendations of Al Miossi. The IBD interest was to grow, to get bigger. That wasn't necessarily the bank's interest.

George Baker had one distinction. He had never left Chicago or the Midwest. Omit George from the promotion list, and you omit those others who have never left Chicago, the heart of the bank. Those who didn't sign on for the foreign lark.

He was a true Continental banker, a Continental "Profile," someone you could trust.

The true Continental bankers were still the credit men.

George was given the title before the cold weather ended. There were plenty of inventive explanations for the unusual break in the Bank's protocol, each suited to the views of the author, but no one knew what had been said in that meeting between Roger Anderson and George Baker in the winter of 1972.

Nobody backed Roger down, that was certain. And nobody changed his mind. Once Roger was convinced of something, he stuck it out under any circumstances. Later events showed just how resolute he was. Once Roger Anderson made up his mind, nothing could change it.

So maybe the explanation of the strange promotion of George Baker was that Roger had not made up his mind about the grand promotion list, was not satisfied with its definition of the values of the Continental Bank. He had known since his first days at the 1946 bank of Walter Cummings that the core bank, the Chicago bank, was the bank. His years of foreign duty hadn't changed his mind about that.

The December promotion list had forced an issue that protocol had long let lie.

George's promotion wasn't a wavering of Roger's will; it was a confirmation of it.

SIX

*T*HE BARCELONA MEETINGS turned out to be the closing ceremony of the Continental's international banking period. But
who among those gathered on the top floor of the Banco Atlantico building that April night would have dreamed it? The spirit of the
enterprise was at its peak. Even the president of the bank, Tilden
Cummings, the voice of Chicago conservatism, the sternest of the skeptics about Dave Kennedy's vision, had come around, had acknowledged
that it was a good thing.

Just when the global bank seemed an irrefutable fact, it slowed. It
was unexpected. Yet it was fitting, because in 1972 the American
Challenge itself moved to a climax, and the challenges of the others –
the Japanese, the Arabs, the Germans – took its place.

In the summer of 1972 Don Graham announced that he was leaving
the post of chairman of the Continental Illinois Bank.

In his public statement Don said he was doing this because of a desire
to leave the heavy rigors of the job. He was fifty-nine years old, and
he would take early retirement.

The new chairman was Roger Anderson.

John Perkins, happy to be president of the bank, would soon accept
the nomination to be the president of the American Bankers Association as well. In any event Roger would create a "corporate office" that
shared management with John and with Don Miller, the head of funding.

The commercial banking department was satisfied with the selection; everyone now said they had figured it out in advance anyway. The international banking department was elated.

Telegrams and letters of congratulation to Roger came from bankers all over the world. They were warm, personal messages from people who knew him: Julio Gomez in Argentina, Guillermo Banares and Pepe Ferrer and Jesus Laucirica in Madrid, Prince Jean d'Arenberg in Brussels, and dozens of others.

He answered every one of them with a personal note.

The commercial department now had a credit man as chairman, as tradition ordained.

Don Graham, true to the code of the corporate banker, placed the bank above himself and passed the gavel with grace in April, 1973.

"The heavy rigors of the job" was sufficient public explanation. It was deemed appropriate for the man and for the bank that Don Graham retire into the quieter history of the Continental, where he would be a footnote to the notable bankers who preceded and followed him. There was no brochure of the kind when Dave Kennedy left, no special salute.

Future reporters would be told by unnamed colleagues that Graham was a lawyer by training, not a credit man. He had lacked experience. He had been a less than dynamic leader, had lacked a forceful personality, had seemed the stereotype of a small-town banker; he could not cope with the banking revolution.

A period was about to begin in which ironies rained on the Continental. Don Graham's place in history was the first of them.

The fact was that he was the most successful chairman the Continental Bank had ever had. During Graham's four years the Continental grew to half again its size – beyond the magic ten-billion mark for the first time. The loan losses of his bank were the lowest in the industry. Its profits were historical records for every year that Don Graham was its chairman. Not even Dave Kennedy had had such a profit record.

It was under Graham that the bank created its holding company laid the groundwork for the expansion that followed, and it was in this same period that the Continental opened up its lending presence in the New York corporate market, its strongest lending group outside Chicago.

Don Graham had been a spectacular success.

And he had done something that was probably unique in the institutional society – certainly in the business society – of his times.

He had succeeded a visionary and had managed to hold the course. Neither Lyndon Johnson nor Pope Paul VI had seemed to grasp what the man before him was all about, and both their institutions reeled as a result. In American business, where the "not-invented-here" syndrome had become obligatory, where you couldn't do what the other man did no matter how good it was, what Don Graham accomplished was singular.

More midwestern than Chicago, most at home in the University Club, Graham had kept it going. By the time he was through the Continental had sixty-one branches and subsidiaries in thirty-four countries on all six continents. He had completed the multinational bank.

"We thought of it as the only real bank outside New York," an expert on the banking industry said at the time. She was one of the real experts, a bond trader at Chemical Bank.

There was a second irony about the day Don Graham passed the gavel to Roger Anderson.

Graham had created the energy lending group at the Continental, the bank's most celebrated group; but he had been trained as a lawyer and by implication would be remembered as not having had the experience to be chairman.

But now upon his departure, the commercial department had a credit man as chairman, as tradition ordained.

That was the second irony. In the modern history of the bank, from Walter Cummings on, Roger was the only credit man who was ever chairman of the Continental.

"It was primarily his performance," one of the board members, Keith Potter of International Harvester, would tell a reporter some time afterward, "primarily in the overseas area."

SEVEN

"*I* ONLY HOPE THAT whoever becomes the next chairman is better prepared for the job than I was."

Roger, the best prepared of all Continental chairmen, said this often in the mid-1970s. The bank under Walter Cummings and Dave Kennedy had been simply a bank. But it wasn't just a bank anymore; it was a holding company. All the big banks had become holding companies in 1969 and 1970. Regulations did not allow a bank to own nonbank businesses, but someone realized that they did allow a holding company to own a bank and nonbank businesses, too. So the bank formed a holding company and sold itself to the holding company by an exchange of shares; then the holding company got into leasing, real estate, merchant banking, and the like. More opportunity. More complexity.

Roger took over the chairman's job on March 26, 1973. Almost as if on cue, one thing after another happened in the market, that strange and enveloping outland beyond the six columns on LaSalle Street, that unpredictable mix of humans and numbers that only economists think they can understand. Over the next couple of years many of the dangers that Walter Cummings had warned about, and some that even he hadn't dreamed of, afflicted the banking industry.

In 1973 there was the OPEC oil boycott, which jolted everyone in the country, and a huge rise in the price of oil followed. There were long gasoline lines. People thought that filling their tanks was going to be the main problem, but the main problem was going to be inflation. Before it was all over most of America would be using the term *money market account,* and people who had always been happy with four and a half percent on their savings accounts would get used to earning ten or fifteen percent and would think that the only thing that had changed about the economy was that they were making more money.

For the money-center banks, the main immediate question in 1973 and 1974 was about the new oil money. Each new barrel of oil now generated several dollars for each single dollar it had generated before 1973. What would this mean for their international funding and lending? The fear was that Saudi Arabia or Iran might deposit so much money at the Chase Manhattan or at the Morgan Guaranty that if either got mad at the U.S. government it could sink the bank with a sudden withdrawal. Senator Frank Church formed a committee to assess OPEC deposits in the big U.S. banks. Almost incidentally the Church Committee also asked how much money the big banks were lending overseas. The committee found that the Arab deposits were no threat but that U.S. banks were lending a mountain of money to Latin American countries and that that could be a threat.

Wall Street analysts were concerned about the banking industry but were not quite sure which way to go. Uncertainty about the new conditions might cause bank stocks to fall. On the other hand the Arab money might mean a boom for them.

The main business of the new one-bank holding companies in New York and Chicago and San Francisco was real estate. The novel term was REIT, or real estate investment trust. In the first two years that Roger Anderson was chairman of the Continental Bank, the United States was hit by one of the biggest recessions since the 1930s, and it whammed real estate developers harder than anybody. The REITs were blasted. The New York banks took hundreds of millions in losses, with Chase Manhattan leading the charge.

Wall Street analysts were worried about the industry. Everybody was talking about the "sheep" effect, by which no one bank thought for itself; every one of them just watched to see what the others would do and then did the same thing. This meant that in banking more than any other industry, what was bad for one was going to be bad for all of them.

A New York disk jockey cracked, "The First National Bank announced today that it is jumping off the Brooklyn Bridge. Other banks are expected to follow shortly."

In 1974 an important and venerable German bank, the Herstatt, went out of business. It closed its doors because it couldn't come up with the money to make its international payments. This rocked the banking industry, particularly the U.S. banks, because it dramatized the flaw in the international payments system: international payments are made in dollars. For the system to work at all, payment orders have to be honored whether a paying bank has balanced its account or not, and some of them ran hundreds of millions of dollars in what was called "daylight overdrafts." It was all trust and convention. If a bank were a member of the payments system, that bank was unimpeachable. Only with the Herstatt crash did the idea surface that the system was only as trustworthy as any single major bank of any nationality.

Because it looked as if it might wreck the whole payments system, the Herstatt crash was scary. The next disaster, the biggest bank failure in American history, was less scary.

The four-billion-dollar Franklin National Bank of New York failed in 1974. It was a matter of foreign exchange, not REITs. The Franklin was an old and respected Long Island bank, the Island's largest. It had been acquired by foreign investors – our old partner in Italy, Michele Sindona – with the idea of making it into a major money-center bank in New York. But the expansion lending was vigorous and unwise; the Franklin captains, including our old European division head, Peter Shaddick, tried to cover their shortages with a spectacular bet in foreign exchange. The bet failed; the bank failed.

And this happened in the first two years Roger was on the job. Analysts now worried loudly about the banking industry. There were rumors of other bank failures. In a letter in the 1975 annual report, Roger commented,

> Throughout 1974, the banking industry was affected by rumors of impending industry-wide problems resulting from the difficulties of a very few U.S. Banks and others in Europe. These rumors have been intensified recently by a spate of irresponsible articles in various periodicals.
>
> In our opinion the industry – while facing a number of uncertainties – as a whole is sound. . . .
>
> The small number of highly publicized but isolated banking problems do not justify concern about the stability of the system.

This was right, and it was true.

The press is always a problem, willing to believe the worst and to publish it. That is why businessmen, and not journalists, manage businesses. On the line you know you are always going to face problems, to have to deal with them. It doesn't help to have all that shrieking going on. The press does this every time. They think it is their obligation to the public.

EIGHT

N OT ALL FRENCHMEN WEAR BERETS, and not all bank managements were party to the sheep effect. Walter Wriston never was.
The people at Morgan weren't. The Continental Illinois
definitely wasn't.

The Continental Bank, never part of a flock, did well during the difficulties of 1973 and 1974. The Continental had made some investments
in REITs, but they were conservative and the losses were minor by
comparison with the Chase Manhattan. The reaction to the Herstatt crash
was caution, and the payments system was closely examined, but business went on. Committees studied the effects of the OPEC move on the
Eurodollar market, in which the London branch was a prime participant. The Franklin affair had no direct effect except to further distance
the bank from Michele Sindona. (Only Al Miossi maintained personal
contact with the beleaguered Michele – loyalty in the extreme.) In both
1973 and 1974 the Continental reported record earnings. That was the
bottom line.

There was a serious setback for the Continental Bank, though, one
that Roger had to take personally, for it was purely a Continental Bank
mistake. His bank's mistake. It was the biggest one the bank had made
in a long time.

(As you envision the thousands of bankers at their Reuters monitors in 1984, when billions of dollars are fleeing daily, the amount of money involved in the problem of 1974 seems almost trifling.)

It was only $12 million, but at that time it was the most prominent, most widely publicized loss in the modern history of the Continental Bank. 1984 was still ten years away. In Don Graham's last year as chairman, net charge-offs on the whole loan portfolio had been $4.7 million. *The Wall Street Journal* picked it up. It was an embarrassment.

And it was personal.

The problem arose in Continental Illinois Limited, the London merchant bank that had been created only a couple of years before as a holding company venture. The business – merchant banking – and the market – London real estate – were both new to the Continental. The investment had been made by the book; pros were hired to run it and big capital was committed to it so they would do it right. The pros blew the whole show in no time at all.

When you're new at something and you have a reputation to protect, you try extra hard to do it well. You don't want people to say you don't know what you're doing, to say you should stick to your own business. So when something bombs so quickly, it's especially cutting.

It was also embarrassing because the bank had been warned. Wayne Allen had spent all his time at the Barcelona meetings talking about how bad the whole merchant bank operation was to anyone who would listen to him. But Wayne tended to dramatize; he didn't have much credibility, as they say. That it was Wayne who was doing the warning probably strengthened, rather than weakened, confidence in the merchant bank operation.

Even though the Chicago management didn't place much faith in what Wayne Allen said, it was prudent to review the operation. So Chuck Hall was sent over to check things out. It also was an opportunity to give Chuck – who was thought to be in line for the top job in the future – some more international exposure. Chuck came back to Chicago and wrote a report that confirmed Roger's opinion that things at Continental Illinois Limited were as they must be, given market conditions.

That was another thing that made the case special: Chuck Hall's report.

Later, after the Limited hit the fan, any number of people in Chicago allowed that they had expected it all the time. "Those guys didn't even know the rental market," somebody said. "One of them paid thirty percent above the market for his own apartment." There were some good laughs about it.

171

Wayne Allen's name never came up. But somebody made copies of Chuck Hall's report and circulated it around the bank. Chuck was no longer in consideration to be the future chairman of the Continental Bank.

It was time for somebody to step in who really knew banking, somebody who could once and for all straighten out those turkeys at the merchant bank.

George Baker was sent off to London.

Careers are made on tests. Chuck Hall hadn't passed the test.

George passed it.

It was George who fixed the situation at Continental Illinois Limited, London. There would be no more embarrassing reports in *The Wall Street Journal* and only one last mention of the Limited in the next annual report.

> Our London merchant bank, Continental Illinois Limited, was adversely affected by difficulties, primarily within the British real estate market. The merchant bank had made provisions for possible future loan losses of principal in the amount of about $12 million. The loan provision and similar reserves for interest on related loans, is being offset by an additional capital investment of $15 million.

In this same annual report George was pictured – hatless at an airport, the open sky beyond – in his new position: executive vice president for International Services. It was the first time international services was capitalized, and this was meaningful. The international banking department was something else.

It was quite a change from Metro Midwest to International Services, but it proved a point. If you are an able manager, you can manage anything. If you are an able banker, you are an able banker anywhere.

These are business axioms, self-evident truths. Another business truth is track record. Track record is results, and results are bottom line.

George had repaired the situation in London. Other people might have talked about it, but George repaired it. That was track record.

NINE

T HE FIRST CHICAGO was still close on the heels of the Continental. Big changes were taking place at the First.

In 1974, the year of Franklin and Herstatt, the year George Baker took care of the Continental's London problem, the venerable chairman of the First National Bank of Chicago, Gaylord Freeman, was preparing to hand over the reins to younger management.

Some said the succession plan came from the Harvard Business School; others said it came from Alfred Hitchcock. It made the bank's three top executives equal deputy chairmen for the year 1974; the year was allotted to determine the fittest.

So the financial community of Chicago watched with fascination during 1974 as Dick Thomas, Chauncey Schmid, and Bob Abboud made their moves.

When Freeman retired in 1974, Robert Abboud was made chairman.

Abboud was an ex-Marine, a Harvard MBA, a fighter, a winner. His favorite saying, according to his colleagues, was, "Nothing pleases me more than to take a deposit on a new account and the check is written on the Continental Illinois Bank."

He was also the city of Chicago's favorite banker.

Mayor Richard Daley was the city of Chicago. And his bank was the First Chicago. So the First had Bob Abboud, the mayor, and a new sixty-story building. Sixty-stories is perception. And perception, the business consultants were starting to say, is the only reality.

Abboud, both before and after he became chairman, made a major mark at City Hall for the First Chicago. As Bob Wilmouth busied himself with the technical end of things and managed the bank's colossal move into the new building, and Dick Thomas worked out the holding company and the London Eurodollar operation, and Chauncey Schmid worried about portfolios, Bob Abboud saw to the bank's preeminence at the center of influence.

It was mainly due to Abboud that the First displaced the Continental Bank as the primary bank – as bank, agent, and adviser – for the city.

There had been no calls from Mayor Daley to the chairman's office when Gaylord Freeman was in it. There were many, and they were routine, when Abboud was in it. As far as the mayor was concerned, Abboud had credibility.

With Abboud at the First, the Chicago economic development commission belonged to the First. This was a high-profile group concerned with the civic priorities of Chicago, development projects that united the will and resources of city government and business. The commission merited the mayor's physical presence at its meetings, and it included the very top corporations of Chicago. It was symbolic of primary corporate citizenship.

John Perkins, Continental's president, was a member of the commission along with Abboud. But the chairman was Tom Ayers, head of Commonwealth Edison and a member of the First's board. Sweetest of all, the meetings were held in the bold new First Chicago Tower.

Everything about the new First Chicago seemed to confirm its primacy among the city's banks.

The imagery was powerful. The tower commanded the center of the Loop, the major architectural marvel in a city noted for architectural marvels. There, for any visitor to Chicago to see, was a bank. And inside with the city's economic development commission was Mayor Daley himself. John Perkins had to walk over two blocks to get in on the party.

Mayor Daley was struck down by a heart attack early in the afternoon of December 20, 1976, while riding in a limousine on Michigan Avenue near the Drake Hotel. The car stopped, and an emergency medical team from nearby Northwestern University Medical Center was there in minutes.

While the mayor was being treated, a call was made on the limousine telephone to City Hall. Right after that, calls were made from City

Hall to a dozen key numbers in the Loop. One of them was to the office of the chairman at First Chicago. Robert Abboud wasn't there. He was at the moment on a tractor in Barrington, a northwest suburb where estates were big enough for tractors, at his home. A call from the bank got him off the tractor. Not long after he finished dressing in business clothes, his own limousine – which had been at O'Hare Airport – arrived there to bring him into Chicago. It was quite an operation.

So as Richard Daley, the mayor of Chicago for twenty-one years, breathed his last at the age of seventy-four, a meeting in City Hall was already discussing who should be the next mayor. A dozen men were there. Ten of them were professional politicians. One was a private businessman. One was a banker.

The First Chicago, by all indications, ruled the roost.

When Abboud acceded, Dick Thomas remained at the First as president.

"But he never really had a role after this," A First Chicago officer said. "Abboud saw to this. Thomas was no doubt the best banker in the corporation. He accepted this. He was quieter; he was focused on the business of the corporation. He didn't want to fight about it."

Chauncey Schmid went west to run a bank in California. Bob Wilmouth, the fourth early candidate who had been eliminated when the others were made deputy chairmen, had gone to California the year before.

Many of the First Chicago officer corps left the bank right after the succession: Thomas's men, Schmidt's men. Folklore had it that two hundred left in a year.

Continental people knew people at the First. They were friends; it was a friendly rivalry. They didn't like to see this happen to them.

The styles of the two banks had always been different. The First looked east, emulated the New York banks, and accepted the moral authority of New York; the Continental was of Chicago and was pleased with midwestern traditions.

But the character of the two banks – the Continental and the First – had always been the same. They were solid, traditional, feet-on-the-ground pillars of the city. They were banks.

What happened at the First in 1974 seemed not to have much to do with banking: the purpose, the traditions, or the institution.

But there was a sense that it somehow did have to do with modern business. There was a sense that a business school plan of some kind was at the base of it. All the competitors were Harvard MBAs. Maybe it was something they had learned out there, people said.

There was a sense that perhaps the rules were changing.

People in the First Chicago went through a lot of distress and confusion. But there are business sayings that apply to any emotional situation: *If you can't stand the heat, get out of the kitchen. This isn't personal; it's business. Hard-nosed and no-nonsense businessmen are calling the shots. They're paid a lot of money to do so, and they must know what they're doing. Unless you're in their shoes, you can't see the big picture. Do what you have to do. Bottom line.*

These are intimidating sentences. People accept that their distress is personal; they can't argue with business priorities or business sayings.

It remained that the traditional chairman of the First was gone and that there was not only a new chairman but a new order as well.

What happened at the First Chicago wasn't the Continental's style. But in the dizzy banking world of the mid-1970s the First's methods commanded attention, attracted curiosity. You might rattle off the business sayings and make fun of them, but people in business take them seriously. There is truth in every cliché, particularly those in business management.

A lot of eggs were cracking over at the First Chicago, but it looked as if they might be making a hell of an omelet. Abboud, whatever you wanted to say about him, had all the credentials. He had all the tools. He had a staff of MBAs from the best schools. He had the mayor. He had the building.

Chicago was changing. Banking was changing. Everything in American business was changing except one thing: speeches about change. Business people who had never read the book were quoting *Future Shock*. Some IBM people were using entire sections as sales pitches.

Maybe they know something we don't know.

It was no time to rely on tradition.

TEN

A MONG THE NEW YORKER CARTOONS that satirize the upper middle class at their dinner parties was this one in the mid-1970s. Two banker types, one white, one black, are standing in conversation in a living room. Their wives are talking in the background. The white banker type asks the black banker type, "What are you people calling yourselves these days?"

They were *New Yorker* types; it was *New Yorker* humor. The blacks in fact were having a hard time deciding what to call themselves in the early 1970s. *Colored* was out, but the NAACP refused to change its name; *Negro* was borderline; *black* was in, but it smacked of 1970s hip, and some older blacks had trouble with it; *Afro-American* wasn't making it at all.

Blacks weren't the only ones with the problem. Let the black guy in the cartoon speak the line, make the other guy the banker, and you could have used the same caption: "What are you people calling yourselves these days?"

Bankers weren't sure what to call themselves those days, either.

"Carl isn't a *banker*," said a young senior executive at Wells Fargo, referring with admiration to the bank's new chairman. "He's a *businessman*."

The new bankers weren't sure they wanted to be called *banker*. There was a connotation to that term that some found negative and discomfiting. There was something old, static, drab, and certainly undynamic to the term. A *banker* sat behind his big desk in carpeted quiet, sat on the money and didn't get the message.

A *businessman,* however, was with it. *Executive* was okay; it was transferable across industry. *Financial services* was often used in place of *banking,* and *financial industry* was favored by some over *banking industry* because it put you at the same table with investment bankers and merchant bankers and brokers and underwriters, and these were the glamor areas of finance – the dynamos, the doers – and that was where you wanted to line up.

The pecking order had always been there. Investment bankers – the deal makers, the movers of industry – had always looked on commercial bankers as nine-to-five drones, only one step up from federal bureaucrats, one step over from Con Edison. They were slow, complacent, and sitting on it.

The old bankers were able to live with that, but the new bankers weren't. They wanted to be on the fast side of things. The deal-making side of things. "Relationship banking" was for the less imaginative, for those who had to depend on tradition. It wasn't business oriented.

Mergers and acquisitions. Leveraged buyouts. The stuff of investment banking was coming over to the money-center banks. It was fast track.

Credit man seemed to stick, to hold its own. It was a secondary term, a qualifier, and it meant you knew your business. It was okay.

But *banker* meant the other guy, the guy whom life was about to pass by.

In the eagerness to adapt change, it seemed that the old-time banker – and the old perception of banking – was the main target.

The old axioms, the old traditions were mainly *old.* And to be old was to be unchanged and invalid.

ELEVEN

TONY GRINA FOUND THAT THINGS IN CHICAGO HAD ALREADY CHANGED by the time he got back from Frankfurt. An operations manager who had been in on the first wave of the European expansion, Tony had opened and managed the Frankfurt branch in 1968. He came back to Chicago in early 1971. So things were already changing in 1971, well before the management consultants arrived.

"It was already much harder to get in to see people. It was harder to have direct conversations. The buzzwords were all over the place." *Buzzwords* were business school words.

The banking business was now being called "the service business." But the service business was really the knowledge business. And the knowledge business was cloaked in the mystery of its terminology. No average banker could walk into a meeting now and expect to understand what was being discussed. It took trained management professionals to understand the language. The emblem of the trained professional was his language – a language available not in Frankfurt but in the laboratories of business science. The language of the new management pro, like the knowledge, was complex.

"Everything was buzzwords. Before they started calling it that, we had been a real service business. Everything was for service to the customer. Now the division managers were spending all their time together, analyzing internal data. Operations was setting profit goals and cutting services that didn't meet the goals. Before that, it was a full-service approach. We could respond to what the customer asked for. The profit was in the relationship.''

In the bank's 1975 annual report ten full pages were devoted to "corporate strategic planning." This is where the essence of scientific management was to be found. The science had now developed – with computers, advanced methods of financial analysis, and business education of power never dreamed of – to the point that "the invisible hand" itself could be gloved.

This was an article of faith. It had credibility.

> It is possible . . . to single out a management function that pervades every sector of our organization, giving each a disciplinary framework within which its duties can be carried out in successful interrelation with the total corporate effort.
> That function is planning.
> Planning is a complex process at a large institution like Continental, and it is made even more so by the fact that we are part of an industry that must be ready to accommodate rapidly shifting social, economic, and regulatory demands. Moreover, planning has a somewhat complicated language of its own that can make it difficult to describe to those not familiar with the process.

Ten pages.
Times had changed. There was much to be done.
Bottum was in charge of it.

For Ed, it was the other end of the stick. It was a long way back from Brussels, from that funny old building, from the customer types who would never make it to the Mississippi, from the calling officers with six different accents, from the problems sorting out commercial exchange rates from financial exchange rates, and from crises over seating arrangements.

He had had to deal with the differences among all those people, the distances between all those places and cultures.

His new staff function, corporate management, was as far from the line as Chicago was from Brussels.

His special relationship with the European division continued; almost every one of the field people who came to Chicago would stop by to see Ed even though he didn't have anything to do with their business anymore. Most would make visits out to see Ed and Joyce in Winnetka – old friends.

But the atmosphere of the bank was changed when he got back. The business was changing. It was more complex.

It was harder to talk to Ed in the business framework. He had a way of talking in which his eyes would go up, seeming to look not above you but to look at something inside his own head. Maybe he had had this mannerism before, but you hadn't been aware of it. It was as if he had the entire Harvard B School curriculum posted, just inside his forehead. You would speak to him, he would check the format, and the format would reply.

It was harder to converse now. A conversation had to have two sides. Some conversations were exasperating. It was hard to get into a specific subject because partway through a buzzword would show up ("You're talking about the layering process. Aha. You might check with the Asian division people.") and he would stamp it, code it, file it, dismiss it.

Things were more complex.

Management was a science now. A situation in New York, you came to realize, wasn't really a situation in New York, but a generic event that had a standard origin and a standard finish.

It was nice to remember those simpler times in Brussels. But they were gone forever.

His speech patterns were interesting. Ed was now fond of talking about "the Erik Jurgensens of the world" or "the Dave Taylors" of the world, rather than about Erik or Dave.

He wasn't the only one who did this, of course. It was a fairly common tendency in the 1970s and on into the 1980s. You hear some of the play-by-play announcers do it from time to time: the Mike Ditkas of the world. The Larry Birds of the world.

You had to wonder about it. It seemed to assume that the type of people you had, and the type of work they did for you, and the type of attitude they had toward you were all generic. That there were no differences. That they all had the same willingness to work, to spend eight or ten or twelve hours there. A production quota. In the past, there had been differences. Some were better at this; others were better at that. Some were smarter; some were steadier. Patience varied among them. There was attitude. There was the loyalty factor.

There was another new word: *fungible.*

Fungible was a commodities word. Wheat, barley – it meant that one thing was interchangeable with the next. Coffee.

There was a feeling that maybe people were fungible now.

In modern management the annual corporate planning exercises took weeks. Every group, every department presented detailed information. It was management by objectives, asset goals, profit goals. It was all run through computers.

You couldn't really argue.

They knew so much more than they had before. There were so many more tools – if you only knew the language.

When the new pattern of things became clear, some of the young lending officers in Group H-N, the eastern division's office in New York, blamed it all on the old domestic-international differences.

"If someone had been able to get Gene Holland and Al Miossi to sit down at the same table," said one of them, "then none of this would have happened."

But he might as well have said that if Europe and the United States had reconciled their differences, then the Japanese would not have taken over the world's trade.

By 1974-75 it didn't make any difference anymore whether Al Miossi, the senior man in IBD, and Gene Holland, the senior man in the domestic CBD, sat down at the same table. By now they were like generals on the eve of World War I. The old protocols, the old conventions, the old marching orders, the old rivalries had all been superseded.

Some of Gene's most loyal admirers were beginning to wonder about him.

"Did you hear what he did for the planning exercise?"

"No, what did he do?"

"He brought in some penciled notes on a piece of paper. Said 'This is about as close as we think we'll get to it.' "

"No! Is that what he did?"

That penciled piece of paper was no doubt the best piece of planning to be turned in by anybody during this glorious corporate planning era. Old Gene – true to the core.

TWELVE

*E*ARLY IN 1975, the word got around that the bank was thinking about hiring McKinsey & Company.

In the knowledge industry the best companies were those that knew the most, and management consulting firms apparently knew the most. More top business school graduates went into the consulting industry than into any other. (Commercial banking was on the low end of the list.)

McKinsey was one of the biggest management consulting firms, and for banks it was the most important. McKinsey had been seriously one-upped sometime before by the Boston Consulting Group, an envied rival in the knowledge industry, when Boston had come up with a "matrix" approach to marketing. Much fame and business and coining of business axioms and terms (*cash cow* was a good one) had come to the Boston Consulting Group as a result.

McKinsey had responded with a matrix of its own for management of service industries, in which the product is intangible. The product, in fact, is management itself. McKinsey shaped a matrix that applied very well to banks, and they sold it to Chase Manhattan and Citibank, among others. So McKinsey's work – its authority – was accepted at the highest strata of American banking.

The rumor about the Continental and McKinsey didn't have much credibility at first. On the one hand you could say that it made good sense since the Continental was now competing head-on with banks like

Citibank and Chase all over the world. ("If we're going to play the game," one fellow said, "we'd better know what we're doing.")

But on the other hand, if we were already competing head-on, then maybe we already knew what we were doing. More important, it just wasn't the Continental's style to bring in either outsiders or "experts." The Continental style – in fact, the style of Middle America – was self-sufficiency.

All the top people were lifelong Continental people, and that would not change. Although the Continental had led the way in new electronic technologies, it had resisted "trendiness" in business fashions. The First Chicago had seen fit to throw up a sixty-story glass and metal show-piece-of-Chicago tower at Monroe and Clark. Continental had had the self-sufficiency to retain its twenty-three-story landmark at LaSalle and Jackson (and to acquire another architectural treasure, the Rookery, next door, for a personal financial center).

That showed the ultimate confidence in one's own traditional way. Only Morgan had done the same in New York. For European bankers the two most celebrated banking floors in the United States were Morgan's on Wall Street and the Continental's on LaSalle.

With this tradition it was unlikely that the Continental would bring in a management consultant to tell them how to organize their business. It gave too much credit to academics, to trendiness. This was still down-town Chicago banking.

"If it ain't broke," Jones said. "Why fix it?"

The announcement:

In July 1975, Continental's chairman directed the formation of a Global Task Force to provide a "comprehensive and systematic approach" to this subject [organizational structure] which will posture us to best serve our customers in the years ahead.

George R. Baker, Executive Vice President, International Services, was given responsibility for directing the planning study through a steering committee made up of officers drawn from several bank departments. Baker appointed Leo C. deGrijs, Senior Vice President, International Banking Department, to head a subsidiary project team composed of bank members and outside consultants chosen for their knowledge of organizational development work relating to commercial and international banking.

The word was that Tom Dowen, who was back from Europe and sitting around IBD waiting for a job assignment, had been offered the task force job and turned it down.

184

Dowen would never be forgiven for that. Leo deGrijs, a good soldier, accepted the task force job and with it the job that Dowen might have had, head of IBD.

For the next eighteen months the McKinsey people were in the bank, all over the bank, all over the world, doing the study.

It was something called "the process." They went through the various floors of the bank building in Chicago. They came to New York, to the office at 277 Park Avenue and to the subsidiary at 1 Liberty Plaza.

The way "the process" worked, the McKinsey person would isolate a group or unit manager by appointment and go down a list of questions, writing all the time in pencil on a legal pad. They probably asked the same questions of each one: of Jack Finke in New York, of George Conrad in Frankfurt, of Dave Anderson in the eastern division. Some of the McKinsey people were assigned to the project for the duration of it; they became familiar figures around the bank, and you could remember their names.

"Those stony-faced guys," Dave would say later, "all over the place."

McKinsey had started in Chicago, but it came out of New York now. McKinsey people were the kind of professionals you saw walking on Park Avenue rather than on Wall Street. New bank buildings were uptown in New York now, along with Seagram's, Lever House, the foreign banks, the law firms, and the Mercedes-Benz dealership in central Manhattan. Investment banks. McKinsey collars soft and loose, like William F. Buckley's. Ivy-related. Serious business but with a touch of removal, so as not to be confused with the form-fed legions of the commercial banks and the companies themselves.

The McKinsey people seemed a little wistful, maybe bored. They thought a lot, going down the list of questions; they noted the answers, but more with patience than with curiosity.

Because obviously they *already knew* the answers. They had been there before. The framework, you came to realize after a time, was one not of information gathering but of the multiple-choice test – to see if you knew the right answer.

There was little to be argued. The preeminence of American management science was inarguable. And the people who knew it, truly knew it, were the people who made it their one single specialty.

Stony-faced guys. Impassive. Probing. Doing a highly professional job. Everyone was subject to questioning – except those on the task force, of course, headed by George. There was the customary but subtle line of jurisdiction: there would be evaluation of how everyone *else* would do, and not of those who were party to the task force.

Joe Anderson, of the Continental Illinois Limited episode, was on the task force. Around the world. At the branches. Asking the questions: how things worked – or rather, how *you* were working them. The audit. Consciousness raising.

And something happened, even in that transitional time. Things got to be secretive.

In banks you have confidentiality. That's your trust.

But secrets are different. Among the bank corps it wasn't a familiar condition. Even the way the groups had been laid out, on open floors rather than in closed offices, lent to openness. It was a tradition, going way back. Everything was out in the open.

But now something was going on. Who knew what was going on? On the line, on the edges, you couldn't really know. Only what you heard, and more than half the rumors originated in the what-if speculation of some rim player, in his imagination.

There was a period of eighteen months of secret knowledge, of behind-doors movement. The open platform had been the motor of the bank, but now it was abandoned, stranded. People out there knew nothing.

Officers started to position themselves to find out what they could.

It was that thing that hadn't been there before, that air of remonstrance – of *knowing*. Somebody – a lot of people now – knew something that you didn't. And they weren't going to tell you what it was.

At the end of the eighteen months, after many thousands of hours, after many hundreds of thousands of dollars, McKinsey recommended to the Continental Bank that it do the same thing the Chase and Citibank had done.

Form a new organization with matrix management.

THIRTEEN

January 17, 1977

Reorganization at Continental has been guided by a research effort conducted with the assistance of an outside management consulting firm over a period of about 18 months.

Some 60 key managerial assignments announced today by Executive Vice President George R. Baker will be implemented during the next several weeks.

The announcement of the new bank was a media event. After it hit Chicago, the presentation – with charts and names of management selections – was taken on the road. In New York securities analysts and journalists joined the several hundred customers invited to the presentations.

In the new Continental Bank primary business growth would be with multinational corporations.

According to the five-year plan created by corporate strategic planning, the Continental's goal was to become one of the top three U.S. banks to the biggest companies in the world.

A multinational bank was to be created. The best of the bank's skills in corporate lending and global services would be combined in a new multinational banking department – the MBD – which would have two large divisions in Chicago and a European division with headquarters in London.

The commercial banking department would handle domestic business.

International would handle the technical operations of overseas branches and would deal with local banks and companies in foreign countries.

In New York there was a cocktail party and buffet at the Hotel Pierre for the foreign banking community, for the foreign banks that had banks and branches in Manhattan. There was a slide presentation on a huge screen of the new business strategy, showing the organization chart with its executives.

Roger Anderson was not at the party. George did the talking, easy and emphatic, and if ever in the past the Continental had felt traces of diffidence, of out-of-townism, in the centers of glitter, they were a vague memory that evening.

It was the first time George had spoken to a large group of foreign bankers. It was easy. If they had been his senior class at Coe College, it would have been no harder. With George talking, few there could doubt that this was the final analysis and that the bank would reach its goal.

He introduced the bank executives who were there. And with his natural audience sensibility he made special reference to Al Miossi. There was abrupt applause, a spurt of recognition, when Al's name was mentioned.

"And of course you all know that the man who will be in charge of International Services in the new bank will be Continental's 'Mister International,' Al Miossi."

Mister International. The tone was droll.

A few of the Continental people looked at each other. There were a couple of nods. But none of the Europeans – much less the Japanese – picked up on that nuance. They thought Al had been promoted.

It was a new world, a new banking industry, and the new bank reflected the "changes taking place in the environment for banking and financial services." It brought to bear the ranking consultants and the most advanced knowledge of management techniques, strategic planning, information systems.

Here comes Continental Illinois.

The change was not an easy one; that was true. It made some people happy, and it made some people unhappy.

Some of the guys who a few years before had told funny anecdotes about the Walter Cummings bankers were left aside by the new changes and were now moaning the most.

There was grumbling about George. He had been expected to come out in good shape; after all, he had managed the reorganization project. But no one foresaw just how well he would come out. In the

McKinsey matrix-management format, George was put in charge of almost everyone in the bank except for the corporate office and Marge Hallinan. Marge was Roger's secretary.

That distressed some people. Al Miossi was upset, for sure. Gene Holland, until recently the top commercial banker in the house, couldn't have been too happy.

But this was no time to take things personally; executives are paid well enough to overcome their hurt feelings. Even they had to admire the sheer business sense of the structure and the intelligence that went into it.

The word *services* in the title meant that the new bank was modern. Walter Wriston of Citibank had introduced the term into banking. When Walter Wriston spoke, bankers listen; they thought Wriston knew something they didn't. The new term, *financial services,* was the modern successor to the old word *banking.* One was an old building with columns and some green eyeshades. The other is steel and glass towers, global electronics, and holding companies. Now we know about financial services. McKinsey knows about it. *Services* gave the new structure instant credibility.

It also solved another problem. Not only did the new bank move George ahead of Gene Holland and Al Miossi and Ed Cummings (Walter Cummings's son), the three lending chiefs who had left him behind in the famous promotion list of 1971, it even moved them out of the mainstream. Now that they were the senior officers of banking services, George could make somebody else head of the banking departments. Gene and Al and Ed were to run nothing, spend their time in committee meetings and outside functions, and be in color photographs with George – everyone smiling – in the annual report.

These three were not business-oriented men. They were bankers, with all that went with that term. They were the reason why McKinsey had confirmed the term *financial services,* the reason for the reorganization itself. The world had changed; banking had changed. It was a *business.* These men – their generation, their kind – hadn't treated it as a business.

If you were committed to that idea, if you had the eyes to see what was happening in the market – at the First Chicago, at Chase Manhattan, at Crocker Bank – then you did what you had to do.

The rules had changed. Holland, Cummings, Miossi, and their generation of gentleman bankers would never have put business – the bottom line – first. They would have observed many customs first, many traditions. They took the bank too personally and placed too high a value on personal loyalty.

They were the bankers who told trainees that "banking is a business of people," giving them the impression that it was some kind of humanitarian effort.

Banking was a business of people. What business wasn't? But business – any business – was finally measured by the bottom line. The old-line bankers just couldn't get that through their heads.

So some people were unhappy – some of the Miossi people, the Holland people. There was grumbling about the senior jobs in Europe going to George's old pals from the Metro Midwest days. But what did they think George should have done? He had a huge job ahead, and anybody who wants to get it done has to work with people he knows, people he trusts.

It was nothing personal.

It was business.

FOURTEEN

THE IMAGE OF THE NEW CONTINENTAL BANK SPREAD QUICKLY. The new design was presented to customer groups and financial analysts both in America and in Europe.

Roger Anderson, whom some had faulted for not making more of a media figure of himself, went to Europe in early 1978 and gave press briefings in London, Amsterdam, Brussels, Frankfurt, Paris, and London.

In September Roger went to London and formally dedicated the bank's new European headquarters building at 162 Queen Victoria Street. He unveiled a commemorative plaque in the company of the Lord Mayor, the Sheriff of London, and the editor in chief of Thomas Newspapers Limited, which had once published *The Times* of London on the same site.

And Mayor Bilandic of Chicago planted a "35-foot Chicago tree" at 840 South Canal in a well-photographed ceremony dedicating the bank's new operations building.

The results of the reorganization were simply remarkable. And they were immediate.

Late in November 1978 the new bank held a meeting for security analysts to put the whole thing in perspective. There was a full house. More and more analysts were coming to these meetings now. More than eighty of them came to 231 South LaSalle Street.

Twenty-two months into its reorganization, the Continental was the hottest bank in America. It had just been selected one of the nation's five best-managed corporations by the most prestigious of all the business magazines, *Dun's Review*.

At the meeting, against the background of a full-color, wall-size photograph of the seat of Chicago finance, the bank's executives charted the remarkable results.

There were charts comparing the Continental with its eight peers, the largest banks in America. There were presentations on how resources were used, and why; on the automation of the Continental's operations, which was state of the art; on vast new electronic information systems; on the new managerial talent; on expansion; on philosophy.

And Roger talked about history.

That was unusual, and it was a highly personal part of the program that day. For business people history is four quarters long. History for credit analysts is maybe three years of operating results on a spreadsheet. *History* is a word for academics; maybe it is the main thing that makes them academics instead of businesspeople.

Roger welcomed the group of analysts and made the first slide presentation.

"I would now like to look at three very different banks."

Three slides of figures were flashed on the big screen. The numbers shown denoted millions of dollars. ($2,900 means $2,900,000,000.)

SLIDE ONE

	Bank A	Bank B	Bank C
Total assets	$2,900	7,400	23,000
Equity	$ 261	480	965
Asset leverage	10.5 times	15.4 times	23.9 times
Net income	$ 25	46	143
Return on assets	0.87%	0.62%	0.62%
Return on equity	9.00%	11.00%	14.9 %

SLIDE TWO

Loans	$1,100	4,100	15,800
Deposits (demand, savings)	2,600	4,000	5,400
Loans to assets	37%	56%	59%
Loans to deposits (dem., sav.)	42%	105%	290%
Demand deps. to assets	79%	47%	15%
Govt. securities to assets	29%	9%	2%

SLIDE THREE

Total manpower	3,800	6,918	10,339
Assets per employee	$ 0.75	1.00	2.6
Officers	214	465	1,195
Vice presidents and higher	62	112	346
Officers/manpower	5.6%	6.7%	11.5%
Vice presidents/manpower	1.6%	1.6%	3.3%

Roger discussed each slide as it was shown, going down the numbers, the comparisons.

If you have ever wondered about the secrets of financial analysts, these slides may provide a simplified key.

Analysts look at gross amounts, pure size, and they look at ratios. They focus on the ratios.

There are three kinds of ratios: leverage, liquidity, and profitability.

Leverage is the essence of banking. It means how much of other people's money – deposits – the bank collects and lends on public confidence in the bank's own money: its capital.

Liquidity is how much of its money a bank has on hand, in its vault or in somebody else's vault. The government requires all banks to keep some cash with the Federal Reserve.

Profitability ratios affect the other two ratios. A profitable bank can increase its capital, so it can take more deposits and make more loans.

Analysts figure the key specific ratios like this:

Return on assets: income divided by assets.
Loan/deposit ratio: loans divided by deposits.
Equity/asset ratio: capital divided by assets.

They look, too, at a "quality" ratio that doesn't pertain to the three basic kinds: loan loss coverage (loan losses as a percent of profits and loss reserves) and charge-offs (loan losses as a percent of total loans).

These last two ratios weren't covered in the slides that day; analysts could find them in the operating statement. At the Continental Bank they were too low to speak of.

Roger went on. "One would have to agree that these three banks – varying dramatically in size, in asset and liability composition, in earning power, in leverage, in manpower totals and manpower mix – are very different institutions. And, indeed, they are."

Bank A was the Continental Bank in the year 1958.

Bank B was the Continental Bank in the year 1968.

And of course, Bank C was this "same" bank today.

"How much is going to change in the next ten or twenty years?" He concluded, "What we know is that we must plan for change – substantial, structural, pervasive change."

It was quite a show: it showed a space-age machine, a model for the 1980s. Where GM or Ford might pull back the showroom drapes to unveil the latest and most advanced product of line, power, dimensions, and technology, a bank can unveil its new lines only in the relief of historical distance: 1968 and 1958.

Bank C dwarfed the others. Its profitability – which increased the dividends to its owners and the bank's own capital base – was of an entirely different order.

The modern bank made more loans and relied less on customary deposits. The 1950s bank had used just under half of its deposits for loans, but the 1980s bank used deposits for only a third of its loans and funded twice that much from the new money markets.

Although the names of the men involved were not on the slides, the dates showed the main personage of Banks A, B, and C. 1958 was Walter Cummings's last year. 1968 was Dave Kennedy's. There stood Walter on the left, Dave in the middle, and Roger – and the corporate office – on the right.

And there with them stood the banking industries of their times.

Legend had it now that Walter Cummings had been such an old-time banker that he had placed all the money safely in government bonds and lent none of it to people and companies who needed it. This was not

193

true. If you look at the Fed figures for the 1950s, you see that his balance sheet is typical of the rest.

The bank of Walter Cummings, like those of Dave Kennedy and Don Graham, was ranked seventh or eighth largest in America. His ratios were like those of other banks of the time.

The 1958 bank's return on equity, 9 percent, was the norm of the Big Ten that year. Three were higher, six were lower, and seven were within decimal points of each other.

The 1958 bank was a measure not so much of Walter Cummings's unique eighty-year-old conservatism as it was of the mind of the U.S. banking industry. And that in turn was a measure of U.S. industry.

The three key years showed the attitude of an entire country, not just its banks, which were only the scorekeepers of industry. Money isn't capital; it isn't accumulated wealth. It is the measure of capital, the account. To lend more money on less capital took American confidence, not bank confidence. There were countries where banks were still held by law to the ten-to-one ratio of Bank A. If the slides had shown international loans, that would have been an American attitude, too – all big banks were trying to get into the business.

The officer ratio was an American phenomenon, too. There were more American kids graduating from college now than there had been in 1958 and 1968.

If you were an officer in Bank A, you were one of twenty. In Bank C, you were one of eight or nine.

That was true everywhere. It was happening all over. There were more officers and more managers.

Because, it was agreed, life was more complex.

It was a new bank. Financials couldn't tell you about the people in it, but that was assumed. Tradition guaranteed it.

The "same" bank was not the same bank.

FIFTEEN

*D*un's Review 1978: The Five Best-Managed Companies.

    Boeing
    Caterpillar
    Continental Illinois
    General Electric
    Schlumberger

Not long after the *Dun's Review* selection, the bank sent commemorative paperweights to all the officers. They had been made in Italy of fine white marble, three inches square. On top of the marble, in small blue letters on a white background, was the legend written above. It was circled with a gold plate, and there was a gold trumpet pictured above the company names. It was nice.

The selection was important. Bankers by definition cannot be exuberant, but in an approval-oriented industry this was very high public approval. All your peers and publics would be aware of it. Roger adhered strictly to the code: all for and of the bank; no personal glory. He publicly gave credit for the honor to the entire management corps.

In the entire decade of the 1960s there had been one major article on the Continental in the heavy financial press, the 1966 piece in *Fortune*. From 1970 through 1976 there had been nothing.

A lot of articles were coming. Just as it had suddenly become a multinational bank, the Continental was now also suddenly the darling of the financial press.

"Banking on Fresh Growth" appeared in *Barron's*. "Continental Moves Up a Shelf" in *Euromoney*. "Continental Shakes Up the Competition" in *Institutional Investor*. "Wildcatting With Continental" in *Forbes*.

Financial World, Commerce & Finance, Banking, and the other next-level magazines also had articles. "Dream Bank" was the title of one of them.

Businesspeople like these things. They like the attention, the recognition. It is human. Your picture is in the paper, something to show your aged aunt who had never understood what work you do, anyway. Your high school history teacher. ("I knew that boy would do well.") Perhaps there was a personal side to business after all.

It was written about as if it all had happened just yesterday. This was the *Dun's Review* lead.

> A decade ago, Continental Illinois . . . was known as a conservative but expanding Midwest bank with a handful of foreign branches scattered about the globe. At the time, its greatest distinction was that its chairman, David M. Kennedy, was tapped to be the first of the Nixon Administration's many Treasury Secretaries.
>
> What a difference ten years can make. Today . . . Continental . . . is an international money-center bank offering services across the entire banking spectrum.

It was as if the Continental had become a multinational bank by the stroke of a pen. As if the ageless rivalry with the First Chicago had been turned into a rout.

The First Chicago was in chaos. The financial community of Chicago was now eager to salute the Continental as the city's premier bank.

The three-way fight at the First for the right to succeed Gaylord Freeman as chairman, which had been won by the tenacious Abboud, had produced a disaster. The lending policies were now confusing. Some of the large customers of the First, particularly the Pritzker group, had been won over by the new Continental, and that was public knowledge. There were more power struggles and conflicts among the board of directors, and all of it was in the press. The profitability of the bank sank to the low end of its peer group.

The First Chicago managed to hang by its mural to its top-ten position, but it hopelessly lost the big game, the effort to be the biggest bank in Chicago. At the end of 1974 the Continental weighed in at $19.8 billion in assets and the First at $19.1. By the end of 1979 the Continental Bank was more than five billion dollars bigger than the First.

And this was only three years into the new matrix-management organization. In the new age of electronic banking the Continental was a "dream bank," rebuilt with a management system that was the best the knowledge industry could design and equip.

Those were heady times, the late 1970s, the beginning 1980s. The bank was at the top of the industry. There was continuing press coverage; one paper's story encouraged another's. But after a while they seemed superfluous. There was nothing more to prove.

But inside the bank you had a feeling that something important had been traded for all this; some essential part of the substance had been exchanged for the perception.

People talked about it. Everything looked good, so there was nothing to put your finger on. But there was a sense about it. One of the young officers in the eastern division said one day, "You know, when you used to hear about how good the Continental Bank was, you thought it was because it was us. Now you find out it's some system."

PART

SEVEN

*The
Sign*

SIXTEEN

NEW YORK AND CHICAGO.

At the beginning of Wall Street is a church – Trinity Church, black and vigilant. It looks straight down Wall Street at Irving Trust, Morgan, and all of them.

At the beginning of LaSalle Street is a bar, The Sign of the Trader.

The Sign had been a favorite spot for Continental people for years. It was an all-day bar. The traders from the commodity exchanges in the Board of Trade building would finish early in the afternoon and go down to The Sign. Then the Continental people would come over from across the street between five and six P.M.

King Arthur's Pub was nearby on Wells; it was sometimes used for parties. But The Sign was the place. A lot of IBD people went over there, particularly when someone from one of the overseas branches was in town. You'd gather up a group at the end of the day and take Jorg or Jorge over to The Sign. It was easy to gather up a group. The open platform in a commercial bank is inherently convivial.

The Sign was a kind of officers' club, with a midwestern touch. There were senior officers, junior officers, trainees there. Some of the secretaries. Secretaries were not subordinate at The Sign. In a local bar rank depends on how well they know you, and some of the secretaries had higher rank at the bar than some of the officers could ever hope to.

Besides, they knew more about what was going on than anyone else did; a key function of the bar was to circulate gossip.

It was a midwestern bar, anyway, which means that nobody was subordinate. The Sign was neutral ground. It was after hours. You took off your captain's bars.

At The Sign, you might hear Rosie Potock, the long-time Latin American group assistant, saying, "Cut the crap, George," to George Baker, the highest ranking bank officer who frequented The Sign. George had a certain sense of humor, and he liked to tease Rosie and Pat Poulakos, Al Miossi's secretary, and some of the other regulars. All these people had been at the Continental Bank for a long time.

It was from The Sign of the Trader that George ran the bank.

It was his style. It was a business style, a Chicago style. Sleeves rolled up. Down on the shop floor. Cut through the formalities. Get it done.

In the after-five atmosphere of a dark bar, away from the Sunday-school propriety of the bank, people relaxed, revealed more of themselves, and said what they were really thinking. People went there with people they chose to be with, not with those they were assigned to be with. The conventions were toned down there. The department lines, the chain of command, were muted. It was person to person at The Sign of the Trader. Office conventions didn't help you there.

At The Sign you saw who could hold his or her liquor. You saw who said too much when they got too many drinks in them – or even before that.

You saw who mouthed off, who could take a ribbing, who could give it back in the right style.

You could learn more about people in an afternoon at The Sign than in a year on the platform.

It was style. There were a number of precedents for it. The tradition of the squadron leader who stuck close to his men, the city newspaper editor and his reporters, the foreman and his hands.

It all depended on whether the squadron leader or the foreman could hold his own with the best of them, man to man. He had to know how to drink, how not to let the situation get away from him. If he could do all this, he increased his authority with the squadron; he made it personal as well as official.

George, for sure, never let the situation get away. He controlled this situation just as he controlled the one across the street. You had to respect him for it.

The Sign of the Trader wasn't dreary if you were there with friends. Not dreary at all. Dark, yes. It was in the Board of Trade building, first floor, right across Jackson. You went in the revolving door, then straight ahead; it was the first door on your left.

To the right, as you entered, was the bar. Straight ahead through an entryway were the tables and booths, a large room of them on the right, a smaller room, partitioned, on the left. The rear booths in this smaller room were as far away as you could tunnel into The Sign. Not everybody could see you there. Out in the larger room there was a clear view of every booth and table, of every group.

George inhabited the large room, with occasional rounds to the bar area and the small room.

He would usually arrive with one of the senior officers, Joe Anderson probably. Even though Bergie – Gerry Bergman – was known to be George's choice as the next president of the bank (when George was formally made chairman), Joe nevertheless remained his closest confidant. It had been Joe, then the controller, whom George had taken with him to handle the merchant bank problem in London. When George was knighted for that job, he saw to it that Joe was knighted, too, with the department-head job for multinational.

Joe always wore a white shirt, always looked good. He had an Irish face and a personable smile. He would have looked right in City Hall or in a Kennedy family portrait. You had the idea that Joe watched himself, that he knew what to do, that he made sure he did it. Joe couldn't become the president of the bank; he didn't have the edge. But that was okay. George would take care of him.

There were a number of other senior regulars. Bergman wasn't there much after he remarried, but he was there when he needed to be. Ken Rudnick was close. Hollis Rademacher. Most of those who knew that George was already running the bank, the department heads who came to the top after McKinsey, were there.

It was a ceremony of sorts. It was logical that it began with the seniors; that's who George would finish the office day with. They would walk across Jackson. A group of them, discussing the day, around the bar. It had a clique effect. A necessary interlude to remind people who the insiders were, the inner fraternity.

Then there was a one-on-one phase, for genuine business left over from the office day.

The genuinely important bank business was done in the end booth against the east wall. There you would see George in one-on-one talks with Bergie or Rademacher or Joe Anderson. You knew the discussion had to do with deals that hadn't been concluded during the workday. There you could argue about them in the right atmosphere. Time wasn't pressing. It was dark. It had a thoughtful air. In the early days you would see Jones there from time to time, sitting across from George in the business booth, papers in front of them. Or perhaps one of the other senior officers for whom The Sign was not a scene but a business place, an effective way to wrap things up.

Jones didn't hang around long; he just came to end the business. Dave Taylor used to come over while he was going through his divorce and have a few drinks, but only in that period. Gerry Bergman went through the same thing. Modern life. There was a rumor for a while that George was getting a divorce, and he heard about it, and it upset him. The word was that he told Bergie to get it squelched, but fast.

And in the last part of The Sign scene George hung around with the junior people. Sometimes he'd end up going to one of their parties on the Near North Side or on the lake side of the Loop.

By the early 1980s the routine was well known through all the groups. It was early knowledge for the new trainees. You knew where things were happening; you picked up on the style. Some stayed away from it, but there was always a crowd at The Sign, every day.

"A lot of credits got approved in The Sign of the Trader," one of them said later, "if you knew what to do."

"You mean the young guys were presenting their own credits over here?"

"The young guys. The young gals."

SEVENTEEN

O F ALL THE NEW TERMS THAT CAME WITH THE NEW BANK, Bank C, the one with the greatest impact was *manager*.

Yes, you had always had managers. The people who headed the lending groups in the original organization had been managers. They had coached the young officers, they had looked after customer accounts, they had coordinated the calling, they had overseen the credit approvals, they had kept track of the loan and deposit totals.

But after McKinsey, the word, the title *manager* meant something different, something more. It wasn't merely *manager;* it was *Manager,* capitalized. In the old bank the function of managing had been much simpler. The old managers were simply bankers who were managing other bankers. This complex new period called for Professional Managers who could Manage anything.

People didn't want to be bankers anymore. They wanted to be Managers.

At Northwestern University the School of Business, which Dave Taylor had attended and which Roger Anderson had attended as the School of Commerce, now called itself the School of Management.

There was an elusive "beyond," another realm of knowledge, that Managers had access to.

In the earlier days the "beyond" had belonged to the international people. They knew the secrets of the world that lay beyond your own

205

experience – the mysterious, the Casbah. Now management was science, and the secrets were in the laboratory—the business school.

"Busyness" characterized the new organization. Task forces abounded. They were proofs of mainstream. There were more committees. There was electronic mail. Information systems – "manual" in Bank A and B days – were all computerized.

There were more layers in the organization. Four different departments now conducted business, independently of one another, in Asia.

Like the old word *manager,* the old words *busy* and *meeting* assumed new meanings. As did the old term *credit man.*

The image of the traditional credit man – that magus who understood character and credit, people and numbers, equally well – had always been romanticized. In reality you ended up with more emphasis on numbers than on people. But still the image of the all-round credit man – the man with a special instinct for character and a special faculty for reading the true fiber of the customer remained intact in banking folklore.

This romance was no longer necessary.

What had tipped the balance altogether was the computer. There were many more numbers to analyze now. There were new ratios to invent, and formulas for understanding that escaped the old low-tech banker. With the computer the variations on a company's numbers were great beyond imagination, and numbers were infallible. The technology was too striking to resist.

Now the materials of individual credit analysis – annual reports, Form 10-Ks, spreadsheets, and lengthy prose-and-numbers reviews written by graduates both of business school and of CR&A, the bank's new and advanced credit training program – might produce a stack of more than one-hundred pages. No detail was omitted; no variable unexamined.

What had taken an earlier generation weeks to compile and consider might now be done in days, sometimes overnight, and with a degree of thoroughness unknown to the elders.

And it was this capacity that permitted the new bank to decide, to act, and to grow so quickly.

But there was no high-tech system for character, for people evaluation. There were still just the same old unscientific impressions that had always been used.

In the new bank as in the old, people evaluation was done the way it was done in most small midwestern communities, which were as approval-oriented as big banks were. There was private opinion; there was public concern.

A lot of times your opinion depended on other people's opinions.

206

Opinion was like the prime rate. It could hold for a year, or it could change without notice. But while it stood, it was powerful. Opinion was the maximum committee.

Multinational – the five-year plan – was the fast track at the Continental.

People were positioning themselves. Something remarkable was happening. People were starting to quote George—not just to repeat things he said but to quote him, quote his sayings.

"George's concept is 'the universal banker,' " you heard someone say one day. "If a man is a good banker . . . it doesn't matter if he's a Korean doing business in Argentina, . . . or an Iowan doing business in Korea, . . . or an Argentine doing business in Iowa. He'll get the job done."

Someone else quoted the same saying.

These were IBD officers. They were worried. Repeating fashionable truisms had been standard at the bank; it was a favored way for people to show they were with it. But to quote the source: "George says . . ."

It was as if they thought that by doing this they would subtly fit into the plan, be One of Us again, even with something as nutty as "the universal banker."

"Do you realize what you're saying, Bob?"

"What?"

" 'The universal banker.' Have you thought about it? You're saying that if you know how to read numbers, you don't need to know anything about Argentina, anything about the Argentines. If you can do a discounted cash flow, you don't have to know anything about the people you're dealing with. Do you believe that?"

"It's the new concept."

"It's the old concept. It's what the American automobile industry and television industry has been doing for years now: you make a good car or a good television set, and it doesn't make any difference whether it's Argentina or Korea, people will buy it. What's a good car? They want you to design cars for them. That's what the Japanese are doing, Bob."

"Times have changed. You've got to live in the real world."

"This is the unreal world."

The language was nutty and masterful. In an environment of change those who knew the terms defined the rules. "The universal banker" disposed of the international banker as the word processor disposed of the typewriter.

The international types complained that the only thing universal about "universal banks" was that they had grown up in the Metro Midwest divisions, unblemished by experience outside Chicago.

This may have been true, but it missed the point. In the new banking, just as in the new business, the debate was not between theory and experience or between the staff and the line. The debate was between *kinds* of experience. Now that business was raised to a science, through technology, equipment, methods, systems, and training, the experience of the laboratory superseded the experience of the field.

"How does it feel to be part of the foreign division?" George asked Pat Poulakos at The Sign. It was a standard ribbing George liked to pull on her. People who had been at the Continental Bank for a long time could kid each other.

"It's not the foreign division, George. It's the international banking department."

"It will always be the foreign division."

EIGHTEEN

*T*HE SIGN HAD BEEN NEUTRAL GROUND, an after-hours place. You took off your captain's bars there.

For the Chicago people based outside Chicago – those in the MBD group in New York or those doing a tour in a foreign branch – The Sign was home base. There could be long intervals between trips home; getting oriented to a foreign city meant getting disoriented from

Chicago, its landmarks and rhythms as well as its people. And back in Chicago the days inside the bank were spent in meetings and silent work at temporary desks. But The Sign was where you got the feel back. It was where you heard all the rumors. The counterpart of numbers work was still an extraordinary interest in common gossip. That was part of the appeal of The Sign. You found out what everybody was up to.

But the atmosphere of The Sign changed with the McKinsey bank. It now had an edge to it. People who worked together drank together, so you would go over together after work, two or three people or maybe the whole group. It was groups. And there was a growing difference between those groups now. People, distanced, exchanged looks that you hadn't seen in the Continental Bank before.

There were "in" groups and "out" groups now. Some people seemed to know who they were; some people didn't.

The guys coming in from out of town couldn't seem to grasp it. They thought the bank was still the bank. They heard the stories. They still didn't get it.

For those based out of Chicago the trips back to LaSalle Street weren't as much fun anymore.

People you had known for years, good guys, were guarded now. They were careful. Many of them seemed to know something. But they weren't telling what it was. Others were worried or frustrated. They were good guys, too; the same people you had known for years.

The biggest change in Bank C wasn't in the financial statements. It was in the look of the eye.

At the old Continental what had characterized the people was the real look of interest in their eye. Curiosity. Anticipation. Interest.

It was a midwesterner's look, open. It went with the open platform. It was friendly.

That look was rare now.

It was as if the eighteen-month McKinsey period of secret conferences and closed-door planning had started a permanent mode.

People had the look of the McKinsey people now, of those stony-faced guys. People knew something that you didn't. And they guarded it.

It was as if the curiosity had been removed. There was no need for it now. All the answers were known.

There was a system now, a management system. It had replaced the other stuff.

The Chicago people based outside Chicago returned to find a baffling atmosphere. More and more, people looked just above your eyes when they talked to you.

"What the hell is going on around here, John?" one of the New York staff said to a friend. "Who's running this bank, anyway?"

Looking down, not even above: "George Baker is running this bank."

NINETEEN

*I*T WASN'T THE SAME BANK, some people said, although it appeared to be.

Gene Holland was still there. Ed Cummings and Al Miossi were still there. They were executive vice presidents in charge of the commercial, multinational, and international banking services, respectively.

Except that none of them had much to do. Gene held his title and his office, but the business of commercial banking was done by the metro, national, and special-industries department heads selected during the McKinsey turnover. Ed Cummings had no voice at all. His MBD title was an honorific made necessary after his job – real estate – was assumed by the noisy and colorful James Harper, who had been brought in from California to modernize the business. There were so many layers in multinational that one more went unnoticed.

Yet they were there, the old Continental leaders, parties to all the ceremonies – credit committees, policy committees and senior customer functions. This lent to the bewilderment. These were men who had generaled regiments, and many of those who had modeled their careers on them and had sought their counsel over the years were confronted with an elusive situation.

210

At First Chicago the case had been clear, the sides overtly expressed. Here the issues were tacit, masked by the continued presence of the chiefs.

It was slower and just as bewildering.

These were very tough times for Al Miossi.

He had spent twenty-five years working to create the broad view, the world view, for the Continental Bank. "The only thing that Bangladesh and Brazil have in common," Miossi had said in speeches to economic groups in Chicago and New York, "is that they both begin with the letter B." He feared now that the distinctions would be lost.

The best man on Miossi's staff, Gerry Keeley, had spent years in London developing the bank's first Eurodollar operation. He was gone from IBD now. He was a senior vice president on George's staff. But he was never consulted anymore. Gerry didn't complain; he kept the code. But others in IBD came frequently to Al's office, asking for the inside story. Al couldn't help them. He was neutralized. He spent his time traveling and attending committee meetings.

Matters of international policy – sovereign risk or country exposure – were now overseen by the new regime. The list of countries was reviewed, name by name.

At one country limit meeting presided over by one of the senior "universal bankers," late of Group 4, the Africa-Middle East list was under review. He read the names.

"Well, let's see. The next country on the list is . . . Nigger. Is that the way you pronounce it – Nigger?"

A veteran international officer, watching Miossi, saw him turn pale. There was silence.

"Well," said the new committee chief, straight-faced, "who wants to say something about Nigger?"

Al sat there, not responding to it. Someone else finally said, "I believe it's pronounced *Niger.*"

The committee chief looked at the paper for a moment, then looked up solemnly. "Maybe you're right. It's only got one g."

Miossi's long-time friend, the venerable Renzo Polito, was the bank's representative in Rome. He listened as a young officer in the European organization said to him, "I think you'd do well to realize that this is not Al Miossi's bank anymore. This is George Baker's bank."

He said it in the manner that had become common in some parts of the bank by now: the direct language with indirect eyes. It was businesslike, knowing, patient, and unpatronizing. *You would do well . . .*

It was a confidence shared. And it required acknowledgement.

Everybody knew it had never been Al Miossi's bank. Only a few of the Europeans, the old-timers, had ever thought it was.

But it didn't make sense to call it George Baker's bank now, either. Because Roger was still the chairman. If it was anybody's, it was Roger's bank.

To Roger, the bank wasn't his. The titular head of the bank saw the bank as a team with no superstars, not even himself; he had gone so far as to share the prestige of his office with John Perkins and Don Miller.

But across the street were a man and a group that seemed determined to make it known that it was this man, this one man, who was running the bank.

There were two codes.

In a back booth at The Sign of the Trader, one vice president said, "Somebody should tell Roger what's happening."

TWENTY

THE CONTINENTAL BANK WAS AT THE TOP OF ITS INDUSTRY, and no one was more aware of it than Roger Anderson.

The long-planned and carefully implemented realignment in 1976-77 has more than met its objectives since, and in 1978 further strengthened our position as one of the top U.S. banks for corporate customers.

It was the tenth consecutive year of record earnings. In a slow loan market filled with strong competition – there were now forty-nine foreign banks in Chicago, not to mention those in New York – the new bank increased its loans to U.S. commerce and industry by more than 21 percent. The bank moved closer to its goal of "some 400 U.S.- and foreign-based multinational corporations." It now served more than three hundred of them, more than one hundred of them in substantial ways.

1979 was the eleventh record year. Domestic commercial and industrial loans grew almost 25 percent, half again as much as the New York competition's.

The third year in the five-year multinational plan again brought a head-of-plan performance, and the Greenwich Associates research firm showed that the financial officers of more than a thousand companies rated Continental among the top three U.S. banks.

Somebody ought to tell Roger. . . .

Roger was now doing what people had always said a chief executive should do: he was delegating the operational tasks; he was acting as the Continental Bank's statesman to the city, the country, and the world.

The bank had taken the lead in the Chicago 21 Plan, the vast community development design to prepare the city for the twenty-first century. The bank dealt with the issues of world trade and human rights, now a focus at every shareholders' meeting. There was constant interchange with the city government and with the statesmen of the Federal Reserve System.

In the annual report photographs of 1979 Roger stands on the Great Wall of China after establishing the Continental Bank's relationship with the Bank of China. John Perkins stands behind a podium at the American Bankers Association, addressing the membership as its president. And Don Miller stands behind another set of microphones, again in a public expression of the Continental Bank.

On the cover of that report is the picture of a downstate Illinois farmer who had held stock in the Continental Bank since 1929. It was a reminder of where the basic strength of this bank came from.

In creating the greater Continental Bank, Roger was enlarging Chicago's importance as a world financial center. It was not beyond the imagination that Chicago could someday be the financial capital of the United States.

TWENTY-ONE

T IMES HAD CHANGED SINCE THE CONTINENTAL "PROFILES" OF 1966. F. Scott Fitzgerald's famous line "There are no second acts in American lives" was out of date now. There were second acts and even third acts.

A lot of Americans who had married their high school and college sweethearts, had married them for life, for the American Dream, lost those sweethearts in the male-female wars of the 1970s and 1980s. Women once went to Northwestern for a "Mrs."; now they went there for the MBA.

In 1966, when the "Profiles" brochure was made, the "Profiles" were all white boys, your basic World War II bomber crew. The pride of the community, what you wanted your kid to grow up to be in the post–World War II world. There was moral superiority in those faces. They were the faces that had liberated Europe and saved the world.

There were different American images now. In about the mid-1970s the first of the business-oriented self-help books started selling big, ones like *Looking Out for Number One* and *Winning Through Intimidation*. Be a winner, don't be a loser: it was a 1970s notion. Not long after that John McEnroe first played at Wimbledon and an investment group controlled by George Steinbrenner acquired the New York Yankees. No more Mr. Nice Guy.

And there was in the mid-1970s the disremembering of the Vietnam war.

Losers.

World War II types. Yokels who had bought the press release, who had been gullible enough to go over to those swamps. People were discomfited to speak to them now. The American image and self-image of the 1980s were a long way from the "Profiles."

It wasn't easy to get a grip on "American," and it wasn't easy to get a grip on "the bank" anymore, either.

Times had changed. Times had blurred the old image of "American." Times had changed "the bank" as well. You couldn't blame everything on George Baker and his pals.

"This is not the same bank," someone would say. "Someone's got to tell Roger what's happening."

Tell Roger what?

The Continental was at the top of the industry. Things were never better.

Be number one.

There was a feeling, an atmosphere of new ownership, of a new corporate culture, one as different from the old bank as The Sign of the Trader was different from the columned main banking hall on the second floor.

Somebody else owned the bank now.

It was a private ownership.

If you wanted to be a player-coach, there was an advantage in owning the Continental Bank instead of the New York Yankees. George Steinbrenner couldn't do what he really wanted to do, put on a uniform and put himself in the lineup. In the Bronx, he would have been maimed if he did that.

But George Baker could put on the uniform, get right down there on third base, replacing Graig Nettles, therefore becoming – by implication – the best third baseman in the league.

At The Sign. In Europe. On the South American trip. On the Asian trip – there were new travel stories.

But the new hard-drinking, hard-travelling, hard-living stories made the fond anecdotes about Dave Kennedy and Roger Anderson seem quaint. Friends would smile. Nod. *He's something else, that George.*

One story about a Far East trip with Saul Steinberg went all over the bank. The Continental managers received the party at all of the principal airports in Asia; a blond cookie kept appearing at them. Who was she with, Saul or George? Everybody was disappointed to learn she wasn't with George; it spoiled the story. Still they liked to talk about it – the image.

Up on the sixth floor the tight-assed IBD types were buzzing to each other. Shock after shock – that was the fun of it. And of course they'd exaggerate everything.

The story came back that on George's Buenos Aires trip he'd made a move on some Argentine chick and that Dave Lenz, the Continental resident there, had intervened to save her.

"Totally untrue," said Lenz. "Nothing like that happened. Nothing out of the ordinary at all."

But it was too good a story. You'd hear it over and over again. It entered the folklore.

Brazil: An arrival scene at the airport, broken booze bottles at the taxi area.

Chile: Appointments with high government officials; the local manager is left there alone; the high-level visitors from Chicago fail to show.

Scenes around Chicago. Colorful stories.

Curiously, George didn't seem to mind them at all. He seemed to cultivate the image. The only rumor he tried to stop was the one about his divorce. It was false, and it upset him. He told Bergie to squelch it. Such was the control of the new regime that he could do just that.

The other stories didn't seem to bother him. Maybe he enjoyed them; maybe he didn't give a damn.

He seemed to be playing: Down on the field. In full uniform. On third base. Around the horn. The fun part.

Maybe a big, traditional commercial bank was too ripe an element for the "mainstream," "fast-track" concepts of the advancing 70s.

It had always been an approval-oriented bank.

People here had been used to working for good grades, for percentile rankings on the SAT and GRE. They were used to taking multiple choice tests in which the people giving the tests knew all the answers.

It was all mixed: the team concept, the mainstream, the core, the fit. It was important to fit in. There were courses in improving vocabulary, in dressing for success, in speaking to the media, in reading the personality of your boss, of your employee. Gaining approval.

The personality-based Bank C produced a clone effect that the old bank had never required.

This was the late 1970s. You started to hear the term *survivor* now. It wasn't an American term. American tradition honored fighters –the men at the Alamo, Butch O'Hare, Patrick Henry – not survivors. Survivors were the guys on the edge of the crowd.

"Oh, I'm a survivor. I'll land on my feet."

"What do you mean, 'land on your feet'? What the hell are you talking about?"

"These are not decent men," someone in the Mexico group would tell you. *"Son cabrones."*

Some of these guys – your buddies – were actually starting to walk like George, to talk like him. Some of them started smoking cigars. Some actually seemed to *look* like him.

There was a certain smooth manner. W was starting to stand like G, who was known to be on the fast track, holding his hands in front of him, rocking back and forth a little bit when he talked. There was similar diction, similar phrases. People would laugh at the same time, at *exactly* the same time.

And all of them – *all* of them – were starting to look away. To avoid eye contact. That was what you did when walking around New York City.

There was a different rhythm here now.

Somebody knew something.

"What's happening here, Erik?"

"It's not the same bank. You've been away too long."

An acknowledgement was required. You were to acknowledge this, to assent.

There was a smell of acquisition, of new ownership. There was in The Sign a new corporate culture, one as different from the traditional bank as the bar itself.

It was as if by acquiring the IBD, you settled the business of the foreigners themselves, did away with their idiosyncrasies, put them in line.

Among the Continental people, there was knowledge of such power plays. Everyone knew what had happened at the First. But they disbelieved that such concepts, such power plays could happen at the Continental Bank. Years in the presence of Dave Kennedy and Roger Anderson had confirmed the special character of the Continental. No matter what you saw happening in front of you, you still believed in the bank.

The point was not that the new concepts were dominating one big corporation after another, nor that people were acting tough about them, acting as if they were unaffected by them, and calling them "the real world."

The point was that you didn't think they would happen *here*.

It wasn't our style. It was someone else's style.

It was what They did, not Us.

TWENTY-TWO

THE MOST BAFFLING THING WAS THE RELATIONSHIP BETWEEN ROGER AND GEORGE.

Roger was still there. Roger was still Roger.

But one by one, the men who had been closest to Roger Anderson during his thirty years at the Continental Bank, those who had held him in highest esteem, those who would have put their hands in the fire for him – his friends – were being eliminated.

And he stood by and did nothing while it happened.

Years in the foxholes. Years of crossing the barbed wire, of putting the thing together, making it whole.

He seemed oblivious.

He was making the same speeches, using the same language. It was as if he thought the bank was still the bank. As if he didn't realize whose bank it was. And he was the only one who seemed not to realize it.

When you looked around this vastly changed place to make sure you were at the right address, it wasn't the address you were looking for.

The global bank – the bank of the American Challenge, that had knit so many diverse types together – had its valedictory in April of 1980. The event was Debbie Miossi's wedding at St. Joseph's Catholic Church in Wilmette. She married Mike Niebruegge, an attorney at Mayer, Brown & Platt, whose address was 231 South LaSalle Street, Chicago. The reception was at the Indian Hill Country Club.

218

Debbie's wedding reunited the Continental's international corps. It was particularly nostalgic under the circumstances. Woody Everett was there from the Philippines. Luis Calero came up from Mexico. There were a dozen people from Europe. Gerry Keeley. Joel Smith. Erik Jurgensen.

Deb, career lady of modern America, was a cutie of a bride, as blond as her mother, straight to the point, the darling of the corps. With the help of Pat Poulakos, she had put Al Miossi in bluejeans.

Roger was there, with Mari. The weather was superb that Midwestern autumn, outdoors at Indian Hill.

Roger was standing near the bridal party, looking over the gathering. "It's like having the family all together," Roger said.

For a moment it looked as if there were tears in his eyes. You looked again. Yes, there *were* tears in his eyes.

That was the bafflement of the period. Roger was still Roger. You couldn't doubt it; the man had not changed. In the speeches, the letters in the annual report, he said the same things he had always said, promoted the same beliefs. But in the light of what was happening at the bank you had to ask yourself if he really meant it, if he hadn't been converted to the public-posture expertise that was now being recommended for executives. Saying the right thing the right way.

But Roger meant it. He actually thought it was still the same.

That was what being an officer meant, what being the captain meant.

You must do your duty, and because this means doing things that may hurt people you care about, you have to keep your distance. The captain is alone. He must do what he has to do.

It was as if Roger had to guard hmself against his own sentiment, against whatever instincts in him might conflict with the analysis, the science, that business required.

Business was business, and personal life was something you kept apart.

Business required a different kind of discipline, a different kind of education.

You couldn't let one interfere with the other.

TWENTY-THREE

O F ALL THE PRESS COVERAGE OF THE CONTINENTAL BANK during the five-year period in which it was the darling of the financial press, the *Institutional Investor* article of October 1980 stands out.

The article was one of those pieces of journalism wherein the writer's personal reaction is as fascinating as his subject. Neil Osborn, an Englishman who knew international banking, was the magazine's lead writer on the theme. He was well spoken and well tailored and far better educated than most of the people he had to interview.

The winds of the multinational era had brought Neil to work in New York and live in New Jersey, both far from the one true financial center, London. Then they had sent him into the American Midwest. He was to do a story on a bank in Chicago that somehow had become hot copy.

One prepares. One gets the bank's most recent annual report, the one with the eighty-three-year-old farmer on the cover who has owned stock in the bank for fifty years.

"It wasn't a big buy, I'll say that," Rell Small recalled in the annual report, "but $690 was a lot of money then, I'll say."

Blimey! The American prairie, the stockyards – the isolation.

How to relate this to international banking? How to translate it for The City?

The title of the piece was, "Continental Illinois Shakes Up the Competition – Roger Anderson has proved you don't have to be a dynamic idea-generator to create a banking power in America."

> Last year's annual report from Continental Illinois Bank has a toothless old man on the cover. His name is Rell Small and he's a farmer in Illinois. He also symbolizes, Continental suggests inside the report, the All-American virtues of hard work, thrift and clean living to which all good citizens should aspire. This uplifting message struck a chord with more than one shareholder and farmer. Small received a number of letters praising the report. He even received one from the "Far East," he later told a bank officer. "The Far East?" asked the officer. "Yup," replied Small, "Philadelphia."
>
> Sure, that's a corny Midwestern story about a corny Midwestern bank. But lately nobody's been snickering too much about Continental and its hokey country ways. That's because in the past five years or so, Continental Illinois has transformed itself from a decidedly prosaic institution, the second bank in Chicago, the Second City, into what one competitor has called "the most feared bank in the United States."

It was the damnedest magazine article. There were six pages of photographs, drawings, facts, gossip. *Institutional Investor* was the leader at this, the *People* magazine of the banking industry. It was a 1970s creation that, in the best business tradition, had found a need and filled it. There were lots of personal profiles, color caricatures of banking stars, titillating personal rumors that tradition forbade mentioning but that the players were delighted to hear someone else say.

There were references to a high-ranking officer who held on to his job despite his drinking problem; to senior officers squabbling over seats of honor at the lunch table; to "a drunken exhibition" by bond department officers at a party; and so on. Such things had been hushed up at the bank. People were shocked and pleased to see them in print.

On the one hand, the story was about a big, corny Midwestern bank run by a big, dumb guy. It was unknown to the rest of the world but was now making a big noise in the domestic market.

> The vestiges of the bank's parochial origins are reflected in the bank's low stature in the international banking market. . . .
>
> "We're a country bank," bubbles executive vice president Melick. . . .
>
> If Anderson appears a colorless man, it should be remembered that he has spent his entire career in what used to be a fairly colorless institution. For years, particularly in the 1960s and early 1970s, Continental lived in the shadow of the First Chicago, a more glamorous and prominent bank in almost every respect. . . .

Indeed, it's fair to say that Anderson is a less than awe-inspiring figure at first glance. His suits tend to be a little shapeless, he favors large, woefully outmoded tie clips and, as he crosses from his desk to greet visitors, he sometimes feels obliged to hitch up his pants before shaking hands.

The fact of the matter seems to be that Anderson has a talent for delegating authority. He may not have many ideas himself. . . . But he's prepared to let his subordinates implement their ideas.

These were things to be expected from a bank with an eighty-three-year-old farmer on its cover.

But on the other hand, the story was about the "most feared bank in the United States." Because the big, dumb guy was letting his smart guys do the work.

Since 1975, Continental's commercial and industrial loans have expanded from $4.9 to $9.6 billion, and it has joined Chase, Citi and BofA at the top of the market. Indeed, in the first quarter this year, Continental passed Chase and became the third-largest lender in the nation.

This is the achievement of George Baker Jr., 50, a fast-talking, streetwise, cigar-waving executive vice president in charge of Continental's "general banking" division. . . . Armed with no more than native cunning and an undergraduate degree from Iowa's Coe College when he joined Continental 29 years ago, Baker has risen to the fourth most important position in the bank. . . .

Perhaps all this has something to do with Baker's engaging personality – corporate chairmen and treasurers are as susceptible to blarney as anyone else. There's nothing Baker likes better than draping himself over a chair and rattling out unbankerlike comments on his business. (The difficulty of controlling a nationwide network of lending officers is a favorite topic, for example: "If you have a bunch of turkeys out there, you end up with a lot of bum credits," he avers). . . .

If Baker wants to do business with a corporation badly enough, he's prepared, quite unashamedly, to buy his way in. . . .

Like chairman Anderson, Baker believes in giving his men a remarkably free hand. He himself seldom looks at loan proposals. . . .

"I wrapped up a $150 million deal in an hour-and-a-half not long ago," says one particularly chipper Continental youngster. . . .

The mystery . . . is how chairman Anderson, cautious and conservative by nature, and nurtured for years in a humdrum environment, could not only tolerate but actively spearhead this kind of aggressiveness. . . .

"People complain that Roger is too slow and deliberate in dealing with matters they bring to him. My answer is, don't take things to him," says one officer. . . .

Continental doesn't have big plans to become a more prominent international bank. . . .

Anderson wants still more loans. "We intend to continue to increase our share of the U.S. loan business," he says.

Money-center bankers are not allowed to be astonished. It is very bad form. So the officers of the Continental Bank kept their cool after reading the *Institutional Investor* article. That it baffled the corps, the outside world was not to know. Cautious inquiries from the international customers of the bank were tactfully laid to rest.

Has Roger actually seen this?

If Roger hadn't seen it, he soon would. There were media experts at the Continental who knew how to handle very touchy situations. The article was reprinted immediately and routed to every officer in the bank.

Months afterward, what Neil Osborn, the writer, most remembered about Roger was that he hitched up his pants.

Back in New York, he still talked about that. It had impressed him deeply.

"The man actually hitched up his pants before coming around the desk."

Midwesterner impressions, all confirmed.

But that is one of the things we loved about him, Neil.

TWENTY-FOUR

"**M**AYBE GEORGE HAS SOME COMPROMISING PICTURES OF HIM. Do you think he has something on him?"

That was a crack around the bank then. It got laughs.

"Seriously. Do you think he does?"

Nobody really thought George had pictures of Roger. He didn't need them.

Someone should tell Roger what's happening to the bank.

It was a quaint thought, heard now and again.

Someone was telling him. John Perkins and Don Miller were telling him.

Year after year, the three members of the corporate office – Roger, John, and Don – would meet to review the names of senior officers who would form the management succession. Each time, Perkins and Miller would delete George Baker's name. Each time, Roger would put him back in.

Roger had read the *Institutional Investor* article, yet he was still convinced.

Even if Roger had hung around The Sign and heard the cracks over there, he probably still would have been convinced.

But George wasn't as convinced about Roger.

All the Roger nicknames – and there were a lot around the Bank now – were coming out of the same place.

"Snow White."

"Eagle Scout."

Size 13s. (For his shoes.)

The Bank C guys laughed at this. The Bank B guys – the Kennedy bank guys – didn't laugh, of course. They listened to the laughter. That was part of the fun of it for the Bank C guys, watching the pallor on the faces of the Bank B crowd during Roger cracks. It was almost as much fun as watching Al Miossi's face when you called Niger "Nigger."

> The mystery at Continental is how chairman Anderson, cautious and conservative by nature . . . could not only tolerate but actively spearhead this kind of aggressiveness.

In early 1980 a rumor went around The Sign that George had faced Roger down again. The word was that it was a palace revolt. The young Turk deal makers, exuberant at the success the new policies had brought them, wanted even more such policies. They demanded them.

But this time people believed the rumor. For those who had read John Steinbeck, it wasn't George and Roger anymore; it was George and Lennie.

By mid-1980 no one in the commercial bank was waiting for the atmosphere to return to normal. There was a new norm, a new character.

But in a bank, all seems stable. The columns, the flags, the daily rituals. All the people doing their jobs, neatly and thoroughly. Tellers. Vault people. The guards. The procedures. Lock and key.

This doesn't vary: The daily rounds. The carpets. The silence. The reassuring, guaranteeing silence.

The quarterly reports.

TWENTY-FIVE

*I*N 1980 THE EARNINGS OF THE BANK EXCEEDED $200 MILLION. It was the twelfth consecutive record. A location map showed Continental offices in sixteen American cities.

> Success in efforts to build commercial and industrial loan market share . . . reflects a fundamental commitment to domestic wholesale banking. Emphasis here has expanded the commercial loan portfolio by more than 100 per cent since 1975.

"Basic Strengths" was the caption to that section of the annual report. Pretty soon the Continental Bank would be number one in commercial lending to domestic customers.

The success exceeded even the plan.

No one was saying, "Somebody ought to tell Roger," about this.

In 1980 the commanders of the old bank were officially taken out of the line management. Gene Holland became chairman of the credit policy committee. Ed Cummings became the area corporate officer for Europe, and Al Miossi the director of international affairs. Each of them could thus wind down his career in the place he preferred: Gene in Chicago, Ed in Europe, and Al in first-class travel accommodations.

As before, Gene Holland, Ed Cummings, and Al Miossi were listed under George's name, but now they were listed as members of his staff, a role that Gerry Keeley had had to himself until then.

Gerry left the bank in 1980 to take a job in Philadelphia. He had been at the Continental Bank since graduating from Notre Dame in 1956 – half his life. There was a good-bye party for the Keeleys in Kenilworth, and many of the old-bank families were there. George Baker couldn't make it. Marianne Baker came alone.

Gerry went by on his last day to see Roger, but there wasn't much time to reminisce; Roger had a train to catch.

Roger had more time when Bill Anderson resigned. With Bill, veteran of the campaigns of Spain, Greece, Latin America, and Michele Sindona, the good-bye was quiet and personal. He and Roger talked about the old days, about Bill's new job in Minneapolis.

"You know," Roger said as they sat there, "that they'll talk about you when you're gone."

It dropped in there, the comment. Philosophic. Plaintive, in a way.

As if Roger had no idea what they had already said about him.

Whoever they were: maybe the They of the mysterious and impenetable bank that he had joined in 1946, that permanent, ponderous, and powerful entity. It was as if they were still beyond him, incomprehensible, although he headed the entity itself.

Chuck Hall resigned in 1980 to become president of Rollins-Burdick-Hunter, a Chicago firm.

And John Jones went to work for Chicago Bridge and Iron.

When John Jones left, it stunned Roger.

John was the classic of all the Continental "Profiles" of 1966. The all-American, as all-American as Roger himself. Maybe Roger's relationship with John Jones was the closest he had ever come to trusting his people instinct over what he read in the balance sheet.

Roger spent a long time with Jones. When Jones left, it hurt him.

There were others who left. All the "Profiles," the originals, the hard currency, the 1967 dollar, of the Continental Bank left. Gerry Pearson left. Pearson was the heart of Group U. He was the symbol of the oil and gas division of the bank. He was famous in the industry.

He was the last of the old Group U line officers, the last of the fabled group that had distinguished itself by going out en masse every day at ten A.M. to the coffee shop when coffee breaks had been forbidden and auditors from the bank were scouring neighborhood cafés for offenders. They went partly for the coffee and partly for the auditors.

Group U had also distinguished itself as the leading banking group for the independent energy industry of the United States – coal as well as oil and gas – for over thirty years.

One of the field vice presidents who was in from New York dropped by to say good-bye to Pearson. He stayed to talk with some of the oil group afterward.

"This is too great a blow," he said. "The Continental Bank just can't afford to lose people like Gerry Pearson. Jones, and now Pearson."

A young vice president, a nice guy, was standing nearby. He was wearing a light brown suit and a pale yellow shirt, emblematic of the division at that time. He said, "Well, Jim, you probably should keep in mind that Gerry Pearson's departure is going to open the way for several young people who are ready to move forward."

His tone of voice was the thing. Slow, correct phrasing – a quiet admonishment. *You are missing the point,* it said. *You are out of the mainstream. Things are happening here, they will continue to happen, and that's the name of this game.*

You guys just don't get it.

Tradition had proved that no one person was indispensable at the bank. But tradition had also proved that the strongest officers of the bank never left it. They had always stayed. Until now.

In the new bank, others waited – anxious, well trained, capable – to move ahead. The human resources, if not fungible, were boundless. Here was a new generation of "universal bankers."

TWENTY-SIX

WHEN IT WAS ALL OVER, there would be a thousand explanations for what had ruined the great Continental Bank. They would all have to do with numbers, and there would be numbers to prove each one of them. The explanations with numbers would all be voiced by experts; they would all be validated by business terms.

But the crucial relationship between Roger and George was the enigma that no one would ever explain. Numbers could not describe the enormous differences between the two men, between the Continental Bank symbolized by Roger and the Continental Bank created by George.

Maybe it had to do with faith in numbers, especially Roger's faith in numbers, the conviction that numbers can be trusted more than people. People can fool you, but numbers can't; not if you truly analyze them. There was such a huge responsibility in banking; you had to know what you were doing.

Maybe it was Roger's need to know, to be absolutely sure, to guarantee.

Maybe after all those years of filling that huge brain with the numbers, of analyzing the details of ten balance sheets while most men struggled with one, of carrying the bank home in his briefcase for years, of touching all the bases, of coming closer and closer to grasping it all, of getting every bit of it down on the spreadsheet, getting a glove on the invisible hand itself; maybe after all the years of doing that, Roger realized that he would never know enough to be sure.

"I want to be sure that the next man in this job is better prepared for it than I was."

He had said that in the early 1970s. It had been modesty; he was the best prepared chairman the bank would ever have. But there was so much more to know. There was the "beyond."

The one ideology that mattered, the necessary wisdom – true knowledge of the "beyond" – lay where he had been told it lay when he had first stepped inside this wondrous and most honorable of institutions as a young naval officer in the America of 1946. The "beyond" lay in the core bank, in real banking; it lay with the credit men.

And perhaps he always felt that he had been denied true knowledge when duty had taken him away from the core bank, had taken him into the international phenomenon, and had left him there for twenty years while those in Chicago had obtained the knowledge. While George, there at the core, had obtained it.

A sense of family prevailed among those who had gone through the foreign campaigns with him, who had taken the bank around the world. But these good friends could not know, either, for they had done the same thing he had – international banking. Roger knew their limitations; they, too, had been denied the real bank, the core bank, where one might know.

George knew. George had been there. He had the track record. His manner showed that he knew.

John Perkins and Don Miller would rule Baker out. Roger would rule him back in.

"Jones should have told Roger," Al Miossi said later. "He always listened to Jones."

But what could John have told him? That the Continental was rated the best bank in the country? Roger already knew that; he read the papers.

Or should he have told him that it was "a skyscraper built on sand"? That was the *Wall Street Journal* headline, only the *Journal* didn't print it until long after 1980.

In 1980 the Continental didn't look like a skyscraper built on sand.

On the cover of the 1980 annual report was a photograph of two workmen at the construction site of the Continental Bank's new building in New York City.

The Continental had signed the biggest leasing commitment in dollar value in New York's history: 260,000 square feet of space for thirty years in the skyscraper being built at 520 Madison Avenue between Fifty-third and Fifty-fourth streets. It would become the Continental Illinois Plaza. The annual report said,

> Madison Avenue is a long way from Rell Small's Walnut Farm birthplace and Gardner, Illinois, home town, where he still looks forward to putting out a few tomato plants again this spring in his eighty-fourth year, and still husbands some of the Continental stock that he bought a few weeks after the crash of 1929 and held to make stockholders of his children and his children's children over the years.
>
> The difference between then and now, or New York and Gardner, could hardly seem greater.

1980 was a record year. The bank went from $35.8 billion to $42 billion in assets and earned profits of $226 million.

Tell Roger what?

1981 was another record year. The Continental was now a $46.9 billion bank, the sixth largest in the country, ahead of Chemical. The profits were $254.6 million.

1981 was the last record year.

TWENTY-SEVEN

THERE WERE TWO GREAT FLAWS IN THE BANK C REORGANIZATION. The first flaw was the new organizational form itself. Matrix management was already a dead idea even before the Continental bought it. The second flaw was the market rationale. The bank reshaped itself to accommodate the banking business from multinational companies. But that business wasn't growing; it was shrinking.

By January 1977, when the new Continental Illinois Bank was unveiled, the McKinsey people were gone. They missed all the excitement in Chicago.

But they had other fish to fry. In the executive offices of McKinsey at this time there was "a general concern with the problems of management effectiveness, and a particular concern with the nature of the relationship between strategy, structure, and management effectiveness."

So the McKinsey people formed some internal task forces of their own. "One was to review our thinking on strategy, and the other was to go back to the drawing board on organizational effectiveness."

The leaders of the second task force were Thomas J. Peters and Robert H. Waterman, Jr. Out of it came America's all-time business best seller, *In Search of Excellence*. It was published in 1982, the ominous year of the Penn Square failure. By 1984, the year of the Continental "disaster movie," the book had sold 1.3 million copies in hardcover and another 1.5 million in paperback.

The McKinsey people put even more time into their own internal task force than they had to the Continental Bank's task force. They talked "extensively to executives around the world who were known for their skill, experience, and wisdom on the question of organizational design." They found that these executives "shared our disquiet about conventional approaches. All were uncomfortable with the limitations of the usual structural solutions, especially the latest aberration, the complex matrix form."

Especially that aberration.

"Our next step in 1977 was to look beyond practicing businessmen for help. We visited a dozen business schools in the United States and Europe (Japan doesn't have business schools). The theorists from academe, we found, were wrestling with the same concerns."

It was some task force. Peters, of course, was not your average consultant, and had left McKinsey & Company by the time the book came out, in deference to the third principle of the study. It found it didn't have to spend all its time in Japan to find out about business excellence (something that the business Academy had resigned itself to by this time). It based its findings on forty-two model firms in the United States. The book's subtitle was *Lessons from America's Best-Run Companies*.

"Our findings were a pleasant surprise. The project showed, more clearly than could have been hoped for, that the excellent companies were, above all, brilliant on the basics. Tools didn't substitute for thinking. Intellect didn't overpower wisdom. Analysis didn't impede action. Rather, these companies worked hard to keep things simple in a complex world. . . .

The eight attributes that emerged to characterize most nearly the distinction of the excellent, innovative companies go as follows:

1. *A bias for action,* for getting on with it. . . .

2. *Close to the customer.* These companies learn from the people they serve. . . . Many . . . got their best product ideas from customers. . . .

3. *Autonomy and entrepreneurship.* The innovative companies foster many leaders and many innovators throughout the organization. . . .

4. *Productivity through people.* The excellent companies treat the rank and file as the root source of quality and productivity gain. They do not foster we/they labor attitudes. . . .

5. *Hands-on, value-driven.* Thomas Watson, Jr., said that "the basic philosophy of an organization has far more to do with its achievements than do technological or economic resources, organizational structure, innovation and timing." . . .

6. *Stick to the knitting.* Robert W. Johnson, former Johnson & Johnson chairman, put it this way: "Never acquire a business you don't know how to run. . . .

7. *Simple form, lean staff.* As big as most of the companies we have looked at are, none when we looked at it was formally run with a matrix organization structure, and some which had tried that form had abandoned it. . . .

8. *Simultaneous loose-tight properties.* . . . For the most part . . . they have pushed autonomy down to the shop floor or product development team. On the other hand, they are fanatic centralists around the few core values they hold dear. . . .

Most of these eight attributes are not startling. Some, if not most, are "motherhoods." But as Rene McPherson says, "Almost everybody agrees, 'people are our most important asset.' "

January 1977: task forces in search of excellence. It was nice symmetry.

As you went down the list in 1982, you found that all eight, point by point, described America's bank, the Continental Illinois.

The problem is, they described it as it was before the experts reorganized it. McKinsey had sold us matrix management, the very snake oil that the excellent companies avoided. They had sold us layers, secrecy, "universal bankers," the customer equivalence of Argentina and Korea, of Belgium and Iowa, business orientation, buzzwords, and Them and Us.

McKinsey had sold the Continental Bank its obsolete equipment.

TWENTY-EIGHT

THE SECOND FLOW IN THE BANK C REORGANIZATION WAS THE
MARKET RATIONALE.
The legitimacy of creating a "multinational" bank – that is, of
giving it the name, of creating a special organization, with dozens of
new titles, the works – was the extraordinary success of the Continental's commercial banking group in New York.

This was the celebrated Group H-N.

Before the American Challenge of the 1960s the bank had been as
tentative about a resident lending group in New York as it was about
branches in Europe. For twenty-five years, the commercial banking
department had deemed a one-man representative office to be a sufficient presence in New York. The job of the representative was to arrange calls for officers from Chicago.

Continental Bank International opened in 1963, but the law under
which it was created, the Edge Act, limited it to foreign business. Its
accounts were the banks and companies of Europe and Latin America
and Asia who traded with the United States. It was an international
presence, not a New York presence.

The bank didn't really go into New York until the very end of the
Kennedy period, the beginning of the Don Graham period. It was Gene
Holland, whose style and thinking set the standard for the commercial
department at the time, who finally decided to take the gamble.

Gene Holland thought enough of Don Myers, a quick, open-mannered young guy who had worked for him in Group H – the eastern division – to let him set up a New York group in 1968, manage the existing customer accounts, and try to get some new business. The group took some space in the building being used by Continental Bank International at 71 Broadway and then later moved to the Chemical bank building at 277 Park.

Don Myers and the hand-picked group of Chicago boys he took to New York between 1968 and 1974 had given the Continental the missing link between its overseas network and the multinationals. This innovative group – Dick Hughes, John Brubaker, Mick Friedman, Kirk Hagan, Mike Murray, Bill Gunlicks, Dave Anderson, Bob Griffin, and Bob Holland – produced an unexpected volume of new business and did so in industry's most sophisticated market.

But it wasn't a success in business volume alone. It was a success in style. The Continental's customer events – the receptions, the economic presentations – outdrew those of the Chase in its own city. The men in Group H-N, most of them under thirty, not one of them yet thirty-five, covered three hundred major companies and had more than half of them on the books.

Ninety-four of the largest hundred U.S. companies and 318 of the Fortune 500 were accounts of the Continental Bank in 1973. Annual report writers saw fit to note that commercial banking officers "generated substantial volumes of business . . . for the international banking department." Although some of the IBD people snorted, this was entirely the case. The Big Ten bankers in New York had made a mark.

It was a case in which the success of a venture so far exceeds expectations that corporate planning has to conclude that the market did it and that they – the planners – had merely underestimated the market.

The conclusion was obvious: the real multinational market remained to be tapped. It was time to plan for it, to get some real pros in there to maximize it, to do it right. So it began.

The problem was that the multinational companies had become banks themselves.

Exxon's cash management operation was superior to Citibank's, which was superior to that of any other bank. Exxon operated in dozens of countries and had no idle funds in any of them, which meant no free deposits of the kind that had made the company such a valued friend of bankers. Other companies, if not at Exxon's level, were more than adequate. There was little for banks to tell them and little for banks to sell them.

Exxon's foreign exchange trading was as good as its cash management.

If companies could move funds quickly from cash-surplus to cash-deficit subsidiaries in other countries, it meant they borrowed less from banks.

Prince Jean d'Arenberg had written a long memorandum from Brussels detailing other aspects of the multinational problem in 1975. U.S. multinationals were no longer expanding in Europe; they were, in fact, contracting. He urged a more European strategy for Continental Bank, S.A.: a Hausbank approach to relationships with European countries; less rotation of account managers, with emphasis on continuity and adaptation by the Continental to local practices.

The young calling officers in the Continental's New York office also were discussing a problem with the multinational market. It was a new problem, and a greater one.

Something that had started in 1974 had an enormous impact on big banks' dealings with the big companies. It was the year of the Franklin and Herstatt bank failures – headline events. But this event didn't get a headline. Yet it would have a far greater effect on corporate banking than the famous bank failures.

The ninety-day note began to disappear.

The ninety-day note was the basis of commercial banking. It was to commercial banking what washing machines were to the Maytag company – the lead product.

The ninety-day note was what defined them as commercial banks. They financed commerce, the manufacture and transportation and sale of goods.

A company figured to move its seasonal production in 180 days. It would borrow from its banks to finance the goods – as inventory, as accounts receivable – until the buyer paid up.

The bigger a company was, the more it sold, the more it borrowed from banks. Billions of dollars of business.

A few companies borrowed more than a billion by themselves. These were companies who used several lead banks, because no one bank could lend that much to a single customer. U.S. law limited a bank to single-customer credit of 10 percent of your own capital. So even a huge bank like the Continental – with capital of $1.75 billion – could lend only $175 million to Sears or International Harvester or General Motors.

A whole set of banking conventions went with the ninety-day note. Short-term borrowing was done under a line of credit. The standard condition for a line of credit was that the company keep demand deposits – "compensating balance" – with the bank. The formula was called "ten plus ten." To have the line, you kept deposits equal to 10 percent of it. If you used the line, you kept deposits equal to another 10 percent of what you used.

So if a company had a $10 million line, it put a million in the bank. And if it borrowed the whole $10 million, it put another million in the bank.

Everybody did this. It was the convention. It was one of the reasons why big corporations were such good customers.

The ninety-day note defined commercial banking. There were still countries in the world whose laws limited commercial banks to short-term loans; Spain, for example, had an absolute maximum eighteen months, strictly controlled, and no mortgage lending of the American style.

Modern U.S. banks did much more, of course, not only home mortgages but term loans as well. *Term* meant more than one year, and it had been getting longer and longer. Three, then five, up to seven and ten. Some were now twelve or fifteen years, loans that only investment banks had done in the old days and then only as middlemen.

But the ninety-day note was the basis.

The big users, the big companies, began to use it less and less in 1974. Because they didn't need the banks anymore.

They could now issue their own ninety-day notes, called commercial paper, and broker them to the public for lower rates. The public, in turn, earned more on this paper than it could on bank deposits; the companies paid less than they would for bank loans.

The commercial paper market didn't need much time to grow big. It was huge from the outset; it just got huger.

The companies who could take advantage of this were the big ones, those with the best-known names: the multinationals.

TWENTY-NINE

*I*N THE RESTRUCTURED CONTINENTAL BANK OF 1977 – Bank C – multinational banking was advertised as the "mainstream."
There had been a subtle scramble for position during the last months of the McKinsey period. "Fast-track" career people knew they had to be in the mainstream. But the word soon leaked out to the lending groups, to those on the main banking floor, that multinational banking wasn't going to be it after all.

After all the excitement the MBD divisions had the dullest jobs in the bank. They were still just Metro Midwest, signing off on routine line renewals to big companies, reading activity reports on lock-box deposits.

It was the work of the old-time bankers. It was the same thing the three-six-three crowd, the Bank A and Bank B fogies, had done in the days of cobweb banking.

So although the public progress reports on "the multinational bank" were as vivid as before, the fast-track people on the inside were keen to the reality. The MBD was not mainstream; it was dullsville. The big new organization chart was obsolete as soon as it was published.

The place in the Continental Bank where the deals were being done, where the new banking was being developed, was in a new department

238

on the tenth floor. The mainstream, without doubt, was Special Industries.

Lending for mining projects. Aircraft and shipping finance. Leasing deals.

And above all, lending to oilmen.

The Bank C organization – once you peeled off the layers and unscrambled the language and the titles – turned out to be a gussied-up version of the Bank A organization.

The foreign division was back where it belonged, under domestic banking, where it had been in 1955.

This brought an unanticipated problem.

The bank could by edict domesticate its own foreign division management, but the edict didn't work on the foreign customers. The European banks and the South American companies just wouldn't fall in line. They were as foreign as ever. They still wouldn't do business exactly the right way.

When it became clear that more good multinational business wasn't going to materialize, the only available global business was still "foreign" foreign.

The sharp new "universal bankers" now in the international department were fast-track people. They knew what their peers in Special Industries – the guys and gals they had just come through the training program with – were doing. They were doing deals. They were making bonuses.

The new kids in IBD wanted to make deals, too. And the new managers had to keep them happy if they were going to keep them in the Bank.

The Continental Bank's foreign lending grew as it had never grown before. Loans in Asia, Africa, and Latin America doubled in the new bank. In 1981 alone assets in Latin America grew by a billion dollars, half again as much in one year.

The old international department was gone. Not one of the companions of Roger Anderson during the American Challenge period was still in place.

Not one of the senior managers in Brazil, Chile, Argentina, and Mexico spoke the local language. In Asia four different Chicago departments carried out independent business operations, all under Managers. Nobody knew anybody over there anymore.

But it wasn't the "universal bankers" in South America who had the biggest problems in the fatal year of 1982. IBD wasn't all that had vanished in Bank C.

By 1980, most of the men of the originating multinational group – Myers, Hughes, Brubaker, Hagan, Anderson, Griffin, Friedman – were gone.

And all the veteran lending officers of the old Group U – the oil group on which the Continental's energy-lending reputation was based – were gone.

The senior officers for Oklahoma didn't speak the local language.

It was the "universal bankers" in Oklahoma who had problems in 1982.

PART

EIGHT

The Penn Square

THIRTY

THE PENN SQUARE BANK, N.A., was a second-level bank in Oklahoma City, where the old-line Bank of Oklahoma and the First National Bank and Trust Company of Oklahoma City dominated the traditional assets and deposits of the city and the state. On the morning of Tuesday, July 6, 1982, customers of the Penn Square bank who dropped by to cash checks, to look into their safe deposit boxes, or to make deposits found the bank's doors locked. They learned that a group of government bank examiners had spent the weekend inside the bank and had decided to close it the night before.

It was because of the neighborhood customers that the closing got some television coverage. In America it had been a long time since people had actually lined up outside a failed bank to try to get their money out. The media – television and print – carried pictures of those lines.

Without those lines there probably would have been little if any television coverage of Penn Square's closing. Such bank failures were business-page items, but they weren't national television news. There had been ten bank failures the year before, in 1981, and who could remember the name of one of them? The Penn Square Bank was bigger than any of the ten banks that had failed in 1981, but it was no bigger than the West Texas banks that failed in 1982 and 1983 and attracting little public interest outside their local areas.

But there was something special about the Penn Square Bank, something that neither its checking-account customers nor *The Wall Street Journal* nor Roger Anderson would have thought possible.

Penn Square, with $33 million in capital of its own, had managed to obtain a lot of money – deposits, loans, participations, call it what you like – from some of the biggest and best-known banks in New York, Chicago, Detroit, and Seattle.

Rumors that some big banks might suffer because of Penn Square moved through the banks before they hit the press. The word at the Continental was that the bank might be involved. It could be embarrassing for the energy division.

The first thought, naturally, was for peer consequences. The energy lenders – known to be the top pros in the bank – would get grief from the other groups. And the Continental would get grief from New York bankers who were already sore about the bank's "best-managed" reputation. It could be embarrassing.

In a perverse but very human vein, lending officers in the other groups might lay it on the energy guys. They had been flying high too long. They deserved it.

But on the other hand, it was unlikely that Continental was involved in other than a minor way. Among the 2,600 correspondents of the Continental Illinois National Bank of Chicago, Penn Square ranked somewhere in the middle. Continental was a wholesale bank, preferring big companies and big banks as customers. A big bank was one with more than a billion dollars in deposits. There were just over four-hundred of these in America, and 95 percent of them were customers of the Continental. With $33 million in capital, Penn Square was about the size of a large Bolivian bank or a second-level bank in Peru or Argentina.

John Perkins may have heard of Penn Square; he was president of the American Bankers Association, and he had a superior memory for names. But maybe he hadn't; even skilled memory people had a hard time associating the "Penn" with Oklahoma. If Roger Anderson had been president of the ABA, he would have known where the Penn Square Bank was because his memory was even more awesome than John's. As it was, however, Roger had no reason to know of the bank before July 1982.

The story hit *The Wall Street Journal* on Wednesday, July 7, the morning after the Monday holiday closing. It wasn't about an isolated Oklahoma bank failure.

PENN SQUARE'S FAILURE BODES LOSSES FOR MANY

OKLAHOMA CITY – For the first time in many years, large numbers of uninsured depositors and creditors stand to lose money in a big bank failure.

Late Monday, federal regulators closed Penn Square Bank, one of the biggest energy-related lenders in the Southwest, declaring it insolvent because of large loan losses. It was reopened yesterday as Deposit Insurance National Bank of Oklahoma City.

Continental Illinois Corp., whose Continental Illinois National Bank & Trust unit purchased about $1 billion of Penn Square loans, said yesterday that it expects a second-quarter loss because of a special charge to cover losses from those loans. Chase Manhattan Bank of New York, Seafirst Corp.'s Seattle First National Bank and Northern Trust Corp.'s Northern Trust Co. unit also face charges against earnings.

Continental didn't specify the size of its special charge. But analysts estimated it at $120 million to $200 million before taxes.

A billion dollars? Could we have given a *billion* dollars to this little Oklahoma bank, the one that just failed?

THIRTY-ONE

ROGER ANDERSON LEARNED OF THE PENN SQUARE PROBLEM on June 29, 1982. One week in advance of the failure, officers inside the Continental learned from the Washington bank examiners that there was trouble in Oklahoma.

It took some time after that for the energy division to put together some figures. By the time the Penn Square failure announcement was made the Continental staff was fairly confident of the figure for the aggregate of loans bought by the Continental from the Oklahoma bank.

The aggregate was $1,056,000,000.

Neither the lending group that had made the loans, nor the division it belonged to, nor the loan department of the bank, nor the computer information specialists, nor the auditors had before this time computed this total under the caption "Penn Square Bank."

So there were two surprises for Roger Anderson on the July 4 weekend. One was the existence of a bank in Oklahoma with the unlikely name of Penn Square, and the other was the fact that the Continental, in effect, had lent this bank a billion dollars.

Within days of the July 6 Penn Square failure Roger Anderson put together a three-man team to start an investigation inside the Continental. He reached Ed Cummings in Europe and asked him to head it. He telephoned Bob Ruwitch, a veteran lending officer recently retired from the bank, and Bill Plechaty, a veteran of the old bank auditing system, now in charge of personal banking services.

How much of the billion dollars would be lost – definitely unrepayable – couldn't be known right away. Only $30 million had been a direct loan to the failed bank. The lending officers had a best estimate: $200 million. There could be more, but the lending officers said they didn't think so. They deemed a $200 million write-off liberal, more than would probably be lost. It was better to be conservative.

The job of the three-man investigating team wasn't to assess the losses but to find out how and why so many loans had been made to the Penn Square Bank, to uncover the human error in the process.

During the second and third weeks of July calls from the press and from securities analysts poured into the Continental Bank. The bank declined to comment, and pique at this as much as anything else started rumblings among the experts.

The bank wasn't ready to speak yet. It held them off.

The Chase Manhattan Bank took the first hit, on July 19, two Mondays after the Penn Square news.

For the first time since the Great Depression one of America's Big Ten banks reported a quarterly loss. Due to dealings with a small New York securities firm, Drysdale Government Securities, and a small Oklahoma Bank, the third largest bank in the country acknowledged a loss of $16.1 million in the second quarter of 1982.

An executive vice president, a senior vice president, and seven other officers of the Chase lost their jobs. Another executive vice president was demoted.

There was still no announcement from the Continental.

In Chicago the next day Roger Anderson sent a memorandum to the Continental staff, preparing them for the loss. He told them that the bank had learned of the Penn Square case only a week before the failure.

On Wednesday, July 21, the sixth largest bank in America announced its results for the quarter.

An operating loss of $60,950,000.

An addition to the loan-loss reserve of $262,000,000, of which $220,000,000 attributed to Penn Squares'.

Actual credit losses, charged against reserves, of $82,200,000, of which $45.1 million attributed to Penn Square.

An increase of $456 million, to $1.3 billion, in nonperforming or problem loans.

$151 million of the problem – nonperforming – loans were related to Penn Square.

The Penn Square debacle was a unique case for the Continental, as it was for the other big banks involved.

The overall increase in problem loans had been due to accounting rules pertaining to the Continental's emphasis on domestic lending.

Foreign loans had been a subject of concern among New York banks for months. There was broad leniency in U.S. accounting principles for treating problematic foreign loans, but there was no such leniency for loans to Americans.

"In addition to the massive and continuing examination of our loan participations with the Penn Square Bank," Roger Anderson announced, "we have also reviewed other elements of our loan portfolio. As a result, we believe that the Penn Square loan participations represent a unique problem."

Continental was the largest domestic, commercial, and industrial lender in the United States. A higher percentage of nonperforming credits made sense. It was credible.

The reaction was mixed.

"To take losses like this is incredible. Maybe they're trying to be conservative, but it does raise questions about their whole credit policy," said Larry Fuller, one of the most quoted of the bank analysts. "It sounds like they threw the kitchen sink in."

Some analysts said they were concerned about the problem loans, but others liked the conservatism in the move: take the hit now, be over-conservative in the problem-loan area, and get it out of the way early so you don't have to do it again later.

It was a conservative bank. It had always been. Its style was to face up to mistakes at once. The fact was that the great Continental Bank had made a blunder. Such things can happen. Nobody knew how or why Special Industries had put so much money into the Oklahoma bank, but it had.

Bank analysts agreed that problem foreign loans do not show up as nonperforming because banks can merely roll them into new loans.

The Continental would have earned $51.2 million without Penn Square. The total assets of the bank were $48.6 billion.

Mainly, it was embarrassing. Everybody in the industry was embarrassed. The loss had been totally unexpected. Chase Manhattan's trouble with Drysdale had been in the press for weeks. No one had been surprised. Chase Manhattan had made the same mistake, but the industry expected mistakes from Chase.

Roger made the public announcement on July 21. John Perkins and Don Miller made a private trip to New York to sit down with New York bankers and give them the straight inside story.

That was good form. We had stubbed our toes, and we knew that we had embarrassed not just ourselves but the industry. We owed the New York banks the visit.

When John and Don were at Morgan Guaranty, Morgan offered to be of assistance to the Continental if they were needed.

That was good form, too.

John and Don declined with thanks.

On August 2 John Perkins, George Baker, and Dave Taylor were with securities analysts in New York. The press was barred from the meetings. The Continental offices explained that their earlier silence had been in deference to an Illinois law that prevented public discussion of loans. They said the Continental was still trying to determine how it had become so deeply involved with the Penn Square Bank.

They disclosed details of many of their large credits to financially troubled companies. They were "eager to talk . . . they volunteered information about some loans without being asked," an analyst said.

The "decline in confidence" arose from the uncertainty created by the earlier refusal to discuss the difficulties rather than from the actual and potential losses. Despite their size, analysts considered the losses manageable for the country's sixth biggest bank.

"The disclosure gave me comfort," another analyst said.

They just wanted some direct answers. No one was worried.

Roger made his first press appearance in Chicago the next day and gave the same presentation. Everything was out in the open.

> We have no intention of pulling in our horns. . . .
>
> I believe our basic philosophy of lending is sound, but it's apparent our system broke down. . . .
>
> You go almost ten years with virtually no problem loans and there's some tendency to let one's guard down. . . .

Continental still has not fully unraveled how it got into the Penn Square situation and why it had not been detected. To find out, the bank has about twenty-five of its own people stationed in Oklahoma City.

A listing of the most prominent problem loans of the bank was given to the press. It was a rare show of openness and of confidence by a big American bank.

On August 30, after an eight-week investigation by the Cummings Committee, the Continental made sweeping changes among the executives involved in the Penn Square losses.

John R. Lytle, a vice president in charge of Oklahoma lending, was fired.

Gerry Bergman, head of Special Industries, resigned.

Jack Redding, head of the oil and gas division, took early retirement.

Patrick M. Goy, a vice president under Lytle, resigned.

This was the end of phase one of the bank's investigation.

"Our investigation has shown that strong measures must be taken to reinforce both the discipline and the management structure at Continental," Roger Anderson announced. "Our actions are responsive to this requirement."

There were hearings before the House Banking Committee in September. John Perkins spoke for the Continental. "Our problem in Penn Square was with human error, not the bank's procedures," said John.

John Lytle said, "They are trying to make me and the others scapegoats."

THIRTY-TWO

*I*T WAS AN INCREDIBLE STORY.

A mature, highly respected bank chairman had turned his bank over – carte blanche – to a fast-talking, cigar-smoking, irreverent, colorful deal maker. The captain of a ship had surrendered the conn to a lieutenant who ran its engines to flank speed and then steered it into an iceberg.

A *Fortune* reporter, first to arrive on the scene, wrote: He took the bank "on a lending spree as wild as his personal style – and shook the pillars of the financial community."

Now the chairman of the bank wanted you to believe he was surprised.

"I had a concept," the chairman told a *New York Times* reporter. That's all he could say; he said he could not say more on the advice of counsel.

It was an incredible story, Penn Square.

The chairman, Bill P. Jennings, had put together a group of investors to buy the small bank in 1974 with the idea of expanding the bank through energy lending.

The concept had been to use a knowledge of the market – of the independent oil drillers in the region – to develop a lending business that could be sold to larger banks. It was an investment banking principle. The Penn Square Bank found the loans and took a finder's fee from the big lenders for doing so. As a commercial bank, the bank kept that portion of the lending that the law allowed on its own books.

When Penn Square was acquired by the Jennings group in 1974, it had total loans of $35 million. By 1982 those loans were over $500 million. The legal lending of the bank, however, never exceeded $4 million.

Jennings's lending officers knew the Oklahoma oil industry. Oklahoma was where much of the independent oil industry was. The timing was right. 1974, the year the bank was acquired, was the signal year for what happened in the world energy markets. The unpredictability of the Arabs, the waning of the world's known oil supplies, the widely published concern of conservationists – all pointed to an energy boom, an American oil exploration boom, to follow. Bill Jennings's timing was perfect.

From 1974 on, drilling in the Southwest grew. Oklahoma became dotted with boom towns. It was the only thing that Herman Kahn and the Club of Rome could agree on: the price of oil would never go down again. If you had a corner on this ever-more-dear commodity, you had a lock on business for years to come.

Three years after acquiring Penn Square, Jennings hired a twenty-eight-year-old assistant cashier from The First National Bank and Trust Company of Oklahoma City, Bill G. Patterson. Patterson established a track record immediately. He attracted the interest of the big-money banks from Chicago, New York, and even Washington state. When the oil lenders in the Chase Manhattan Bank turned down the Penn Square program, he managed to convince a different department of that bank – the correspondent banking department – to do it anyway. Before long Patterson was senior executive vice president in charge of oil and gas lending and a director of the bank. Bill Jennings then turned the bank over to Bill Patterson.

By the end of it Bill Patterson was a director of the bank, owned sixteen thousand shares and more than 7 percent of its stock – and was, in the opinion of colleagues, "the son that Bill Jennings never had." He could do no wrong.

Patterson was persuasive at the Continental Illinois. And the presence of the Continental persuaded others. Michigan National came in. First Seattle. It was normal banking behavior. One watches the people who know, the people with the track record, the experts. Expertise in oil and energy lending rested without doubt at 231 South LaSalle Street in Chicago.

Coverage of the Penn Square story was some of the most colorful that financial pages had seen in a long time. *Fortune* and *The New York*

Times had reporters in Oklahoma City soon after the failure; both carried long stories in August.

The Penn Square scenario was a combination of *Cash McCall* and *Animal House.*

There were stories of Patterson's food fights, of Patterson drinking beer out of a boot, of Patterson wearing a German Army helmet to the office and Mickey Mouse ears at other times, and of Patterson mooning the Continental Bank building in Chicago while out on the town. There were stories about Oklahoma oilmen and private jets and huge handshake deals and plenty of good liquor. The common nouns were feature-story gems: *wildcatters, boom towns, rig counts, boots, saddles, limousines.* There was $30 million in personal notes.

There was an energy bank with fast-track, fearless young bankers running circles around the faint-of-heart senior managers who, left behind from another banking era, sat befuddled in the Penn Square offices and cautioned in vain about sound lending practices. Jokes. Laughter.

It ended in a maze of paperwork, desperate last-minute efforts to obtain emergency transfers of money, bank examiners, three thousand loans with unfinished documentation, an unfinished office tower, and Patterson mowing lawns.

In retrospect some affected to be appalled and astonished by the shoddy paperwork, the misnamed deals, the unheeded warnings, the frolics of Patterson, and the couple billion dollars in losses.

But they had to admit that if energy prices had continued to go up – as everyone from Tulsa to Kuwait expected – it would all have led to a great success. The Penn Square Bank might have become the largest bank in Oklahoma. It was well on its way. Bill Patterson might have been the subject of *Fortune* profiles. He might have been a case study for the Harvard Business School. But then again, he earned those distinctions, anyway.

As far as the writers were concerned, there was no story in Chicago. The big blundering bank at 231 South LaSalle Street had covered itself in committees, evasions, ahems, and explanations. Nobody could make sense of any of it, and nobody expected to.

Congressman St. Garmain, the ranking banking industry legislator, summed up the general impression: "Very frankly, these city slickers got taken in by country bumpkins. It's unbelievable and scary, scary, scary."

The stories for the writers were at Penn Square.

Two good books were written about Penn Square, about flashy Oklahoma oilmen and how they took the big-city slickers to the cleaners;

about Bill Patterson, the wildman oil lending chief at Penn Square –
drinking beer out of a boot, Mickey Mouse ears, Wehrmacht helmet,
food fights, and the mooning of the South LaSalle Street bank.

The story wasn't in Chicago. It was in Oklahoma City.

Penn Square Bank may have failed, but it made some colorful history
on the way.

THIRTY-THREE

THERE WERE MULTIPLE INVESTIGATIONS INTO THE PENN
SQUARE CASE.

In Washington the House Banking Committee held formal
hearings, and John Perkins, George Baker, Ed Cummings, and Jim
Cordell – a senior oil-division officer based in Houston – answered questions on behalf of the Continental Bank.

John Lytle, the Continental officer who had managed the Penn Square
lending, also appeared before the committee. In late September he had
been fired; therefore he was speaking on behalf of himself, and not the
bank.

These hearings were public, of course. Also public was a special
investigation made by Goldman, Sachs and Company in July. This report
consisted of detailed interviews with the chief lending officer (George
Baker), the chief funding officer (Dave Taylor), and the corporate office vice chairman (Don Miller). It was first circulated to clients of
Goldman, Sachs and was then made available to reporters and the public.

Also made public were the stories on Penn Square itself and the shenanigans of its colorful crew. *The New York Times* and *Fortune* carried lengthy articles on the Oklahoma bank – on Patterson, Jennings, the oil connection, and the failed concept – in August. Along with losing their bank, the Penn Square principals had lost their privilege of confidentiality. U.S. government officials were pleased to provide reporters with full information.

The investigation within the Continental Bank was not as public.

Inside the bank there was a "two-headed" investigation. The senior management conducted one line of inquiry; the board of directors conducted another. There were three men on each of these investigating teams.

And again there was a heavy irony in this turn of events at the Continental Bank, one that reporters were quick to note.

Ed Cummings, who headed the main investigation, was the son of Walter Cummings, who had given Roger Anderson and John Perkins their starts in banking thirty-five years before.

Bank A was being recalled to take account of Bank C. The old Continental Bank was being brought back to review the new, to examine the "same" not-the-same bank unveiled by its management – at the moment of its election as the best in America – four years before.

Between early July, when Ed rushed back from Europe, and late August, when Lytle was fired and the others were asked to resign, the team of investigators talked with sixty-three Continental people. They were officers and associates from the midcontinent group, from other special industries groups, and from around the bank.

It was grim work. They were grim questions.

Who was involved? Who exactly had done what? What was the background? What did you see? What did people talk about? What were they aware of? Exactly whom do you refer to?

Who knew Patterson? Who went to the parties in Chicago or in Oklahoma? Who else was there? Where were they? What bars?

There were hundreds of files to review, documentation, memoranda. A copy of the letter from John Lytle to Patterson about Michigan National was in the Penn Square file, right alongside the other correspondence.

The personnel records. Examples of appraisals. Criteria of the appraisals.

What was your understanding of the lending policies? What examples did you follow? Whom did you consider a capable lending officer? What were the general opinions of the men in the groups? What did they talk about?

Tell me all you know about this.

It was not easy work, and some of it was not at all pleasant. To uncover the truth junior officers had to talk about the seniors, and seniors had to implicate the people who worked for them.

This was an organization of groups, of teams. Teamwork, team play was the rule, and you could not have this without team loyalty. The report was going to be read by numerous senior people in the bank, by the directors. The source of each comment would be noted.

But it was also a bank, where accountability was the first instinct. And a billion dollars was missing.

THIRTY-FOUR

THE SHORT AND DISASTROUS COMMON HISTORY of Penn Square and the Continental includes the following events.

1974

First Penn Square, a shopping-center bank in Oklahoma City with $29 million in deposits and $35 million in loans, is purchased by a group headed by Billy Paul ("Beep") Jennings, fifty.

1977

Jennings hires Bill G. Patterson, twenty-eight, an assistant cashier at the First National Bank & Trust Company of Oklahoma City.

The Continental Bank implements its global reorganization. Managerial assignments include the transfer of John Lytle, forty-two, from Group 4 (small manufacturers and merchandisers in metropolitan Chicago) to the oil and gas division. A. J. Pearson heads oil and gas lending. John A. Redding heads the new energy and mineral resources group. Pearson and Redding are the principal oil and gas lending officers in the bank. Lytle has a Grade 4 lending authority, $1 million.

1978

John Lytle is introduced to Bill Patterson of the Penn Square Bank by Dennis Winget, a Grade 3 lending officer in the Continental's Oklahoma section.

The Continental begins to buy loans from Penn Square.

1979

Lytle begins serious energy lending. He is a Grade 5 lender, with an authority of $2.5 million.

1980

During the summer Lytle begins a personal borrowing relationship with Penn Square, a $20,000 loan.

At the end of the summer, A. J. Pearson resigns, ending a long career with the Continental.

The oil and gas division is reorganized into the oil and gas group, with four separate divisions: midcontinent, western, Texas (office in Houston), and international/majors.

On September 19, John Lytle is made manager of the midcontinent division and a Grade 6 lender – a $5 million authority. In his division are fifteen lenders and assistants, including two vice presidents, three second vice presidents, and two banking officers.

In November, Michigan National Bank buys $12 million in loans from Penn Square.

At December 31 the Continental's loan purchases from Penn Square are $250 million.

1981

In a January 28 letter to Bill Patterson, Lytle says he assured the Michigan bankers of a Continental "take-out" should they wish it.

In July bank examiners from the comptroller of the currency send a warning to the board of directors of Penn Square about the bank's lending practices.

On July 29, a lending associate in the midcontinent division, Kathleen Kenefick, cautions about the inconsistent documentation of Oklahoma accounts and says, "Corrective action should be instigated quickly."

In July the Continental has about $500 million in Penn Square loans.

Continental auditors go to Oklahoma City to correct the documentation faults. Lytle later says, "These were reporting problems, not credit problems. The matter was reconciling figures for principal and interest payments. A Continental team was sent to Oklahoma to do so." Other testimony, including the Kenefick memo, does not contradict him.

Continental now has several officers from the division in Oklahoma City, operating out of Penn Square. Local bankers kid Bill Patterson about being a Continental Bank loan production office.

In August, Dennis Winget resigns from the Continental and joins Penn Square. Another Continental officer does, also.

In September, Ed Hlavka, the Continental controller, chances to meet George Baker in the washroom and remarks that he thinks a close look should be taken at Penn Square. "It's a pretty frail basket for that big pile of eggs," he says.

In September the Continental has $800 million in Penn Square loans.

Baker reads the Kenefick memo after the auditors have been to Oklahoma and is told the problem has been solved. Kenefick later leaves the bank. One view of this is that she was frustrated by lack of response. Another is that she had a "personality conflict" with her boss. Another is that Bill Patterson dropped pencils on the floor during loan review meetings.

In 1981, Lytle's division doubles its loans to $2 billion and contributes $20 million to the bank's earnings. Lytle's personal compensation has tripled in three years, because of profit incentives. His base salary is $69,000; his total, $125,000.

1982

In January another Continental auditing team is sent to Oklahoma to look over past-due loans. Penn Square's annual report shows an increase in this category for 1981.

In the same month Continental auditors advise management that John Lytle has accepted a loan of $565,000 from Penn Square. The matter goes up through Baker to Roger Anderson. Lytle is admonished but allowed to retire the loan and remain in his post. His comment: "That's the way Oklahoma bankers treated their friends and special customers."

In February total loans purchased from Penn Square amount to $887 million.

The faulty documentation of Penn Square loans is now a heated issue between lending managers and operations managers in the bank. Lytle contends that much of the problem is due to an inadequate computer system. Other managers support his point.

In March, Penn Square receives an unqualified audit from Peat, Marwick, Mitchell & Co. for its 1981 fiscal year.

Energy prices are collapsing.

In April, Baker tells bank analysts that all Penn Square loans meet Continental standards. (He later says, "I was misinformed.")

During the same month comptroller of the currency examiners begin their new review of Penn Square.

In May, Lytle is moved out of the energy lending area.

On June 1 *The Wall Street Journal* carries a front-page story headed, "Big Continental Illinois Suffering Effects of Aggressive Lending." A number of doubtful loans are listed, but Penn Square is not mentioned.

On June 14, Patterson advises Lytle that the comptroller will require Penn Square to charge off $10 million in bad loans.

On July 5 the comptroller closes Penn Square. The bank grew to $525 million in loans, fifteen times its original size, and $490 million in deposits in Jennings's eight years in control. It sold another $2 billion in loans to big city banks. Never did the legal lending limit exceed $4 million.

On June 30 the Continental has between 250 and 300 individual loans on its books that it has purchased from Penn Square. The loans add up to $1,056,000,000.

Michigan National had bought another $190 million, and Chase Manhattan, the Northern Trust of Chicago, and Seattle-First National another $800 million among them.

On the basis of this history John Lytle was fired.

Lytle was the villain of the piece. More than anything else it was the $565,000 loan. John said that he had used it for home improvements, that it was out in the open, that there was nothing wrong with it. When the auditors picked it up, when he was called on the carpet, he paid it off; he sold some assets to do so, he said. Some of his superiors stood up for him and said it was dumb but not unethical.

But among bank officers such a thing violated a cardinal rule, more than even the press seemed to realize. Probably no other officer in the history of the Continental Bank had taken a loan that big – not for home improvement, not even for a mortgage – particularly not from someone it was lending money to.

The rest of it might have passed, odd as that may seem. Many modern managers would be quick to accept that the fault lay with the computers.

The complaints on the documentation? They concerned paperwork, not the worth of the loan. The bank examiners' warning? The comptroller of the currency hadn't told anybody else about it.

The hero of the piece was Kathy Kenefick. She was the first to warn the Continental that it was overexposed in its loans to Oklahoma and particularly to the Penn Square. Her warning memo was the only one. The women's magazines picked up on it.

There was another hero, one only inside the Bank. Among the corps, there was great sympathy for a kid named Pat Goy, who had come in during the 1970s, worked in the metro divisions, and then gone on over to Lytle's group. He had wide respect among the line officers, the kind of respect for talent that had been the nature of the old bank.

Goy wasn't fired; he had been asked to resign. He was the officer who had told the senior management about the overexposure. In August he was called into George's office and he thought he was being promoted. George handed his resignation letter to him.

THIRTY-FIVE

YOU HAD TO HAVE A VILLAIN. That was Inspector Lestrade's first rule: Make the arrest.

For John Lytle it was a great opportunity. He stood at the door of American folk heroism. The billion-dollar man. The genius who had managed to penetrate the computers, the procedures, the systems, and the vaults of a giant and faceless organism for a billion bucks.

Only a year before, a scheming group of insiders and outsiders at the Wells Fargo Bank in California had made the front page of *The New York Times* for only $20 million. Only a few years before that, an officer at the First Chicago had gone over to the bank on a weekend and carried out a million dollars in his suitcase, and that had been good enough for headlines.

But nobody had ever done a billion.

It was hardly believable.

Hardly.

Compared with the oilies of Oklahoma, the great gray bank in Chicago had little to offer in the way of colorful rogues.

The Chicago villain – the culprit revealed by the massive internal investigation, the face-to-face testimonies of sixty-three witnesses – hardly measured up to Bill Patterson.

John Lytle was a middle-aged family man who had worked at the Continental Bank for twenty-three years. The business trips to Oklahoma were the farthest he had traveled from Chicago. Before 1977, his eighteenth year in the bank, he hadn't traveled at all. His work had been with the metro Chicago business groups until then: small businesses and pharmaceutical companies.

He rooted for the Fighting Illini of his alma mater, the University of Illinois.

He commuted from the suburbs. He was friendly. He was a good guy. Everyone knew John Lytle.

But he was the villain. He had removed $1,056,000,000, from the vaults of the Continental and put it in the hands of Bill Patterson and the Penn Square crowd. The investigation had determined this.

John Lytle was fired. He was the only officer of the Continental Bank who was fired.

John Lytle had been there a long time, since the old days.

If you were a lending officer at the bank, even if it wasn't in metro midwest, you knew John Lytle. The bank was the kind of community where everyone knows everyone else. You would see him, as you saw everyone else, around the bank, either on the banking floors or in the dining room. Or if you commuted north, you would see him on the Chicago & North Western, coming in to Northwestern Station, and maybe sometimes you would walk over from the station to the bank with him.

John was not quite a Continental "Profile." He was quieter, a little more tentative. The work, the career, seemed a little harder for John. He had been a little slower to gain the approval of the senior bankers in that approval-oriented society. He seemed not quite as sure of himself or of his decisions as some of the others and was therefore inclined to blend into the committee, to let another make it for him, to see what the group head wanted to do before he said what he wanted to do.

He had joined the Bank at twenty-four and was still an assistant cashier in his mid-thirties. It took him fourteen years – until he was almost forty – to make vice president. He was on the second floor all that time – in Group 5 for years, Group 6 for years, Group 4 for years. His annual raises followed the standard bank pattern; they were as much as most but never the highest.

He was the type of guy who did his job and maybe never really understood why guys like Jones and Myers got more attention and were promoted faster; who was confused and troubled by the promotion lists, those moments of anguish or glory, so many of them disappointing.

John was a team player. He was not a standout, but there were no superstars; no one was indispensable.

It was as if he had to try harder, somehow, to press. It is hard to explain why some guys have to press. But you know it. Lytle was one. Hanging in, holding his job, knowing early that he would never be chairman, maybe never even make vice president. But that was in the American way, too, and it was okay.

But if you wait long enough, something can happen in corporations. The tide can change. What goes around can come around. If you wait long enough, the things that have held you back can suddenly start to work in your favor. You just have to be there.

Sometimes your life changes not because of what you have done but because of what you *haven't* done: not because of medals but because of the absence of them. The environment can change.

In the McKinsey reorganization of 1977 John Lytle's blameless service on the second floor of the bank gave him the status of "universal banker."

One of the key managerial appointments announced by George Baker in those memorable days was John Lytle's appointment in the energy division.

Three years later, after the last of the Group U originals left the bank, John Lytle's career moment had arrived: John Lytle succeeded Gerry Pearson.

The philosophy of the new organization was, If you're a good banker one place, you're a good banker anyplace. No one is irreplaceable. Everyone is the same.

But nobody thought this guy had done it all by himself.

THIRTY-SIX

*T*WO GREAT MYSTERIES REMAINED. How could someone lend a billion dollars to a small bank without anybody else knowing it? How could this happen in the most respected division in the bank?

Those who understood these mysteries kept silent.

Among the lending officers of the Continental the mystery of how such a great amount had been lent, undetected, was no mystery at all.

It had to do with standard accounting procedures and with lending grades.

The billion dollars lent to Penn Square had not been lent to Penn Square itself. The Continental had "bought" loans that the Oklahoma bank had made to private companies. So the Continental loans were booked - accounted for - as loans to those private companies.

It was common for banks for buy loans, or participations in loans, from each other.

Traditionally, such participations had been bought from Chase Manhattan, Citibank, Bank of America, and so forth. It was common practice all over the world; big banks selling off parts of large credits so as to spread the risk. Insurance underwriting was a similar function.

Many of the South American and Mexican credits were bought from the New York banks. It was normal banking.

Once you bought the loan, it was yours.

Citibank didn't owe you the money; the end borrower did. Nowhere in the vast computer information system of the Continental Bank was there a summation of such credits under "Citibank."

Nor was there a summation under "Penn Square Bank," which would have been $1,056,000,000, which was six times the lending limit under law of the Continental Illinois.

Instead of that, there were between 250 and 300 separate credits to Oklahoma companies. All of them were well under the legal lending limit; virtually all of them were under $5 million.

John Lytle's personal lending limit, as a Grade 6 lending officer, was $5 million. His signature, together with that of one other officer in his group, was sufficient under the procedures to disburse those funds.

So the officers in special industries were correct when they said that the problem was due to the computer system. The computer system had not, in fact, provided the answer.

And people could relate to that. Everybody knew the problems with computer systems. It was understandable.

There was no need to mention that nobody had asked the computer system the question.

Inside the bank the matter of how a billion dollars had been lent to Penn Square was no mystery.

THIRTY-SEVEN

THE GREATER MYSTERY was how such a colossal blunder could have happened to the oil and gas division.

The division was the pride of the bank, the best in the industry. And nowhere was the oil and gas group more respected than within the bank. The tradition was legendary: Group U, the mavericks and trail blazers. Easy-moving, soft-spoken, sure-eyed sons of the West. They knew oil people and the oil business as well as George Halas knew the T formation. They had a style. Every morning they went in a group over to Mages Coffee Shop to see who would have to pay. The industry was a game, and no one could play it better than Group U.

The answer to the mystery of Group U was, of course, that Group U was no longer there.

John Lytle, a nice guy from Chicago, was Group U now. He was a good banker, and therefore he was a good banker anywhere – Argentina, Korea, you name it: even Oklahoma. He had gone off to Oklahoma to do business with Bill Patterson, who knew how to treat his friends and special customers.

And a group of the same kind of solid kids who had always come in from Wisconsin and Iowa and Indiana to carry on the Continental bank tradition were in the division with him. They followed the lead and observed the style, having come through the best and most advanced training program anywhere. With the knowledge that the senior management of this bank thought they knew everything they needed to know, they went off to deal with southwestern wildcatters.

("Don't tell me what I said!" the oilman told the greenhorn. "You should have known what I meant.")

The *Fortune* reporter looking back on the case the next February would find to his surprise that the average length of experience of the people in the midcontinent oil and gas division was five quarters. One year and three months.

It came out later that the word had been all over the Southwest, all the way down to Corpus Christi. The word was out to guys with small rigs and big plans: *If you need money, see the Continental Illinois.*

THIRTY-EIGHT

IN 1977, THE YEAR BILL JENNINGS HIRED BILL PATTERSON, the great Continental Illinois Bank was remade by the most approved-of management consultants and was given a new structure and a new style to pursue what corporate strategic planners had determined was its goal: to become one of the top three corporate banks for the multinational corporation market.

But the structure was a known aberration and the market a known decliner. So there was nothing else to do to prove the design except to change the focus, change the language, year by year and bit by bit.

And to do so with such deftness, such business acumen, that the same corporation that had redesigned itself for a future of multinational banking could pile up billions in loans to wildcatters and real estate developers and still think it had met its target.

So that top multinational became top domestic. Smoothly. The subtle difference was unnoticed by the press, the analysts, or even the management. It was all corporate banking, all domestic, real banking – bottom line.

And somehow in this system of comforting, indisputable, inspirational *numbers* where no distinction could be made between a loan bought from Citibank and one bought from Penn Square of Oklahoma, no distinction could be made, either, between the wildcatters and real estate developers – domestic commercial and industrial lending – and the lists of Exxon and Dupont and IBM and Nestlé, whose places they had taken.

A 21 percent growth in commerce and industry loans – ahead of our plan. A 25 percent growth – we're leaving the competition in the dust.

The lost age of the middle 1970s, the strange time that had brought McKinsey to South LaSalle Street and Bill Patterson to Penn Square had deemed *sameness* to be the answer to the complexity.

For "the universal banker," Koreans, Argentines, Iowans were all the same.

Group U was gone, along with IBD, Group H-N, and much of the rest of the old bank, Bank B.

It was as if some new Managers had taken over Coca-Cola, and in their need to invent something of their own, they had decided to get rid of the formula for the product. It was as if they had concocted some other brew, something more like what others were making, and put it in Coca-Cola bottles. It was as nutty as that.

The business had soared.

By the end of 1980, with Pearson gone, it went to $250 million.

By July 1981, $500 million. By the end of the year, $800 million.

And coming full-blast into 1982, racing toward July, when the concern was not with overexposure to Penn Square but was more than ever with growth, Special industries was heading toward $10 billion in assets – a magnificent goal. Everyone was pulling together.

"We are going to have one hell of a party when we hit $10 billion."

The word was out through the department.

In the flush of success John Lytle's pay went to $133,000 – more than $60,000 in bonuses. Others tried to keep pace.

George Baker's pay went to $450,000.

Everything was up, up.

Roger Anderson was the highest paid commercial banker in America: $892,000.

This was proof of the best.

It was an all-out team effort; everyone was pulling together.

Special industries hit $10 billion in July 1982.

The midcontinent division hit $2 billion.

Penn Square hit a billion. Then it disappeared, taking that billion and Bank C with it.

THIRTY-NINE

JOHN LYTLE DIDN'T COME ACROSS as Professor Moriarty when he made his appearance before the House Banking Committee in September.

First, it was a little hard to determine what his job was.

John Lytle was the manager of the midcontinent division of the oil and gas group (worldwide) of the special industries services (SIS) of the general banking services (GBS) of the Continental Bank. Roger Anderson, chairman of the bank, managed George Baker, head of GBS, who managed Gerry Bergman, head of SIS, who managed Jack Redding, head of oil and gas, who managed Lytle, head of midcontinent, who managed the people who were doing the lending to Oklahoma oil companies.

It wasn't Jack Redding's job, as a manager, to get involved in the actual lending, as it had been in the old days. That was bad management practice. Good managers *delegate*.

John Lytle was a Manager, too. In fact, John had other people reporting to him who were Managers – section heads. So for him to be a good Manager, he had to delegate, too.

Except that some of the section head jobs were vacant.

So that John, in the fatal year 1982, couldn't really know what he was.

"Were you designated as a marketing man or market business development officer, or were you a combination of marketing and technician?" Congressman Barnard asked him.

(The House Banking and Finance Committee held hearings on the Penn Square case on September 29, 1982.)

"I am not a qualified engineer," John said. "I think the word *technician* would mean that in the oil and gas area."

"I don't necessarily mean that," Barnard said. "I mean anybody that has been in the banking business twenty-three years has accumulated naturally – in the position that you had – a very important responsibility. You had acquired a general knowledge of the operations of banking, right?"

"Well," John said, "I was the lowest level of management in the lending scheme at Continental. That certainly was important to me, but it is a valid point."

"You managed a portfolio of over $2 billion in loans?"

"Correct. But it must be put in perspective at a very large bank that it was the lowest level of management because there was no section head in the Oklahoma side. Second, I have and had almost no operating knowledge. I don't understand how a loan division works or any of the operating portions of a bank. My entire experience at Continental has been on the lending platform as an officer and then junior manager."

John didn't know operations, didn't know oil and gas techniques, didn't know Oklahoma.

He was a Manager.

He was a Manager of people who had lent $2 billion to independent oil drillers in Oklahoma.

Managers delegate.

Except that there had been no one to whom to delegate, because there was no section head for Oklahoma.

If anyone bears blame in this case, it's obviously that guy – the section head who wasn't there. He was supposed to be Managing Oklahoma.

Nobody thought John Lytle had done it all by himself. Not that guy. The House Banking Committee in Washington, the guys around the bank, the people in Oklahoma, the reporters – none of them thought John Lytle was Professor Moriarty.

The investigators were still trying to find clues that would lead them to the real explanation, to the solution of the case.

The reporters were still trying to get copies of the internal investigation done by the Cummings Committee and of the one done by the board of directors.

Because there *had* to be an answer to this. Somebody had done something. Maybe there had been a plot.

That was the only acceptable answer to this abominable loss of money: that there was a human intelligence behind it. The combined total thefts and robberies performed by the inmate population of every prison in America – a million years' worth of robberies – would not add up to a fraction of what had gone out of this big bank. Who had done it?

It simply wasn't acceptable that it had been done, slowly and methodically, easily and smilingly, ponderously and conventionally, by a big, dumb *system,* to a set of fixed ideas and assumptions whose goofiness would be evident to any single man or woman, but that men and women in *groups* had deemed valid.

Reporters asked for copies of the internal investigations.

The bank refused to release them.

The Chicago Sun-Times and *The Wall Street Journal* filed a joint suit in federal court in Chicago to force the release of the reports.

Something wasn't right. The perception of the bank was clouding.

FORTY

F ROM THE CHICAGO TRIBUNE story on the August 30 firing of
John Lytle:

> The bank's No. 4 executive, George R. Baker, executive vice president
> in charge of general banking services, received an indirect slap. The
> domestic operating units of his group were reassigned to Gail M. Melick,
> executive vice president in charge of operations and management ser-
> vices. But the bank's lending units will continue to report to Baker.

It was the subtlest part of the reaction, the assignment of loan operations to Gail Melick.

Within the culture of the bank, however, this move aroused more
interest than either the firing or the resignations.

The investigation had stopped short of nailing George. This was taken
to mean that Roger was standing behind him. Nobody had been fired
except Lytle, who obviously had to go, and the highest-level resignation
had been Gerry Bergman's. That it had gone that high seemed surprising
to many, and unfair. Bergman had managed three huge groups with
multiple sections under each and an industry variety – mining, construction, engineering, utilities, oil, gas, transportation, and leasing –
broader than anything else in the bank. The Oklahoma part of Lytle's
section had been twice or three times removed from Bergman. Bergman's
removal had to be for political purposes. It was high enough to satisfy
the public and to allow the management to get on with its work.

But in the Bank culture the question wasn't merely who kept his job. The question was always the succession.

The succession was the question even when the institution was losing some hundreds of millions of dollars. The matter of who would be number one ᴜill commanded the attention because the Melick move suggested that Melick was about to pass George on the rail and nose him out at the wire. *The Wall Street Journal* picked it up.

> It was also of interest because of the contest to succeed Mr. Anderson, 61, as chairman. Messrs. Baker and Melick have been viewed as prime rivals. "It's one-up for Melick," one Chicago banker said. "He's gotten his hands into the credit operations."

Gail Melick had been a Continental "Profile," one of the list of exemplary young men from the notable recruiting brochure of 1966.

Gail Melick was a nuts-and-bolts man who kept the machinery running while the smoother cadre saw to the more demanding-of-knowledge business of risk management. Usually people on Gail Melick's career path have no more chance of becoming the top executive of a big bank than a warrant officer has of becoming chief of naval operations.

But Gail was a modern operations officer. The backroom machinery was high-tech computers now, space-age devices that baffled the slow-moving lending people, whose own science was much the same as it had been all along.

The role of operations in banking had changed accordingly. Electronic banking characterized the industry now, suggested its future. At Citibank John Reed, a whiz-kid operations type, was a leading contender to succeed Walter Wriston. And Citibank set the style for what others in the industry would do.

Gail Melick was also a whiz kid. He was a wisecracking, cigar-smoking Chicagoan with an interest in oriental religion, an early MBA, and supreme confidence in himself. He had never been deferential to the tradition that placed lending above operations in the bank. He was the only executive at the Continental Bank whom George Baker hadn't put where he wanted him.

So the implication of this move – neither a firing nor a resignation but a simple reassignment – was that the succession might change, that it might be Melick instead of Baker.

On one side what was significant was promotion – *who* would be selected. It was simple authority, which could be granted on whim, which could be – and often was – granted on political interest, on favoritism.

But there was another side to it that was more important.

It was, who was right?

It was the knowledge industry, and the question was, who knew more? It was a subtle change of moral authority.

Under operations, along with many other departments, was auditing.

Auditors have no function other than to verify the work of other people, to keep them in line. Auditors are the moral authority of a bank.

It was a case of irrefutable moral right. Melick embodied his division. He had been telling the bank this all along. The investigation had revealed months of arguments between operations and lending over the Penn Square documentation, over the mishandling of the entire business.

Lending had not listened when it had been told the truth.

It was because of that that this situation had arisen.

The lending officers had shown that they could not be trusted to manage the operations of their own activities.

The operations people had long thought they were incapable of doing so.

It was proved.

Operations assumed authority.

And with it they overrode decades of supremacy in the bank by the lending officers, decades of subtle and not-so-subtle arrogance.

It was a group accession. And the flavor of it was not unlike the McKinsey plan's leveraging the accession of the metro midwest "universal bankers" in 1970.

The restrained glee with which the metro midwest people had ousted the international types – and their arrogance and self-sufficiency – was not unlike the glee with which operations now put the lending people in their place.

Them and Us.

In the middle of this business war, with shells exploding on all sides, the differing sides of the bank confronted each other once again in the highly formal, highly organized, highly ritualized struggle for who would run things. The institution had already lost hundreds of millions of dollars, and still the focus was on who would be the next chairman.

And there was that feeling again – the one that had come over the bank in the mid-1970s, the one you didn't know the root of or the rationale of until the McKinsey people had come and gone: that something big was being exchanged for this new order.

That something was trust. Trust was being exchanged for it.

And the question was the same as it had been before: If the men and women of the institution can't trust each other, then who would trust them?

Perhaps it is possible that you can be trusted without trusting. Business, after all, is more than simple personal life.

It had been so easy back then to trust and be trusted. It had been so natural, in the days of the Continental "Profiles," that no one had had to give speeches about team play and mutual regard. It would have been like telling someone how lucky they were to be an American in the middle of the twentieth century. They wouldn't have known what you were talking about. They couldn't imagine being anything else.

The next phase of the internal investigation was the formation of a new department to put things right. The new moral order of things would be determined by the credit review and evaluation department, or CRED.

Roger Anderson was still chairman, but the first line of trust now went to operations – to Gail Melick. There was another line of trust, to treasury – to Dave Taylor. Dave Taylor's department was keeping the bank in business, was getting the funds.

The difficulty was apparent. You cannot stop doing business while you get your house in order, but you have to get your house in order.

The knowledge of the lenders had been discredited, not one by one but as a group. The group had failed. Even the lenders who were untainted by the Penn Square involvement were part of the whole and suspect by association. Had Roger Anderson listened to Melick in the first place, everything might have been avoided.

Moral authority – the fact of what had happened – was the real bottom line, was the truth, without argument. The operations people had always thought those turkeys were high handed and high nosed; they had been borne out by the bottom line.

273

FORTY-ONE

THE QUESTION OF WHETHER GAIL HAD ACED OUT George for the succession became academic in November. Ten weeks after the firing of John Lytle and the resignation of Gerry Bergman, George Baker was forced to resign from the Continental Bank.

The board of directors overruled Roger Anderson on this highly charged decision. The Cummings committee had not recommended ousting George. The board committee drew that conclusion from its own investigation and forced the issue.

Within the Continental Bank this was a shocking move, far beyond all the others.

The "St. Valentine's Day Massacre," as Congressman St. Germain had called the earlier personnel actions, was hardly that. One firing and two resignations were nothing compared with, say, what the Chase Manhattan had demanded for a much smaller loss. The removal of George Baker, however, had a much larger impact.

A whole generation, a whole culture had been based on this man. Every important lending job in the Continental Bank had been defined and its holder selected by George Baker. The recruiting program, the training program, what it contained and what it excluded, the lending policies and the style were based on George Baker's view of the world.

That this had been accomplished in only five years was a trivial compliment. It hadn't taken him nearly that long. And the task had been almost effortless.

274

George Baker's removal in November 15, 1982, came as a shock. The whole thing, Bank C in its entirety, had been based on the expectation of George Baker's continuity.

Now people began to talk about Gail in new terms. People began to quote Gail. There was a new interest in oriental religions. "Gail is a genius," people would say. "Gail is another John Reed."

The operations complex that Gail had implemented within the bank – electronic banking, electronic mail, robot messengers, telephone answering machines, the great check-clearing process – now seemed the very essence of modern banking.

What years ago had been as unlikely as a Catholic in the U.S. presidency now seemed an imminent fact.

A great wrong had been committed. Now it had to be redressed.

The moral authority of the bank had to be reasserted.

That was more important now than rapid growth, than flashy deal-making.

Gail Mellick embodied the moral authority.

FORTY-TWO

*I*N SEARCH OF EXCELLENCE BECAME A BEST SELLER and the more notable of its authors, Thomas J. Peters, became an industry in his own right. In speeches and seminars for corporate executives across the country, Peters made famous the adage, "Perception is the only reality."

What once sold the steak was the sizzle. Then the sizzle became more important than the steak. Now it was going beyond even that, Tom Peters told confused American managers in the 1980s. It had gone so far that there wasn't a steak anymore. There was only a sizzle.

The Continental Bank didn't crumble, not during the worst of it. What crumbled was the perception.

The bank had almost $50 billion in assets. The July loss was one-one-thousandth of its resources. There was no danger. The Continental stock actually went up on the day of the loss announcement.

But a loan was a credit. And a credit was a matter of belief, of trust.

The protocol violations, the bad manners, were shocking: a loss by a Big Ten bank, the biggest loss on record, and the absence of an immediate response to questions.

"Because the losses had been totally unexpected, the disclosures had caused a number of analysts to voice fears that Continental might have other large and unexpected bad loans," said *The New York Times*.

It was not the money. The bank made enough money to cover the losses.

It was the embarrassment.

The Continental could cover the lost money, but the banking industry could not cover the fact of a huge error, a misjudgment, one that reflected on the wisdom of all of them. Here, supposedly, was the best of them. It had made a boner to add to the industry's pile of boners: the Chase's embarrassment with Drysdale, the problems of an Italian bank in meeting its international payments, the big losses by the Canadian banks on their loans to Dome Petroleum, and the ever-looming specter of the huge foreign loan portfolios held by the New York banks, those billions of dollars somewhere down in South America that few people in the industry or in the country expected ever to be paid back.

The Continental had called Penn Square an aberration; the next step was for the industry to subtly call the Continental Bank an aberration.

The unquestioned membership of the Continental in the top ten was withdrawn.

Certificates of deposit that the bank wished to sell, which three weeks before had been interchangeable with those of the other big banks, as good as money, now required a premium payment of 20 basis points. Before long, this became a full percentage point – 100 basis points. If the other banks were paying 12 percent, Continental would have to pay 13 percent. Before it was over, the penalty for the embarrassment would rise to 125 basis points.

It was a social punishment as much as a financial one, but the financial punishment was enough to take away the bank's major source of income.

The other big banks instinctively stepped back a couple of paces so they could all look at the Continental Illinois at a distance. If they did not, the public would look at all of them together.

The embarrassment didn't stop with the banking industry.

It wasn't the banking industry that had selected the Continental Illinois as the best managed, most feared, highest quality bank in America. That judgment had been made by the knowledge industry – the analysts, the journalists, whose reputations rested on the quality of their own judgments.

The Continental loss had rifled the notion of the experts' knowledge. It had revealed that none of them had the ability to assess a bank.

This was unforgivable. The other big banks stepped back a pace or two, but the analysts and journalists moved back several blocks.

Just over a week after the loss announcement, the first lawsuit was filed. It was July 20.

Mr. Bernard I. Mirochnick, of Skokie, reported to own one thousand shares, filed a federal class action suit in U.S. District Court in Chicago on behalf of Continental Illinois shareholders. It charged the company and its senior executives with fraudulently inducing the public to buy its stock by masking the company's true condition.

Fraud.

The press reported that James Harper, the executive vice president for real estate, had sold 68,938 Continental shares between April 22 and April 30, at $29.75 to $30 a share – all he owned except for 1,850 shares. Today the stock was 16 1/8, off 3/8.

The suit named Harper.

It also named Roger Anderson, John Perkins, Don Miller, and Gerry Bergman, the head of special industries, the department that had made the loans to Oklahoma.

With 40 million shares outstanding to more than seventeen-thousand shareholders, the drop in the stock price meant a loss of $560 million to these shareholders. Jim Harper had saved himself about a million dollars.

As to the suit, a spokesman for Continental said, "We have not been served with the complaint, so we can't comment on it."

As to Harper's selling of the 68,938 shares, the spokesman was quoted as saying that it was "for the sole reason of realigning his personal investment plan."

Did the bank feel uneasy about the sale?

"This was a personal decision, and the bank doesn't feel uneasy about it."

Did other senior officers sell their shares during this period?

"As far as Continental knows, no other senior officer sold any shares during the period."

After the news of the lawsuit hit the papers, everything changed.

The issue went beyond bad loans. The issue was now public credibility.

There were more questions from the reporters. But the Continental leaders could not repeat the openness of the presentations of early August. Lawyers now intervened. Because officers and directors can be held personally liable for losses, they were advised not to talk. They were charged with fraud, concealing reckless and wholly imprudent loan and investment decisions, those rash actions that had jeopardized the assets, earnings, and net worth of the entire bank.

The press reported that there was a $200 million liability insurance policy to cover the officers, $200 million for the lawyers' fees. Would it take that much?

In early August *The New York Times* broke the story that the Continental had known of the Penn Square problem in 1981. A special report made public by Goldman, Sachs, the Continental's investment bankers, quoted interviews with three senior officers that were held on July 23. George Baker, asked about the contradictions to earlier assurances, said, "I was misinformed."

The Michigan National Bank filed suit, charging that the Continental had misled it, had improperly advised it to buy bad loans from Penn Square.

FORTY-THREE

FROM *THE NEW YORK TIMES:*

For a banking company . . . reputation is more than a matter of pride – it vitally affects its day-to-day operations.

The private visits that John Perkins and Don Miller had made to the New York banks were seen now as casual, lacking in hard answers, oblivious to the problem. Roger now was criticized for not grasping the full import of the Penn Square case.

Roger joined the bank's delegation to the American Bankers Association in Atlanta – John Perkins was still ABA president – and hosted the Continental's customary reception. He was still at ease in the company of bankers, if not in the company of reporters. The reporters in Atlanta were invited to a reception in a separate room. Roger would not meet with them. They noted it.

For the rest of the fall Roger seemed to drift farther and farther from view.

The public relations staff urged him to meet with the press. But the bank had to be seen to first.

Some thought he was simply waiting for 1982, for nightmarish 1982, to be over; waiting for a new year, a new reporting period, to begin. And that might have been true; on December 29 he hosted a dinner for

279

reporters in Chicago, in the Mid-America Club on the eightieth floor of the Standard Oil Building, overlooking the lake coastline. He mingled. He answered questions. He gave opinions.

Some noted that he looked thin, drawn, pale. But then, he was supposed to. People in the bank thought he looked all right.

He looked fine on a closed-circuit television presentation that he gave to the officers of the bank in early February. He encouraged them to hang together, to work as a team toward the goals for 1983.

1982 had been a disappointing year: $393 million in net credit losses. Most of the income the bank had earned during the year went to cover the losses. It had been left with a profit of $82 million. The problem loans added up to $1,937,000,000, 5.69 percent of the total loans. Nobody needed to be told how bad 1982 had been. It was laid to rest.

The goal for 1983 was a profit year of $150 million and a reduction of problem loans by $500 million.

There would be a personnel reduction, but not a big one, and most of it would come from normal attrition - people retiring or taking other jobs. The number of jobs in the bank would be reduced by only 800, to 12,700.

Roger looked good. He sounded good.

He met with some reporters.

There were pieces in *The Wall Street Journal, The New York Times,* in business magazines. *Fortune* did a long one in February.

The perception had cracked. Nothing that Roger or any one of them did now could mend it; not now, not for a long time. Ed Cummings told a reporter, "When you've made a series of mistakes, you have to be humble for a long time."

"I absolutely did not decide to increase the risk level," Roger told A. F. Ehrbar, the *Fortune* writer. "I don't know what has happened elsewhere, but I'm surprised the level of nonperforming loans at other banks isn't higher."

For the objective reporter, it was incongruous: the go-go banking, the conservative sign.

The Continental was suddenly seen as "the weakest by far of the big banks," and its problems were likely to be more enduring than perceived, the writer concluded, cordial though the interview was.

All the while that Continental was adding risks, it managed to persuade the marketplace that it still was as conservative as ever. Many financial publications (though not *Fortune*) lionized Continental as the bank to beat, the one that had magically combined aggressive lending with conservative risk avoidance to become the most feared competitor in the industry.

But not *Fortune*.

It was time for the real pros to make evaluations. In January 1983 *Fortune* published the first of its thereafter-annual "Ranking Corporate Reputations" articles. *Fortune* did it right; they surveyed six-thousand executives, directors, and analysts and put in place the top ten companies in each of America's twenty largest industries.

The best big bank in America was J.P. Morgan.

The worst was the Continental Illinois.

Nothing was heard from *Dun's Review*.

FORTY-FOUR

B ANK STOCK ANALYSTS WERE CAUTIOUS about predicting how the bank would do in the new year. Those surveyed by Zacks Investment Research of Chicago estimated $4.21 a share operating profit, down from $6.58 in 1981, though more than the return in 1982.

Bank analyst Larry Fuller said he expected less: earnings of only $3 a share in 1983, less than half of the 1981 high.

And it seemed that as the expectations got lower, the results got even lower.

By the summer of 1983, a year after Penn Square, the bank had $2.08 billion in nonperforming loans, 6.6 percent of the portfolio.

Nonperforming loans weren't going down; they were going up. The bank had now charged off or listed as nonperforming $842 million of loans associated with Penn Square. There were more problems in real estate loans and loans to other domestic companies.

And the third quarter was bad beyond the worst expectations. Income was down to $20.5 million, almost half below the year earlier.

Weak loan volume, narrow spreads, the high loan-loss provision, the income lost on the nonperforming loans – "Everything went the wrong way for them this quarter," said Kenneth Puglisi of Keefe Bruyette.

Loan losses in the quarter were $90.5 million, more than one-third Penn Square. The problem-loan total was still $2 billion, 6.5 percent of the total. Nearly one-quarter of the problem loans, more than $485 million, were Penn Square.

The Continental didn't make enough on banking in the third quarter to pay its dividend to shareholders, so the bank sold assets to make up the difference. The dividend was sacred; it was paid: fifty cents on each of 41 million shares.

The fourth quarter was little better. The Continental wasn't going to make the Zacks Investment Research estimate, or even Larry Fuller's. In the fourth quarter more securities had to be sold to bring the income for the year above $100 million.

America's most famous business figure, Lee Iacocca, said to the Economic Club of Chicago, "If I had known how easy it was to get a loan from Continental Illinois, I would never have gone to the government." The audience howled.

Perception is the only reality.

Although you were inside the bank, you read the same things other people read – your customers, your neighbors. They asked you questions. They wanted to know what was really happening.

The perception was enormous. Everyone in business, everyone in Chicago, was watching the Continental Bank. The press coverage was more than ever in its history. There were photographs, drawings, graphs, charts. TOIL AND TROUBLE AT CONTINENTAL BANK. CONTINENTAL WORKS TO RESTORE ITS IMAGE. CAN CONTINENTAL BOUNCE BACK?

They weren't going to let it pass.

Roger was withdrawing.

In the bowels of the Bank, the people from CRED were tightening procedures, revising, disapproving the way things had been done before. Retooling.

What had Roger known?

He had known that domestic commercial and industrial lending was the safest – far safer than what the New York banks were doing, that more and more of it was safer and safer.

He had known that the training program provided better and better personnel.

That the information systems were the best available in the world.

That he had the best management in banking, people who *knew*.

That he had the most highly respected oil and gas group in the industry.

He had known what he *saw*. Everything was in place, growing, thriving. The same places, language, and people. Exciting new possibilities. Solid as a rock – and forever.

South LaSalle Street. The 1980s. Credit men. The bottom line.

That's what he had known. But none of it had been true. Events had disproved it all.

And the question was always there – theirs, not yours, but for you to answer nevertheless.

What had he *really* known?

FORTY-FIVE

WITH GEORGE BAKER GONE the job of chief credit officer of the Bank went to Ed Cummings. The cycle was complete: the Continental was formally returned to the standards of Bank A. Walter Cummings had stayed at the helm until he was eighty, and now his flesh and blood was there, perhaps for another eighty.

The personal investigation by Ed Cummings and his committee was completed in December 1982. The board approved the final report regarding the culpability of senior officers.

The internal investigation was now in its third phase. This phase was meant to insure that the Penn Square blunder would never be repeated at the Continental Bank.

The credit review and evaluation division had to restore credibility. Some people saw that – credibility – in the acronym, CRED. But there was a harsh sound to the acronym, too, the sound of police action, of law enforcement, of martial law, of control, of retribution. The sound of the name was clublike.

Loan quality was the inarguable objective. This meant more complete controls, more complete procedures. Dozens of flow charts were designed, reviewed, recommended, and approved. Flow charts to cover every threat, every possibility. More signatures were required to approve a loan; each signature was admonished to take greater care than before.

The credit evaluation procedures were expanded. More analysis was required; more thorough checking of the figures. More figures. The documentation procedures were made absolute, inflexible, and undelayable. After the loans were approved, they would be further monitored. By CRED.

This committee, this CRED, would provide a documentation procedure that would forever guarantee goodness of credit by the Continental Bank.

The key was documentation. The spectre of Penn Square – the reported three thousand undocumented loans in that bank alone - how many Continental Bank loans were undisclosed? One hundred? Two hundred? Three hundred?

If the documentation procedures were correct, this would never happen again; could never have happened before.

Documentation.

Indisputable.

The operations officers at the Continental Bank were now in charge. The lending officers, the highly paid, highly vaunted, highly arrogant crew to whom the bank had entrusted its risk management, had failed horribly and could no longer be trusted.

Melick's men had replaced Baker's men, who had each before them replaced the old men of Holland and Cummings and Miossi. Each new wave had entered with the conviction – and proofs of their own – that the others had not known what they were doing.

Now CRED had to succeed. Because if it failed, there were other men waiting to replace Melick's men, others who for long years had resented the pretensions and the patronizing of the private bankers. Outside, the government regulators waited – the FDIC, the comptroller's people – to step in and do it right.

By mid-1983 the Continental Bank was dead in the water. All its energies were concentrated on exorcising the demons that afflicted it. The mainstream was CRED, and everything else waited, pended, and continged while CRED did its work.

"We have no intention of pulling in our horns," Roger Anderson said not long after the Penn Square loss.

But the language was counterlanguage. CRED could not redesign the people involved, only the system. It was no more possible to have both CRED and growth than to have both 25 percent loan increases and conservatism.

All the king's horses and Walter Cummings's son couldn't put the huge, shattered egg together again.

But the effort was tremendous, was backbreaking.

So many people. So many meetings. So many months.

The banker's basic instinct – accountability – was channeled through the one small opening, CRED, and it created a beam of enormous energy. The impulse of the credit man was to analyze, reanalyze, go over the figures and back over the figures, and do this many times. Somehow this boundless ceremony of repetition of the obvious would make the unknowable disappear.

With CRED, the faith centered on documentation, enough documentation. If all this can be documented, then all will be made well. In vain. Had all the Penn Square loans been documented, the price of oil would still not have met the sixty-dollar projections; it would still have gone down below thirty, then below twenty, then below fifteen.

But still the faith was there, the ritual, a ceremony that went on, day after day, through the one last year of hope, an unending rosary, repeated faithfully: *Mea culpa, mea culpa, mea culpa.*

And unspoken, never mentioned in plain language, was the one enormous, telling fact, so huge and obvious that it permitted no discussion:

Nobody had known the bank lent Penn Square the money.

There were, as the CRED people said, no "aggregates."

The idea that the whole thing could have been avoided by fifteen minutes of computer programming – by asking the question – was unthinkable.

"Do you mean to tell me," said a senior vice president long after the fact, "that you think that Roger Anderson could sit there year after year, looking at loan totals, and not notice the big bulge that was growing up in Oklahoma?"

"He didn't see a big bulge in Oklahoma. It wasn't listed that way."

"In oil and gas, then."

"He didn't look at it that way, Bill. There had never been losses in

285

that area, and there was no one in the world who saw oil going down. He didn't see it as risk; he saw it as success. And in his view to single out one area's success was to undermine the team concept. There were no superstars, remember?''

"Naive, my friend.''

"And true. It was a bottom-line bank, remember. One line. The team result. The truth.''

FORTY-SIX

THE OFFICIAL PRONOUNCEMENTS BY THE BANK remained optimistic. But reporters doubted them. Reporters were talking to people inside the bank now, to individual officers. And they were using that word again: *survivor*.

Report: "Officers from the energy group, going together to lunch at the bank's dining room, have been publicly booed by other employees.''

Gene Croisant, head of personnel: "I think morale is damned good.''

Report: "There is a minor exodus of officers from the bank. Headhunters are receiving stacks of Continental reserves. Recruiters are swarming around the bank.''

Gene Croisant: "Office turnover in the first few months of this year and in 1982 was lower than in 1981.''

Report: "Ten percent of the officers in the U.S. banking division quit the bank in the last quarter of 1982.''

Norman Ross, head of public relations at the First Chicago: "It's a rally-round-the-flag attitude over there. It's been such a good bank that its people are loyal."

Report: "The bank paid no bonuses to its top 450 officers, or profit sharing to anyone in 1982. For the top twenty-five officers, the cut was 50 percent of income."

Report: "For the time being the Continental must labor without much inspiration from the top. . . . One downcast Continental officer likened Anderson to Shane, the gunslinger played by Alan Ladd in the 1954 western. Shane, it will be recalled, disappointed his admirers by temporarily losing his will to fight."

Despite all this the underlying question remained: *How had this disaster come to pass without anyone seeing it before it happened?*

"Mr. Anderson still won't discuss exactly how the bank ran afoul of Penn Square. Litigation is pending against Continental, both by shareholders and by Michigan National."

What had Roger known? Really known? What was in the reports of the investigations by CRED, by the board of directors? What had those sixty-three bank employees disclosed?

"Anderson refuses to discuss what really went on with Penn Square or the bank's other bad loans, saying that any statements could affect the pending lawsuits. The individuals involved have adopted a sort of Nuremberg defense. They either were following orders or were unaware of what was happening."

Nuremberg?

Whether there had been real pressure on Roger was a question that people inside the bank debated. Any time there was a new report in the press, of course, the subject was raised. It had to be. It was the obvious question. Few people inside the Bank thought Roger would leave. The ongoing slurs had made the bank's problem a Chicago problem. The board of directors, Chicagoans, were strong behind Roger. The rash of difficulties seemed to firm Roger's resolve to see the thing through.

It was the press that kept the question alive. Neil Osborn of *Institutional Investor,* the writer of the most-feared-bank piece of two years before, was back in Chicago in the summer.

> Banking houses depend more heavily than most enterprises on the way they are perceived, both internally and externally. When bank chairmen don't put up good fronts, middle-ranking officers become discouraged and therefore less effective.
>
> Indeed, there are those at Continental who believe the institution would be able to move ahead more forcefully if it had a different chief execu-

tive. Says one formerly gung-ho Continental officer, disappointed with the recent performance of the chief executive he once revered, "The best service Roger Anderson could render is to resign." Anderson says he intends to stay in office for the three years remaining to him before retirement, but some high-ranking Continental executives nevertheless expect a change of guard within the next twelve months. . . .

The two most obvious candidates for elevation are treasurer Taylor and executive vice president for administration Gail Melick, the most senior men below 60 years of age in the bank. . . . Outside candidates are unlikely, although John Jones, executive vice president and treasurer of Chicago Bridge & Iron Co., and Charles Hall, chairman of insurance broker Rollins Burdick Hunter, are occasionally mentioned in Chicago circles.

The names of John Jones and Chuck Hall came back into the conversations in the twentieth-floor coffee area. They were Bank B names, the old Continental; along with Melick and Taylor they were the "Profiles" of the great period. Their names were spoken by the old faithful who were hopeful of the return – symbolic or real – of the magic that had been lost with the McKinsey mutation.

What if Jones came back? If Hall came back?

Adrift through 1983, the members of the corps pondered the question, the formula. These were exciting possibilities. One stroke, one key change, might turn everything around. It had happened before.

Roger would stay to the end, no doubt. The press would interpret this as self-preservation at the expense of others. The "people problems" Roger spoke of meant, one writer suggested, "other people" instead of Roger. There was even the suggestion that Roger had gotten rid of George Baker to benefit himself; but Roger had been George's staunchest defender.

He would stay to the end because he wasn't going to let it end this way. He had to get it right. He could not leave the bank until the situation was repaired. It was duty, and he had an iron resolve to carry it out.

"And," said a senior officer long after the fact, "there was the matter of the lawsuits."

FORTY-SEVEN

A LTHOUGH THE EXPECTATION WAS THAT ROGER ANDERSON WOULD STAY FIRM, it was understood that the matter of the succession was to be settled quickly. Three years was not a long time; John Perkins would be retiring at the same time as Roger.

That summer of 1983, the board instituted a special action on the succession, one that the bank had never employed in the past. The two-headed investigation of the Continental's officer corps following the Penn Square debacle had revealed details that had shaken some of the board members and even the investigators themselves.

"I learned things about the senior management of the Continental Bank," one of the investigators said privately, "that I never wanted to hear."

It was with this in mind that the board arranged for a special background investigation of the various candidates for the chairmanship. It was a private investigation.

The question of the succession was settled on August 22, 1983. *The New York Times* reported,

> The Continental Illinois Corporation, the nation's seventh-largest banking organization, indicated yesterday that David G. Taylor, an expert in the bond and money markets, would succeed Roger E. Anderson as Continental's chairman and chief executive officer, following Mr. Anderson's planned retirement in 1986.

Continental's directors tipped their hand yesterday when they promoted Mr. Taylor, now 54 years old, to vice chairman and director. . . . He will report directly to Mr. Anderson. . . . The directors also named Edward S. Bottum to the board, indicating that he would be Mr. Taylor's No. 2 man. Mr. Bottum, 50, had been executive vice president in charge of trust and investment services. He will now shift to general banking services, which is headed by Edward M. Cummings. Mr. Cummings is expected to retire at the end of the year.

Gail Melick hadn't made the cut.

As with the famous promotion list of the winter of 1971–72 – the one that had omitted George Baker – there was once again a private meeting between the omitted executive and Roger Anderson.

But this meeting was before the fact rather than after, and it had the opposite effect.

Roger brought Gail into his office to tell him that he had been ruled out of the selection because of what the board's private investigation had revealed.

The story inside the bank was that Gail had to be carried out of the office, carried out of the bank. On August 15 he was hospitalized.

None of this hit the press. The news coverage was of the selection of Taylor and Bottum, not of the deselection of Melick. But the stories of the investigation, of the meeting with Roger ran through the bank, ran through the world branch network.

Only months later did the press pick it up, as a result of the bank's announcement in a proxy statement of Gail Melick's retirement.

The Bank's announcement also stated that Melick had paid the Continental $272,000 to cover corporate property and perquisites that he had improperly used. He had failed to make a satisfactory accounting. He had also waived his rights to deferred incentive compensation.

There was no elaboration on the story. All the stories stayed inside the Bank. Gail Melick's attorney stated, "Mr. Melick remains under the care of a physician. In deference to his personal health and his privacy, we are reluctant to enter into a broader discussion about the situation."

The Continental Bank leader who had come in nine months before to set a new moral authority was out of the picture in August 1983. It was a shock. Because of the circumstances it was a worse shock than Baker's removal. Shock was now following shock.

In the European network a senior officer said, "It makes me feel as if we were the Wermacht, out fighting the war, and all the time the SS was doing things that nobody heard about, and after it all came out, people made us all feel guilty for them."

The military parallel again. Banks are the most paramilitary of institutions.

The announcement of the selection of Dave Taylor and Ed Bottum appeared in the newspapers of August 23. In the August 29 *Forbes,* there was a picture of George Baker, smiling, and a short item.

> Leaving the bank, where he had spent his entire 31-year career, and the attendant notoriety took their toll. Baker decided to get away with his family for snorkeling in the Cayman Islands and skiing in Aspen. He could afford the break: His severance deal assures him of $22,708 a month through next June. "I didn't have to worry," he deadpans, "about keeping myself in whiskey and cigarettes." . . .
>
> Baker doesn't seem bitter but flatly rejects responsibility for Continental's Penn Square losses. When Penn Square failed, Baker had 4,670 people working for him. No manager, he now contends, could possibly have kept tabs on so many.

FORTY-EIGHT

*T*HE *NEW YORK TIMES* OF SEPTEMBER 29, 1983, reported,

> The human aspect of corporate misfortune was well illustrated yesterday when two top officers of the Continental Illinois Corporation. . . announced that they would take early retirement.
>
> The two are John H. Perkins, president, and Donald C. Miller, vice-chairman. The 62-year-old Mr. Perkins joined the bank . . . 37 years ago. The 63-year-old Mr. Miller joined Continental 25 years ago.
>
> Both men have had illustrious careers. Mr. Perkins, for example, was president of the American Bankers Association in 1978, and Mr. Miller is a past chairman of the A.B.A.'s chief financial officers division.

Until the summer of 1982, the greatest achievement of their careers had been their membership in a team that had turned Continental into a profitable, highly competitive and fast-growing bank. . . . But that vision was shattered following the failure of the Penn Square Bank . . . in July 1982. . . .

Neither Mr. Perkins nor Mr. Miller had responsibility for the problem areas. And both had worked to mitigate the problems. . . . The situation has been stabilized, but both men were tainted by association. . . .

No reason was given for their departures, except that it was "personal." The announcement was made through a bank press release and neither Mr. Perkins nor Mr. Miller would comment.

The reason was personal indeed.

It had been Roger's move; it involved the two people closest to him in the bank. It was them instead of him. In the entire sequence it was the only time he lost his nerve. Overlooked in the flood of news coverage and personnel moves, it was the decision that his peers – the members of the board, those who had worked with him for thirty years – would most remember. It was their moment of disenchantment.

FORTY-NINE

ROGER WENT OUT IN FEBRUARY 1984. Some people say they expected it. He didn't expect it.

A Denver newspaper had published a story revealing that three of the Continental Bank's lending officers owned interests in as many as seventy-eight oil wells that had been drilled by one of the bank's customers, Marvin Davis. They were George Baker, Gerry Bergman, and James Cordell.

For the first time in the history of the bank, Roger Anderson took issue with George Baker.

He did so publicly.

He said he was shocked at the allegations that the Continental's executives had taken such interests.

"Baker, Bergman, and Cordell clearly have violated our code of ethics," Roger said.

Somebody had finally told Roger.

The board met on February 27 and voted Roger Anderson out.

Bank C was officially terminated. Bank B was back on the field to make a goal-line stand.

BOOK

THREE

At this point happened the episode that stands out sharpest among the memories of that day – the flyover. As MacArthur intoned "These proceedings are closed," we heard a drone and looked up. It is difficult to recall now, after years of floundering and blunder, how very good we were in those days, with what precision we ordered things. Four hundred B-29s had taken off from Guam and Saipan hours before to arrive over the Missouri at this precise minute of climax.
- THEODORE H. WHITE "The Danger From Japan," The New York Times Magazine, July 28, 1985

The more I flopped and staggered around, however, the more they went along. I could have been wearing a sandwich board sign saying: STOP ME, I'M DANGEROUS! Even then they might not have done so.
- DAVID STOCKMAN, "The Triumph of Politics." Harper, 1986.

PART

NINE

*The
Home
Game*

ONE

*I*T WAS MAY 1984.

Life itself resembles a matrix. You have different functions, and you have different places in which to do them. If you wanted to, you could draw yourself a grid. Work, family, friends, hobbies, thought: these might be your function columns. Home, neighborhood, city, office, other places: these are the locations. People can't confine one function in one place, not even nine-to-fivers. They all spill over, all the functions, all the places.

You take your work home with you, in your mind if not in your briefcase. You take thoughts of your family to the office. It is a matrix. In ordinary life people don't put that name to it, though. Only in economic life – which is separate from ordinary life – did the idea arise that if you gave a name to it – matrix management – you could control it.

The matrix of thousands of people in Chicago on the weekend of May 19 and 20, 1984, was filled with what had happened to the Continental during the previous week.

It was numbing. You'd wake up thinking about it. You'd carry it with you into the yard, downtown, to the movies. It would come into your head while you were watching the ballgame on television: the Cubs were actually winning their division. Kids were home from college. All the grass was green, all the foliage was grown, the days were warm, the lake was calm and blue, and summer was starting. Then the thought would come back into your head.

The papers were full of it. Long Sunday-edition articles talked about the biggest financial scare since the Great Depression. The television anchorpeople talked about it. What was going to happen next? was their question. Would there be a merger? Would a foreign bank take the Continental over?

The New York Times: HARROWING WEEK-LONG RACE TO
  RESCUE CONTINENTAL ILLINOIS BANK.
  CHILLING SPECTER AT CONTINENTAL
U.S. News & World Report: A BIG BANK FALTERS AND THE
  IMPACT SPREADS
Newsweek: THE CONTINENTAL SCARE
Fortune: CONTINENTAL'S BLOW TO A SAFER BANKING SYSTEM
The Wall Street Journal: U.S. THROWS FULL SUPPORT BEHIND
  CONTINENTAL ILLINOIS IN UNPRECEDENTED BAILOUT TO
  PREVENT BANKING CRISIS

You ran into people, and you talked about it – seriously of course, but with a laugh or two. For the American sense of humor the worst disaster is worth a laugh or two. You can always laugh at yourself if you are an American; you feel that, despite everything, things will turn out in the end.

It was a tough blow, you told the neighbors. But it wasn't over yet, not by a long shot.

But you had no idea what was going to happen. You had no idea what was going on in the corporate office on the second floor at 231 South LaSalle Street – what they were planning, who they were talking with.

And you wondered if anything was going on there. Whether the management of the bank had anything to say about what would happen now. If Washington were in control, then it wouldn't matter what the Continental people wanted to do.

It was a gloomy weekend for a lot of people in Chicago. You looked forward to going back to work on Monday, to find out if somebody else knew what was really happening.

TWO

ALL THIS EFFORT, ALL THIS ACTION. The Mother's Day weekend; Taylor and Bottum never gone; Miossi all over Europe, and deGrijs in Japan; the officer corps working forty-hour days; a worldwide organization – 120 overseas banks and branches in three dozen countries – responding; uncounted meetings and telephone conversations; a labored, carefully drafted statement for public release; the formal allegiance of the sixteen leading banks in the United States. Intense. Focused. An all-out effort.

An effort that failed inch by inch, then failed altogether.

Dave Taylor was the captain of the Continental, the holder of the torch. It was he who led the way through the long days and the strategies, who made appearances on the twentieth floor to reassure the younger people. Events had put him there. Events could have put Bottum there, or Jones, or Chuck Hall, or Gail Melick, or Gerry Bergman; events could have given any of the native-born, minimum thirty-five-year-old members of the Continental tribe – the "Profiles" – the terrible, futile job of steering the institution clear.

All this effort. So many people. So much tension. So many market forces. So many false rumors.

This was the creepy part: It turned out that none of it counted. None of it was primary. It was all secondary, beside the point. None of it was

301

where the action was. What was really happening hadn't involved Taylor or the Continental at all.

Neither Dave Taylor nor the Continental Bank could know that. Neither he nor the others who labored in the great Kennedy office, hour after hour, computer after computer, electronic after electronic, could know that the Mother's Day weekend was beside the point. That the fate of the Continental Bank was being decided in much quieter surroundings.

Washington is a very quiet place.

The speaker was William Isaac, the head of the Federal Deposit Insurance Corporation.

"Last Friday I got a call from Todd Conover asking if I could join him in Volcker's office to discuss the situation at Continental. Their funding sources were starting to dry up in Japan and Europe. It was starting to happen in the U.S., and they were starting to borrow from the Federal Reserve."

(Last *Friday?* The work on the Mother's Day deal hadn't even begun last Friday.)

"We had a contingency plan for this kind of circumstance. . . . The FDIC could infuse a substantial amount of money on an interim basis. We felt the number had to be large enough to restore confidence in the institution – at least $1 billion but no more than $2 billion. The plan included the FDIC's promise to protect all depositers, however big.

"We even had the documents ready, without names and amounts. I called Continental to say we would be prepared to implement steps to begin the capital infusion."

"It was time to bring that plan up from the bottom drawer," a comptroller official recalled for *The Wall Street Journal.*

On Monday, while the press release on the private solution was being circulated from Chicago, while Al Miossi was negotiating with the German banks, while frantic telephone calls were going back and forth between Chicago and Japan, Chicago and Europe, there was a quiet meeting in Washington.

"The regulators began taking charge Monday afternoon," the *Times* concluded.

Conover had gone to the FDIC for a board meeting and had stayed to talk with Isaac. That night he telephoned Paul Volcker. The next morning the three of them – Volcker, Isaac, and Conover – had a meeting.

It was Tuesday now. The story was just hitting the *Times* and the *Journal.* People were still waiting to see what the market would say.

"We had already decided that the FDIC should step in. We believed the bank was solvent, but the markets didn't seem to think so" – Isaac, to *Newsweek*.

The next morning there was a meeting at Morgan's Park Avenue office in New York. Lewis Preston of Morgan chaired it; Isaac and Conover were there. Paul Volcker was there for a while; he had to leave to accept an honorary doctorate at the Columbia University graduation exercises. Principal officers of all the major banks were there to find a solution to the Continental problem. All but one: no Continental officers were there.

"In thirty hours we put together the largest package of this sort that was ever attempted" – Isaac, to Newsweek.

We did it. We did it for them.

After all that effort. With all those Continental bankers. After decades in the trenches, decades of shaping their own destiny, of steering through the free market.

And it turns out that all along it was in the hands of two guys from Washington wearing aviator glasses.

Their pictures were in all the papers.

THREE

INSIDE THE CONTINENTAL there was still strong hope that the bank could come out of the predicament.

At the press conference on Thursday, when the announcement was made that the government was supporting the bank, Dave Taylor had said that a merger partner would be sought. This was what the analysts and reporters were now dwelling on: the merger partner.

The bank has hired Goldman, Sachs & Company to look for a buyer among the world's top 50 banks. A merger involving Continental would be the largest takeover in American banking history.

Bankers surveyed today said that finding an American buyer might prove impossible, and the focus of the search turned overseas.

This appeared in *The New York Times*.

The ranking bank analyst, Larry Fuller, who had been the first to warn about the Continental's problems before Penn Square, told the *Times*, "The most likely merger partner is a major Canadian bank, such as the Royal Bank of Canada." The large Japanese and European banks had to be ruled out because most already had banks in the United States.

The Canadians looked like the ones. The Bank of Montreal had already moved to acquire the Harris Trust, Chicago's third bank.

But it might be a Dutch bank. Amsterdam-Rotterdam Bank was the owner of another Chicago bank, LaSalle National. Where one went, the other was likely to go.

A U.S. bank couldn't take over the Continental unless the State of Illinois changed its laws. Out-of-state U.S. banks were barred by state law from Illinois takeovers. Foreign banks weren't.

It was, in the word of American analyst Richard X. Bove, *outrageous*. Foreign banks had contributed heavily to the near collapse, Bove told reporters from *Newsweek;* it seemed unfair that they should now be able to buy it on the cheap, particularly the Canadian banks.

It was as a hell of a note. There it was again, the nineteenth-century wisdom of the legislature of the State of Illinois. Years had been spent, *decades* had been spent, trying to persuade them to legalize the growth of banking in the state. Long before the crisis of 1984, long before the arrival of the first foreign banks in the city, earnest petitions had been made to open branch banking in the state.

In May 1984, with the assurance that New York was almost two thousand miles away, that Japan and Europe existed only for television viewers, and that things were fine the way they were, the senators in Springfield made sure that Illinois remained the only major state in the U.S. that prohibited bank expansion.

In the largest bank in the state, less money was deposited by people in Illinois than by people on the island of Honshu.

And the people of Honshu had taken it out.

And the local laws forbade out-of-state American banks from making a bid to merge the Continental. People from abroad, having taken their deposits, could take the bank as well.

"All politics," said Tip O'Neill, "is local politics."

By now, any adult member of the Continental Bank family, no matter how naively American, knew that you can't believe what you read in the papers.

Merger? Maybe.

But read between the lines.

Yes, at the press conference the merger search was mentioned. Goldman, Sachs had been hired. But what had been said, exactly?

A merger was a real possibility, Taylor had said. The bank would decide as soon as possible, to "relieve uncertainty."

He also said some other things.

"Merger isn't inevitable. I need to know more about how the aid package is received before saying whether a merger is Continental's only option.

"This bank is not insolvent. It's not about to fail. It just needs a little more time."

As the line officers discussed it over coffee on Monday morning, one point was clear: The Thursday support deal was merely a bigger – but not that much bigger – version of the Mother's Day deal. This one involved the government, yes. But the nature of it was the same. It was meant to calm the foreign markets, to give people time to realize that the problem had been sensationalized, that there was no real danger.

"This says more about the weakness of the market system than about Continental Illinois," Larry Fuller had told *Newsweek*. "Money market and capital-market traders are in shreds this year. Very few of them expected rates to go up as much as this. If the stories about the bank had surfaced six months ago, you would not have had the reaction."

Calm 'em down. Let a little time go by. The public has a memory span of about four minutes. Traders have no memory at all.

If the Mother's Day deal had worked the way we expected it to, if it had restored the "squeaky-clean" image, then the crisis would have been over now. *Okay, it didn't work.*

This one looked like it was working, though. Reporters were telephoning every banker in the world to get a reaction, and the ones they printed – Barclay's, Rothschild, the others – were all saying the right words.

Things are calming down.

"There's no way the Continental Bank is going for a merger if Dave Taylor can avoid it," someone said over coffee on the twentieth floor on Friday morning, the day after the press conference.

"It's a matter of time. How much time do we have?"

"It depends on what the market reaction is. If everything calms down, if the funds come back in, then we've got all the time we need."

"What if the run continues?"

"That won't happen. The government is in it now. That's the price we had to pay for stopping the run. But it doesn't mean they have to stay around."

"What if Royal Bank makes a bid? Whether or not we want it, the FDIC will insist. They're committed to it."

"Royal won't make a bid. Take my word for it."

"Do you know something?"

"Royal won't make a bid."

Whether it was a guess or whether the guy actually "knew something," he turned out to be right. The Royal Bank of Canada was quick to issue a statement declining interest. "The Royal Bank's present business strategy for the U.S. market does not include a merger with Continental." No other Canadian bank's business strategy included it, either. There were no Canadian offers.

In New York traders were speculating on who might make the best merger partner as far as giving the bank a new name was concerned.

If it were Manufacturers Hanover, the new bank could be called ConMan. If Toronto Dominion, ConDom. And if the Continental merged with the Irish national airlines, they'd really have a name to remember.

But the first candidate for merger was none of these.

It was the First National Bank of Chicago.

All politics is local politics.

FOUR

"Two things were important. The first was to be the biggest bank in Chicago. The second was to remain in the top ten of American banks.

"Any time we had excelled the Continental in any category, there was a feeling of elation. People would cheer, applaud."

"Nothing pleases me more than to take a deposit on a new account and the check is written on the Continental Illinois Bank."

It was a half century since Walter Cummings had come to the Continental Bank. Not the biggest kid on the block, but the biggest block in Chicago. A few hundred yards away, the First National Bank of Chicago had a block of its own. They watched each other and watched each other. Maybe there were other people in the game, but they were far away.

For years each tried to beat the other to the punch. Dave Kennedy had done it. He had outbid them, outsmarted them, in taking over the City National Bank in 1961. That had made the Continental number one. They had been number one ever since.

Two impenetrable forts on opposite sides of a gulf.

Now the First Chicago was walking in the Continental's door. On Continental ramparts all defenders had laid down their arms. Not a shot was fired. We watched them come in, dozens of them, the First Chicago types and their attaché cases. For most of them this building had been a redoubt; they had never set foot in it. Now they came in through the Clark Street doors, the shortest route from First Chicago Plaza.

They came to examine us. Anything they wanted to know, we told them. They went through our papers. They noticed the clothes we were wearing, the pictures we had on our desks, the expressions we used. When we laughed about something, trying to lighten the tension, they looked at us speculatively. They wanted to see our guts.

Traumatic was McKnew's word now. He could have used his earlier one, *preposterous*. But if everything is preposterous, nothing is preposterous.

Nightmare. That was Dave Taylor's word.

In a situation like this what is most distorted is time. Time is of one solid piece, with no breaks in between, no change of theme. Not even sleep breaks time.

It was a century's worth of disasters, but no time passed at all. May would surely not pass. A third of May had already been gone when this began, and yet a third of May still remained. Only two weeks ago – incredible to think it – Dave and Kit Taylor had been at sea off Nassau.

More troops of examiners came inside the building. Chemical was considering a bid. Citibank was there. Chemical sent 150 people to do an examination. The FDIC had sent its own team – twenty-eight people – to look at the books.

Press speculation continued. The question now was which bank – the First Chicago, Chemical, or Citibank – was the likeliest to take over the Continental.

The consensus was the First Chicago.

From *The Wall Street Journal*:

> Such a merger likely would appeal to First Chicago's chairman and chief executive officer, Barry F. Sullivan. He took the First Chicago post in 1980 after leaving Chase Manhattan Corp., the nation's third largest bank holding company, about the time another executive won the top post at Chase. "I'm sure he'd love to be head of a bank about the size of Chase," says a First insider. . . .
>
> But there weren't any signs that Mr. Sullivan is in a hurry to make a bid for Continental. . . .
>
> First Chicago and Continental, fierce rivals for decades, have taken different approaches to commercial banking; combining the two would be an enormous clash of corporate cultures. . . .
>
> "First Chicago has the most to lose if a strong competitor takes over Continental," a top officer at a major bank on the West Coast says. . . . "First Chicago may also have the most to gain in the way of cost savings . . . getting rid of Continental employees in terms of redun-

dancies." The Chicago banker agrees. "You've got two banks sitting almost next door to each other. You could combine them in one building almost, and make very substantial personnel reductions. It's an enormus opportunity for expense reduction."

And the State of Illinois wouldn't allow Chemical or Citibank to acquire the Bank if they wanted to. "Illinois legislators," said the same *Journal* story, "said there's no move afoot to introduce emergency legislation to allow an out-of-state bank to buy Continental, especially given First Chicago's interest."

Inside 231 South LaSalle Street, hundreds of numbers people from First Chicago Plaza and Park Avenue and Washington, D.C., were going over the books. Goldman, Sachs, the investment bankers, were coordinating the examinations, passing out what was called "the nonpublic Continental information," seeing to it that the First, Chemical, and Citibank signed agreements of confidentiality.

On the twentieth floor the coffee sessions were more serious even than they had been during the run. The sober teams of outsiders were working in back offices; you couldn't help running into them from time to time. You knew immediately who they were. You didn't have to name them to know which ones were from New York, which ones were from the FDIC, which ones were from the First. They might as well have been wearing uniforms.

If the First Chicago takes over, there's going to be nothing left. If it's the First, we're gone. The building is gone. They'll tear it down and build a hotel here.

The records will be gone. The Continental Bank will be a shoebox full of microfilm. They'll be selling the brass logos in curio shops, like Goldwater-for-President buttons.

"It'll never happen," someone said.

"It could."

"It won't. It won't be the First. Taylor's in Springfield. Every lawyer we have is in Springfield."

309

FIVE

T HE CAPITAL OF ILLINOIS IS SOUTHWEST OF CHICAGO, about
two hundred miles away, on Interstate 55. Springfield is closer
to St. Louis than to Chicago; it is closer still to Peoria, site of
the great Caterpillar company, and to Champaign-Urbana, site of the
University of Illinois. A town of one hundred thousand citizens, it is
about the size of Albany, the capital of New York. Lincoln entered politics
in Springfield.

The site of the world's greatest individual financial crisis was no longer
Tokyo or Frankfurt; it was Springfield.

Dave Taylor made his first formal appeal to the Finance and Credit
Regulations Committee of the Illinois State Senate.

He used banker language – this was a committee with a ten-word title – but it conveyed a down-home message.

*Please change the state law so that an out-of-state bank can bid for
the Continental.*

*If you do, we'll be able to deal with all the possibilities, make the
best of the situation.*

If you don't, the bank may end up declared insolvent.

*If that happens, the Washington regulators are going to force us in-
to a second-rate merger, one that won't be good for our people or for
the State of Illinois.*

"The Continental still hopes to remain independent," he said. "But realistically, the future of the bank may depend on joining forces with another bank."

It was Wednesday, May 30.

Dave Taylor faced a ruling body that had resisted changes in state banking laws for five decades, changes that even the slowest of other state legislatures had made. He wanted them to make a change that no state had yet made: to allow interstate banking in the United States.

The committee listened. They were the "credit committee" now. They asked all the tough questions.

They came through.

Only a week later, on June 5, the committee endorsed – "tentatively," it was true – legislation to allow an out-of-state bank to buy the Continental Illinois. It was a six-to-four vote.

SIX

THE GAME WAS AFOOT.

The First Chicago came to Springfield, too.

Barry Sullivan, a Bronx boy in land of Lincoln, told the committee not to let out-of-staters come in.

"The First National Bank of Chicago is seriously considering buying the Continental Bank.

"It is an in-state solution.

"The combined bank would create a very powerful force, equal to the stronger New York and West Coast banks.

"The simplest way for us to achieve an in-state solution is for you to do nothing."

The Illini solution. *Are we going to let people from New York tell us how to handle our own business?*

The committee scheduled another meeting for June 6 to consider the First National argument.

From *The New York Times,* June 7:

> A legislative battle between Illinois's two biggest banks moved behind the scenes today as a state Senate committee delayed action on a bill to help the Continental Illinois National Bank and Trust Company find a merger partner. Chicago Democrat Jeremiah Joyce, chairman of the Senate Finance Committee, said hearings would resume next week, when the committee would recommend legislation to the full Senate.
>
> Senator Joyce described the delay as "a breather to allow both parties to come in with what will be the final package." . . .
>
> The temporary standoff in the General Assembly came amid "intense" lobbying of lawmakers by the two banks," said Senator Vince Demuzio of Carlinville, a Democratic member of the panel.

Hearings would resume Monday at the earliest, June 11.

The Continental Bank was playing for time. Any delay was good, calm-down time, time to let the market come to its senses. But it was also playing against time. From one day to the next, you didn't know what to expect, or from whom.

Everything was happening in Springfield. Closed-door meetings, open-door meetings, business people and politicians both calling markers, country boys and city boys.

SEVEN

THE AUDITORS FROM CHEMICAL, the First Chicago, and the FDIC were all over the bank. Someone said one of the Japanese banks had sent their people in. But they weren't visible; you didn't know whether to believe it.

On the business floors of the bank the people of the Continental knew only what they read in the papers. The memos coming out of the chairman's office all sounded the same.

Everyone knew, of course, that Dave was out of the bank most of the time, disappearing for one- or two-day trips, time enough to go to San Francisco or Toronto or New York or even London.

The attention of the Continental leaders was still focused on Springfield. Dave Taylor went back and forth to and from the capital. There were more questions to answer for the Illinois congressmen.

The Illinois Senate had to pass the bill that would permit a non-Illinois American bank to merge with the Continental.

But the Illinois House of Representatives also had a banking committee. They had questions of their own. They would be the same questions, of course, but they were *their* questions.

"Do you see an out-of-state merger as the only choice for your bank?"

"We are working on a go-it-alone plan. But reality may dictate merger as the more likely choice."

"You don't think, then, that the bank can go it alone?"

"The Continental would like to remain independent. But we depend on funds from the international markets. It is difficult to restore confidence in the international markets."

Goldman, Sachs was doing the search for a merger partner; they were looking at the first fifty banks. That much was known. But it didn't take much thinking to whittle the list of fifty down to a handful. Cross off the New York banks that had already bowed out, the Japanese banks, the European banks that already had American banks, and the Bank of America, which was having problems because it had acquired First Seattle.

There were five Canadian banks in the top fifty; they were good friends, compatible with the Chicago way of doing things. But Bank of Montreal already owned the Harris Trust of Chicago, and Royal Bank of Canada would not bid. If the Royal wouldn't bid, it was sure the other three would not.

Security Pacific and First Interstate were names that kept coming up, solid California banks and big enough to bid. But no one was ever convinced that there was any real interest by either of them. Talks were going on, but they were about selling individual units of the bank, not the bank itself.

With all these eliminated, there didn't seem to be many left.

"Maybe Goldman, Sachs will buy us," someone said. "With the fees we're paying them to do the search, they can afford it."

Chemical was the ideal one. They had bought the Continental's charge-card business in March. They competed with Citibank for national retail and corporate business. They had sent 160 people in. That showed interest.

You knew only what you read in the press.

Analysts continued to analyze. Was the Continental customer list complementary with that of other big banks? Many of them had the same customers. What of the prohibition against branches in Illinois, the lawsuits pending against the Continental, the foreign loans?

Hans Angermuller, vice chairman of Citibank, said on television that the Continental might have to be split up and sold to various buyers. "It is simply too large to be acquired by a single buyer."

Walter Wriston, retiring Citibank chairman, told an MBA group at Wharton, "I don't believe Continental is going to be merged. . . . It's an unconventional problem that has to be solved in an unconventional way."

It was a strange feeling. You didn't want anyone to take the bank over; you wanted to go it alone. But at the same time, when banks looked

314

at every part of the Continental and then walked away silently, it left a strange feeling. They left with all your secrets, and they left nothing behind. What were they saying in New York?

The grapevine in banking was superior to its computer systems, so everybody in the industry would know soon. The banks had signed confidentiality agreements, but they had sent hundreds of individuals. They would be talking over coffee. When they returned to their own banks, friends would want to know: How bad, really, is it?

EIGHT

T HE NEW YORK BANKERS were marveling at what they had seen. It was an economic phenomenon.

First, the funding.

It had been known that the Continental was taking about $8 billion a day in overnight deposits. That was where the original problem had started, when the Japanese banks had not made the usual one-day renewals.

"But that's not the whole funding problem," one New York banker said. "The funding problem is that just about the whole deposit structure is short term. You've got $8 billion overnight, and you've got $35 billion short term, most of it one-week or less.

"Those Chicago traders were magicians. They were coming up with $35 billion in new money every week, if you want to look at it that way. But they were getting it from the same people every time, mostly from the foreign banks. It was the mystique. I don't think they'll ever get it back."

The $35 billion in short-term deposits was used mostly for long-term loans.

The word going around the banking industry now – quietly, away from the press – was that a lot more of those loans were bad than had been thought before.

The bank had reported problem loans of $2.3 billion at the end of March.

"But there's no way to know how much is bad," a Citibank vice president said. Nobody was willing to guess. Two, three times that much?

"The first thing our people looked at was the loans we had in common with them. There were twenty-one loans we had common participations in.

"Their rating on seven of them was the same as ours. An A rating, for example. Their rating on seven others was a full point better than the rating our loan officers put on them. And seven of them they rated *two* points better than we did. Credits we saw as a marginal C they were rating A.

"Nobody's going to touch it."

It was as if someone came into your house, looked it over room by room, drawer by drawer, letter by letter, and said, "Yech! Can you believe people live like this?"

They didn't tell you. They told each other. But it was your house.

The approval process went on and on. Who was to approve of whom? Whose committee had the moral authority? Who was not to explain, not to complain?

Everybody had a house; but it was your house that was being opened.

The big banks of America were looking nervously at their own houses, too, hoping no one would come inside. A realization was dawning on every one of them: Every major money-center bank was on short-term deposits and long-term lending. Every bank with loans to the American oil industry had graded them too high.

In New York, bankers read the Continental reports in the morning papers and discussed them over lunch.

"The Continental was a good midwestern bank that made the mistake of trying to be a big global bank," said one.

"But the loan losses were domestic," said another. "It was as a global bank that the Continental had its strength."

In New York, the old images were still there, unbroken by years of change. Images of the midwest; images of place.

"If the Continental Bank disappears tomorrow," the banker said at lunch in New York, "it would be like one of those islands in the Indian Ocean sinking into the sea. There would be some ripples for a few days, and then no one would remember it had been there.

"If it were Barclay's Bank," he added, "it would be different."

"Why?"

"Barclay's Bank, my friend, has been in existence since the Seventeenth Century. You cannot compare the two."

"You could use the same rationale on the United States, Jack."

NINE

ON JUNE 11 IN SPRINGFIELD, the Finance and Credit Regulations Committee of the Illinois State Senate prepared to resume deliberations on the Continental request.
And in Chicago the First Chicago issued a statement.
The New York Times reported:

CONTINENTAL LOSES CHICAGO SUITOR

In a surprise move, the First Chicago Corporation announced yesterday that it no longer should be considered a candidate to take over the troubled Continental Illinois National Bank and Trust Company. . . .

In a statement today, First Chicago said that it had decided it would be "preferable for First Chicago to work independently toward its goal of being the premier bank holding company in the Midwest."

The next day, it was Chemical. *The New York Times:*

CHEMICAL WON'T SEEK CONTINENTAL

The Chemical New York Corporation said today that it would not seek to acquire the ailing Continental Illinois Corporation. . . .

"There were a number of positive elements which made a merger attractive," said Walter V. Shipley, Chemical's chairman and chief executive. "But after a thorough analysis we concluded that, on balance, the combination was incompatible with the long-term strategic moves of Chemical."

TEN

*J*UNE WAS RACING BY.

May had lasted forever; June seemed to disappear even as it began. Weeks had elapsed since the merger search began.

USA Today:

So far, no bank holding company has contacted C. Todd Conover, comptroller of the currency, which is ordinarily the first step when a bank is about to be acquired.

But the home game, the battle of Springfield, was won. On June 25 the House of Representatives of the State of Illinois passed the bill that would allow out-of-state banks to acquire the Continental.

ELEVEN

*I*N THE SUMMER OF 1984 the entire leadership corps of the great Continental Illinois Bank was in disarray. The question was survival: individual survival, survival of the corps itself.

Day after day you came in on the same commuter route you always used and went to the same desk, sat with the same group, and listened to the same questions. Somehow the citizenry of Chicago continued to move about the Loop as if nothing were happening, as if the world were still normal.

You thought to yourself, *Some of them don't even know that this is happening.*

You read the papers on the way to work. The *Journal.* The *Tribune. The New York Times.*

MERGER IS LIKELY CHOICE, CONTINENTAL'S CHIEF SAYS
CONTINENTAL ILLINOIS EMPLOYEE EXODUS ADDS TO BANK'S ILLS

"What have you heard?"
"Did you read the *Journal* article?"
"Yeah."

There was something every day. They were starting to write about the people now, about us. People you knew had been getting calls from reporters. They were looking everywhere for quotes, for the real story. Nobody was relying on the press releases. Nobody ever did, not at a time like this.

You felt funny about talking to reporters. You didn't want to say anything that would get out and hurt the bank. The reporters had already done a job on the bank.

But you were caught. They always seemed to know the rumors better than you did. You knew they were trained to do that, to pretend to know something when they don't, to lead you on.

But you felt a moral imperative to resist it, to honor your loyalty to the bank. It was the code, just as it had been during the McKinsey period.

But then you would reflect that the code was an older morality, a dated standard. You were playing by an obsolete set of rules. Others were playing you for a fool. You were caught in between.

There was trauma in the officer corps of the bank.

Everybody knew it. The reporters knew it. They just wanted to know the details.

They'd never get it exactly right. Some things were always screwed up. It was as if the writer had a point to make, a few facts, things that everyone knew were true – and then filled in the rest himself.

The Wall Street Journal:

> Many of Continental Illinois Corp.'s best lending officers, traders and data processors – the middle management backbone of the bank – are leaving.
>
> That's a growing barrier for any remaining hope of attracting a merger partner, as no one wants a shell of a bank, with its major operatives gone. The exodus is also a considerable stumbling block for Continental's other main hope – fashioning a viable independent institution.
>
> And among those who remain, tending to the rumor mill and taking calls from headhunters often overwhelm the task of running the bank – at a time when wary customers and depositors need attention.

"I never even considered that the bank would go under," Bob Holland said. "Never. I always thought it would be a go-it-alone solution. To the last. They'd take a look at us, take a little time, then we'd get back to normal.

"We were having group meetings then. Ed would come down and meet with the groups. He told us, 'We're going to go through some bad times. If any of you are very unhappy, I'd advise you to leave. You can't do yourself any good, or the Bank any good, if you're unhappy here.'

"I went home and thought about it. That's when I decided I'd better leave."

There had been a time – when was it? – when *nobody* had left the Continental. Dave Taylor's father had worked there for sixty years. Look down the platform in 1968 or 1972, and what you saw was an officer corps. Career people. They lived there. They *were* the bank.

But now it was different. "I went over to see some people I knew there. I knew they were going through tough times," said someone who had left the bank before Penn Square, who now worked for Bank of America. "I walked around with this lady I knew from personnel, who was in charge of in-house transfers.

"We stood at one end of the floor and looked down the platform at the guys in the groups, and she was telling me, one by one, what each one of them was planning to do. Who they were talking with. It was like it was a hotel. What day are you checking out?

"There was no secret to it. No stigma. No idea of disloyalty, like in the old days. It was considered smart. The smart guys were the guys who were leaving."

The Wall Street Journal:

> Through a spokesman, personnel chief Eugene R. Croisant plays down the situation, maintaining that most of those quitting are newer employees and that the majority of middle managers are staying.
>
> But by most accounts, that's an unrealistic view. Numbers underscore the extent of the problem. A month-long opportunity to take early retirement expires Monday, and many bank employees estimate that about one-third of the 900 eligible employees will take advantage of it. Many are well-regarded officers who will take their severance settlements and take their service elsewhere.

Gene honored the code. Through the McKinsey period he had honored the code. He believed. He had been with the bank since he left college. He would put his hand in the fire for the bank.

> "I've been here 29 years and I love this bank; I love what I'm doing," says Arthur J. Bruen, Jr., the 55-year-old head of transportation lending. "But I've got a family to think about and I'm looking at a very nice settlement."

Art Bruen – leaving the bank?
Art Bruen?
He had invented aircraft finance. He was the pro, the daddy. He was what Gerry Pearson had been to Group U. Art Bruen was a fixture. He would never go. You couldn't lose people like Art Bruen.

> . . . it's clear that many employees, along with depositors and investors, have lost confidence in the bank . . . Some are more crucial to Continental than its top officers. For instance, Frederick J. Florjancic Jr. is a crack bad-loan "workout" specialist and was chief architect of last

321

December's major refinancing of troubled International Harvester Co. He is leaving to become treasurer of McGraw-Edison Co., a Rolling Meadows, Ill., maker of electrical and mechanical equipment. Daniel T. Zapton, who oversees much of the correspondent-banking operation, has been offered a position at Exchange National Bank, a smaller Chicago institution.

Dan Zapton? Fred Florjancic?

These guys are core. We can't lose these guys. These guys only came around one time. They can't be replaced.

But you were Bob Holland or Dan Zapton or Fred Florjancic, and you read the papers just like everybody else. The papers had a life of their own.

Reuters:

> The Continental Illinois Corporation plans to sell its leasing subsidiary, the Continental Illinois Leasing Corporation, the banking company said. . . .
>
> Continental is also seeking a buyer for its London merchant banking operation, Continental Illinois Ltd, and has explored the sale or real estate it owns in Chicago, market source said. Several bank analysts believe Continental may put its headquarters up for sale.

Its headquarters?

Its headquarters was 231 South LaSalle Street. The building itself was to be sold?

This is where we live.

TWELVE

T HE WORD WAS GOING AROUND on the international banking floor and drifting down to the distraught people on the main banking floor that senior managers in the Continental's European network were attempting their own negotiations to sell the European network to another bank.

These were Chicago boys, weaned on South LaSalle Street.

The idea was that the international part of the bank would be a strong entity if it could get rid of the weak domestic side.

The news made some people flinch.

A few weeks before, just after the change in top management, the talk had been that the way to regain strength was to return to the "core bank" concept – meaning the Chicago bank. Some people thought that if they could get rid of international and other lesser parts, everything would be all right.

People were trying to get rid of each other.

Much of what the Continental Bank had built up during its great global growth period, the American Challenge of the 1960s and early 1970s, was being disassembled now and sent off to the same never-never land where the McKinsey people had taken the spine of the bank in 1977.

The first sale was announced in July. It was appropriate.

Continental Illinois Limited was the first major foreign unit to go. First Interstate had committed to buy the merchant bank. The management went with the purchase price.

It had been Continental Illinois Limited – the meager $12 million loss of 1974 – that had brought George Baker into international authority and that had sealed the decision for McKinsey to redo the bank.

Three branch offices were being closed in Western Europe and Bahrein. Two domestic mortgage subsidiaries were being sold. The Brazilian leasing company was going to the Bank of Tokyo. The Miami subsidiary, with its $100 million in deposits, was closed. The interest in Commercial Continental in Australia was sold. Continental Illinois Switzerland was sold.

The most salable bank enterprises were the ones that were successful. Continental Illinois Leasing, which Gerry Bergman had so ably brought to life in 1972, would be sold to Sanwa Bank for $50 million.

As the hard-won units disappeared, one after another, the one that remained foremost in the rumor mill was the one that had been sold before the crisis: the charge-card division, which had been sold to Chemical in March for a billion dollars. That move had been celebrated by the financial press at the time.

People blamed Dave Taylor for it. The charge-card unit had been one of the best in the bank, a money-maker. It had been a major mistake to sell it, people said, just to meet the dividend.

People were blaming Dave Taylor for a lot of things.

Why hadn't he moved into the chairman's office? Someone said that that showed a lack of commitment.

Dave Taylor's tenure as chairman of the Continental Bank was three months. But people had to have someone to blame.

THIRTEEN

*T*HE BANK.

You remembered how the term had been used. The senior people, the long-time residents, had a way of saying it as if it were a condition, a way of life, rather than merely a corporation. The bank. The navy. The law. The Church. The government. It was a code, a purpose, a corps, an architecture, a history. It had a life of its own, in which you had a part.

What is a corporation? The French and the Spanish both called it an "anonymous society" – *société anonime, sociedad anonima.* Anonymous? What did that mean? Nameless, no individual names.

Was it anonymous because so many people, so many members of the corps, constituted the corporation? And that crowds are anonymous, nameless?

True, Dave Taylor wasn't the corporation. True, Rell Small, the old farmer from downstate Illinois who was on the cover of the 1979 annual report, wasn't the corporation.

A corporation is a legal creation, born on paper. That paper entity owns the building, takes the deposits, makes the loans, pays its employees. Was that what was anonymous – the paper?

Then why speak of *family?* The Continental Bank was a family. People responded to that word; they knew it was true, that it wasn't the paper.

Dave Taylor had asked the shareholders to become members of the team.

If we can add 21,000 stockholders to our team of salespeople, the results could be dramatic. . . . Your positive attitudes can go a long way in assisting us in the rebuilding of our reputation. . . . I'm asking you to join our team.

Earnestly. He was an earnest man. This man spoke straight to everyone.

Now for the first time there was talk that the people who had invested in the Continental Bank might lose all their money.

Lose *all* their money!

Rell Small, the eighty-three-year-old farmer – was he still alive to see this? Did he still have the shares he had bought in 1929?

Perhaps the Rell Smalls of the world did not know that you buy shares in a corporation not to own them but to sell them. He had bought them and kept them. He had thought he was an owner, that he was there to grow with the company, with the community. They were the victory bonds of private business.

Rell Small was not an institutional investor. Institutional investors are anonymous; they are chaired by an accountant who knows why investments are really made: to sell for a higher amount. They were not naive, hokey long-termers. They were sophisticated. The small investor didn't get it.

But the big ones hadn't gotten it, either. The noted Batterymarch Financial Management had bought two million shares at $17 a share in March. T. Rowe Price had a million and a half at the same time; Prudential almost a million. J.P. Morgan had three-quarters of a million shares.

The Teacher Retirement System of Texas had 753,500 shares. Every time the stock dropped $1.33, they lost a million dollars.

A Continental share before the Reuters story of May 8 was worth almost $14. At the beginning of July it was worth about $4.50.

Now there was talk that the shareholders might lose it all.

In 1984 less than half the investors in the Continental were Rell Smalls. But three-quarters of the investors in Bank of America, and all the investors in the fourteen thousand smaller banks of America were Rell Smalls. They were there on faith, there to stay.

People came along later and said you should have known better, you should have read line ten on page thirty-two of the annual report. You were naive.

The Continental had asked them to stay.

Bill Cosby, advertising E.F. Hutton, asked them to stay.

It's a trust business. And whom do you trust? Bill Cosby.

It's America.

It's advertising.

By now July had arrived, the bank was no longer the family that had been so well understood by its members before 1982.

At Batterymarch, at 231 South LaSalle, at the Texas Teachers Retirement Fund they all read the papers.

CONTINENTAL ILLINOIS IS SUED

SEC EXPANDS CONTINENTAL ILLINOIS PROBE TO EXAMINE BANK'S LOAN LOSS PROVISIONS

CLAIMS AGAINST CONTINENTAL ILLINOIS MAKE LONG TERM ASSISTANCE MORE LIKELY

CONTINENTAL HOLDERS OFFER TO SETTLE SUIT WITH SEVEN DEFENDANTS, BUT FIVE REFUSE

What is a corporation, anyway?

Every part of the great bank was now moving against every other part of it.

Was anybody left on the team?

Anonymous society.

FOURTEEN

July 2, 1984

To All Continental Staff

In this same week two years ago, the Penn Square Bank failed and the present unfortunate episode in our history began. It is hardly an anniversary to celebrate but one that I believe we should all note.

This would also be an appropriate week to tell you that a course for our future had been set and we can all now begin to work toward. I will not be able to do that this week. I have little doubt, though, that we are only a few weeks away from some definitive action steps that will remove much of the uncertainty we have all lived with for a long time.

During the last few weeks, your management has been seeking and weighing a number of alternatives. This has been done with an eye to the practical, achievable elements of a solution and has included the interest of all our constituencies. Our success in obtaining legislation in Springfield has broadened the potential options. . . .

Dreams, as we all know, vanish when we wake. Nightmares vanish, too. We then face the reality of coping with this good and bad that the new day offers and must strive to become masters of our destiny. Whatever the future of Continental, it will not be determined by me or a small group of managers. It will depend on you and your determination to rebuild Continental. It will be a time of testing your wits, your cleverness, your salesmanship, your innovativeness, your toughness and, most of all, your belief that we can do it – together.

For many of you, the week ahead has a holiday in the middle. Spend that day with those close to you. They deserve you and need you – as does Continental.

Sincerely, David G. Taylor

FIFTEEN

GOLDMAN, SACHS HAD DONE ITS SEARCH. There was no bank in the world that would make a bid for the Continental Illinois. But there were still friends, people in Chicago who wanted to see the great bank remain there, independent, in its place. There were friends in the oil industry. There were private investment groups.

The New York Times:

In his interview, which was attended by Ed Bottum, Continental's president and No. 2 man, Mr. Taylor said that "at least a dozen people have called us and said they would put up $500 million or $1 billion. . . . We say, 'thank you very much.' "

According to Mr. Taylor, the offers are coming from very wealthy people, some of whom have made fortunes in the energy business, helped by loans from Continental.

The Wall Street Journal:

The prospect of investor groups coming to Continental's aid has brought the names of two former Chicago banking stars, both now in different lines of work, into the spotlight. A. Robert Abboud, fired from his post as First Chicago Corp.'s chairman and chief executive in 1980 and currently president of Occidental Petroleum Corp. in Los Angeles, was said to be part of the Drexel effort. . . .

Meanwhile, George R. Baker, the Continental lending chief who resigned in the wake of the bank's big energy-loan losses, said he has been approached by investors interested in Continental. Mr. Baker currently is a special limited partner at the investment banking firm of Bear Stearns & Co.

Maybe George would rescue the bank. Maybe it would be George's bank after all.

PART

TEN

Of
July 21

SIXTEEN

THE WASHINGTON PEOPLE HAD SET JULY 31 as the cut-off date for a resolution of the affair. But in Chicago some people had a feeling that things would come to an end before then.

One particular date was on the minds of some people at 231 South LaSalle Street: July 21.

July 21 was a scary date in Continental Bank history. When bad things happened, they happened on July 21.

In 1919 a dirigible crashed through the roof of the old bank building in Chicago and killed ten Continental people. It was July 21.

In 1982 the Continental Bank was forced to announce the largest quarterly loss in U.S. banking history. It was July 21.

That same day, a crane being used in the construction of the new Continental Illinois Plaza in New York crashed to the street, killing a man.

You can do much with numbers and computers and personal negotiations. But you are always dealing with the market, and you never know for sure what the market is going to do. The same is true of the force that crashes dirigibles and cranes upon you on July 21.

Small wonder that John DeLorean went to soothsayers, and that economists study sunspots and Super Bowl results, and that Sidney Omar's astrology column is in far more newspapers than Lou Rukeyser's Wall Street column.

Some people were waiting for July 21. There was a creepy feeling that it would all be over then. It made as much sense as anything else in this nightmare.

The Continental affair had gone on too long. There had been too much drama, too many headlines. There had been climaxes and anticlimaxes.

But still it went on. It was July now. The crisis, which had excited public nerves and then dulled them, had to come to an end soon one way or another.

The Washington people would wait until July 31 – no longer. By then the Continental Bank would have to be merged into another bank or be acquired by private investors. If not, the FDIC itself would be compelled to take over the Continental Bank. The U.S. government would nationalize the bank.

Next to the actual liquidation of the bank, that was the worst thing that could happen. For American Republicans, for whom separation of business and government is as fundamental as separation of church and state, it would be worse than liquidation.

In the history of the United States such a thing had never happened.

It happened in Banana Republics. It happened behind the iron curtain. It happened in Western Europe under socialist governments.

It didn't happen here. It damned sure didn't happen in Chicago.

Nationalization was not an American word.

In the meantime the Continental people twisted slowly in the wind. Each new day they anticipated news, searched for signs. They read the press, they watched the stock market, and they read internal memos from the Continental leaders.

SEVENTEEN

"MAN, YOU'D GO TO WORK IN THE MORNING, and you wouldn't know from one day to the next whether you were still in business. Every morning there was some new memo on the computers. You know, they had the electronic mail by then. Every morning, there was some new message that the thing was about to be resolved. What was the name of the guy who was chairman at the last?"

"Dave Taylor."

"Yeah, that's right. Taylor. Every day he'd send a new memo. After a while, nobody was even turning the machine on."

At Continental Bank International in New York, where Louie Ayala was managing the operations of the foreign bank accounts, normal banking business had almost stopped. Everyone was waiting. There were questions but no answers. Around the world, in lesser branches in Europe and Asia and South America, there were periods when all the machinery, even the typewriters, stopped altogether, stopped all at once.

The *machinery!*

In global banking, machinery has a life of its own. It never stops. It is instant electronic communication, it is systems, it is data processing. Whatever else happens, whether a human being is there or not, the machinery lives, pulses, runs. It has to. The bank had traded everything it had for the machinery, for the system.

335

In some of the offices now there were periods when all was still, even the system.

"The first thing you'd do in the morning was to look at the monitor," Louie Ayala said. "You remember that? Electronic mail? And there would be some new memo from the chairman, telling you that they were about to solve everything."

July 16, 1984

To All Continental Staff

A number of us spent last week in Washington D.C. working with bank regulatory authorities toward a final resolution of our situation. In addition, we explored possible involvement on the part of private interests in injecting capital into Continental.

While I can tell you what we were doing, it is just not possible at this time for me to explain what now appears to be the most likely outcome. There are, however, some principles that I believe can be communicated to you.

At this time there is a strong likelihood that through a series of transactions Continental will be structured so that it is both strongly capitalized and has a much higher level of asset quality. We also believe that the "new" Continental will emerge with every prospect of producing a reasonable and growing level of quality earnings. When that ability is proven to the markets over a period of time, I believe we will again be able to regain self-sufficiency in our funding.

The implication of this is obviously important to you. We are developing an opportunity to restore Continental's business and reputation. In order to do this we will have to have a clear vision of what we intend to become and execute our strategies with toughness and precision. It will be difficult because we will have to seek business aggressively with close attention to profitability and quality relationships while at the same time controlling our risks, expenses and overall size. Teamwork and understanding our mission will be principal priorities.

Over the past few weeks we have observed a loss of some of our business and, regrettably, some of our colleagues. Uncertainty has been our enemy and will continue to be until the details of engineering the new Continental are finished and announced. Men and women of good will are working towards that end with a common objective of creating a new, viable Continental. We frequently speak of "negotiations." I prefer another phrase: "mutually seeking a solution." Our week in Washington was

336

not spent in adversarial combat, but rather in cooperative sessions designed to create the new Continental in as viable a form as possible.

I'm looking forward to the conclusion and the ability to tell you and the world about the new Continental. When that happens, however, it will be only the beginning. We will need you more than ever.

Ed and I recognize your impatience because we feel it too. You must recognize, however, that we are working on one of the most complicated financial transactions of the century and it is taking thousands of hours of a large group of people to craft and draft the financial and legal issues involved. We're almost there – so get those chins up again. Don't worry about things you can't control and remember to help those close to you to get through this difficult period.

My best to all of you.

Sincerely,

David G. Taylor

EIGHTEEN

T HERE IS AN AXIOM AMONG STOCK ANALYSTS, and every one of them believes it: "If you get a bunch of people together in a room, anything can happen."
There were a bunch of people in the room now. In many rooms. There were thousands of hours of people in rooms.

337

Anything could happen.

On the morning after the Taylor memo, *The New York Times* printed a story under the headline, RESOLUTION NEAR, SAYS CONTINENTAL. It quoted a banking analyst's speculation that the solution would be for the bank to shed the problem loans, to take on new capital, and to form a "new" bank.

The Wall Street Journal speculated, "Mr. Taylor's statement appears to indicate that Continental would receive a major capital infusion that would allow it to charge off or sell at a loss many of its bad loans."

There still could be a solution.

On July 17 the stock of the Continental Bank, which had been selling at under five dollars a share during July, went up by half a point and closed at 5 1/8.

So as late as that – the hot and rainy Chicago Monday of July 16 and the milder Tuesday that followed – the die-hard believers in the positive destiny of the Continental Bank had reason to believe that the bank would make it. As late as that they had experts who agreed with them: the financial analysts and business writers and investment bankers who speculated in print about a private solution to the Continental affair.

It was more than blind faith, a refusal to face reality. If it had been just us, you could have called it that. But it wasn't just us, it wasn't just the Continental corps. There were authorities – hard-nosed, objective business analysts – who still felt there could be a private solution. As late as July 17, the morning of July 17.

There could be a private group. Private investors could bring in new capital.

The government could lop off the bad loans, separate them into a "bad" bank and try to recover what they could, while leaving the Continental Bank clean and healthy again.

Could there still be a private bank interested in merger? Unlikely, but you didn't know.

You had to wonder what was passing through the minds of people on the main banking floor at 231 South LaSalle Street. Were some of the guys in the old metro midwest groups thinking that George was coming back?

> Another investment banking firm that is trying to find financing for Continental is Bear, Stearns. Ironically, the effort is led by George H. Baker, a limited partner in Bear, Stearns and former executive vice president of Continental, who was ousted when the bank's problem loan troubles emerged earlier this year. Mr. Baker led Continental's aggressive corporate loan expansion in the late 1970's and early 1980's. He is

338

said to continue to be in close contact with a number of leading Middle Western businessmen who might be willing to participate in a capital infusion into Continental. In response to reports, Mr. Baker confirmed that "I am interested in putting together some kind of financing." He declined to comment on whether his firm has made a proposal to the F.D.I.C.

This was in *The New York Times* over the weekend just prior to Dave Taylor's memo on the nearing resolution. According to stories in *The Wall Street Journal,* investment bankers were "scrambling" for private investors for the Continental Bank.

The *Times:*

"Virtually every major investment banking firm is trying to line up financing, but nothing is likely to happen" until the Federal Deposit Insurance Corporation indicates how far it will go in saving Continental, said the head of banking finance at one investment banking company.

Virtually every investment bank. Would that include Morgan Stanley? Kidder Peabody? Merrill Lynch? First Boston?

Goldman, Sachs had been doing the search on behalf of Continental since May.

Bear, Stearns was in it. Unlike the others, Bear, Stearns was a Chicago firm. George Baker was at Bear, Stearns. Who would better know the Chicago-based investors?

Drexel, Burnham, Lambert was in it, right smack in the middle of it. This was the firm that had developed and perfected the "junk bond," the Wall Street innovation of the 1980s, the financial industry's answer to the microchip. Drexel, Burnham had done billions in junk bonds for lesser-known clients; it was logical that they could "package" something for the Continental Bank.

The largest, most powerful, most sophisticated houses of Wall Street were scrambling to arrange one of the largest financial packages in history. Who could doubt their ability to do so?

And with the most famous names in investment banking came names associated with the greatest private fortunes in 1980s America.

Not Carnegie or Vanderbilt or Gould or even Rockefeller; those had passed on to foundations and to universities and – already – to banks. Other banks.

The Pritzker family of Chicago was believed to be in the bidding. Among the Pritzker holdings is the Hyatt hotel chain.

Another name that appeared, both in print and by word of mouth, was that of Larry Tisch. Larry Tisch was a New Yorker; he ran the Loews

Corporation. But Loews owned CNA Financial, the big financial services company out of Chicago.

Carl Lindner, the Cincinnati financier.

David Murdock, the West Coast financier.

T. Boone Pickens of Mesa Petroleum, the Perseus of the Panhandle.

Marvin Davis.

Saul Steinberg.

The Bass Brothers of Fort Worth, Texas, known to be a client of Drexel, Burnham.

According to *The Wall Street Journal,*

> The Bass family, primarily through its Bass Brothers Enterprises, has extensive interests in oil and gas exploration, real estate, hotels and ranches and major holdings in the stock market. It has been estimated that if Bass Brothers Enterprises were a public company, it would rank among the largest of the Fortune 500 companies. Headed by Perry R. Bass, 69 years old, the company also includes his four sons.

There was no doubt that Bass Brothers was in the negotiation. Many believed that the solution suggested in Dave Taylor's memo of the July 16 would come from Fort Worth.

But what if it were George Baker, now of Bear, Stearns, instead?

George was close to the Pritzkers, to Marvin Davis, to Saul Steinberg, to T. Boone Pickens. Everybody knew that.

In the groups of Metro Midwest, the groups that made up the historic core of the Continental Illinois Bank, the groups that had nurtured and formed the banking career of George Baker, there were many who had to wonder. What would you call it if George came back? Poetic justice? Full circle?

Many at the Continental Bank over the previous two years had written George Baker off. Some hadn't even spoken his name. But some were still close friends, still there but "tainted" by their close association with George Baker; they had been quietly isolated within the Bank.

In the culture of corporations, even a corporation that was disintegrating, the most important thing still seemed to be personal promotion. Who would be in charge?

What if – by poetic justice or by cruel irony – George Baker were to end up in the chairman's office on the second floor, the one that Dave Taylor had never moved into?

Some of his close friends had to be thinking about this. And others, the ones who had snubbed him after his fall, had to be thinking about it, the ones who had spilled their guts to the committee that investigated the Penn Square disaster, who had given all the inside details on the scene at The Sign of the Trader.

"We learned things about the senior management of the Continental Bank," one of those investigators had said, "that we would have preferred never to know."

"The Nuremberg atmosphere," the *Journal* had called it. Everybody just following orders. Nobody guilty. Pointing the finger.

The people who had ratted to the committee had to be thinking about the possibility of George Baker putting together the finances that would keep the Continental Bank alive.

What were the images?

George arrives in the limo. George moves into the office. George cleans house, moves Anderson, Perkins, and Miller out of their courtesy offices on the sixteenth floor. George settles the matters he hadn't gotten around to before.

It could happen. If a bunch of people are in a room, you never know what could happen.

NINETEEN

ONE TUESDAY A COUPLE OF MONTHS BEFORE, a nameless Reuters journalist had filed a short report about a rumor in Chicago. The rumor hadn't been true. Everyone knew that now. But it had come true.

There had been other rumors, other reports. These had been fictions, too. And they had come true, too.

341

Battalions of reporters had been working on the Continental story since May. *The Wall Street Journal* and *The New York Times* were in daily competition to get the inside scoop; it was particularly important to the *Times*. One would zap the other if it could, looking for the best story.

When the news came out about the $5 billion asset reduction, the *Journal* said it was a desperate move; the *Times* said it was deliberate, to streamline and facilitate the rescue. The *Journal,* using a source in the safety-net banking group, broke the story on the "unseen" extra $4 billion that U.S. banks were slipping to the Continental through Europe; all the *Times* could do was print the official denial: one paragraph. The *Times* unquestionably had the most knowledgeable banking reporter in the country, Bob Bennett, but Bennett had committed the same error that bank management had; he had made sane interpretations of an insane situation. By July he was but one of several *Times* bylines that appeared above stories on the Continental crisis.

By mid-July the *Journal* had developed its sources within the banking industry – the safety-net group and the Continental itself.

But the *Times* one-upped the *Journal* when it counted. The *Times* was the first to realize, in mid-July, that the Continental affair was no longer a banking story and that therefore sources, good or bad, within the banking industry were no longer primary.

It was a government story now, a political story. *The New York Times* broke the story on the final resolution of the Continental affair on July 18. The *Journal* was two days late.

The problem was, people didn't know whether they should take it seriously. There had been so many false rumors carried in the press; why should this one be different?

But it was. The story said it all. Rumors were a thing of the past. *The New York Times,* with a pipeline to FDIC offices in Washington, had direct access to the only source that mattered. After July 18 the stories were just a play-by-play account.

On July 18, *The New York Times* broke the complete story of the Washington meeting the day before in which William Isaac, the FDIC staff, and a committee of Continental directors defined the plan of the U.S. government to take control of the bank.

The federal government agency was to have at least 80 percent of the Continental; the shareholders of the bank were to forfeit most of the value of the shares they owned. The Bank management was to be turned over to someone other than Dave Taylor and Ed Bottum.

There were follow-up stories each day after that. The main point of interest was who was to be chosen for – and who would accept – the job of replacing Dave and Ed. Would it be Tom Theobald of Citibank? Or Gerald Corrigan of the Federal Reserve Bank of Minneapolis? Or William Ogden, late of Chase Manhattan, a familiar face around Washington? Or Chauncey Schmid or Bob Wilmouth, the ex-First Chicago execs who had left when Abboud was chosen instead of either of them?

The question now, the newsworthy question, wasn't whether the Continental Bank would be saved or not. It was who would get the titles.

Banking is a people business.

Banking is paramilitary.

Maybe it would be Thomas Storrs, retired chairman of North Carolina National Bank.

"They need somebody with high visibility who knows what he's doing and who will inspire confidence in the regulators, the people in the bank itself and the depositors," John Heimann told the *Journal*. John Heimann had once been the comptroller of the currency. He was in investment banking now and was as popular as Alan Greenspan as a source of quotes.

Someone who knows what he's doing.

Somebody with high visibility.

Maybe someone from one of the five best-managed American corporations.

Maybe William Simon, the former treasury secretary, now an investment banker. Nobody had higher visibility than William Simon.

There were follow-up stories every day with headlines like ACCORD IS NEAR IN CONTINENTAL ILLINOIS BAILOUT, but they didn't have much to add. The issue had been defined at the Washington meeting on July 17, and the press had a lock on what was happening. The government was going to take over the bank. It would do so as soon as the paperwork was completed. The only thing to speculate about now was who would get the chairman's title. The Washington people who were managing the press relations now could tell the reporters only what they themselves knew. They were waiting to see who would accept. There were no more false rumors, nothing like the powerful stuff of May.

Well, there was one, but it didn't count for much. On July 18, Dave Taylor issued a denial that there had been a wave of resignations by Continental executives and that the government was trying to back out of its commitment to save the bank. But this was good for only an inch of copy. Reporters weren't concerned about these things anymore. They knew the government was taking over the bank.

They were concerned about the people who would be chosen to run it.

That was interesting.

343

It might be Jim Bere, the Continental director who had worked the hardest to straighten things out after the Penn Square mess. Bere had run Borg-Warner Corporation in Chicago and was "known as a tough boss and a dedicated civic leader." It might be one of the other Continental directors, Chicago people. It might be Blaine Yarrington or Wes Christopherson or Bill Johnson.

"I wouldn't say that it's the best job in the industry," Dave Taylor said.

The question was no longer whether, but when. It wasn't as exciting. People were tired.

And it wasn't as much fun for the press anymore. They didn't have to speculate, didn't even have to investigate. Washington was managing the affair now, and nowhere – with the possible exception of the National Football League – was there greater sensitivity to the importance of published and televised coverage. The press sources were locked. Anything they wanted to know, they were told.

It wasn't as much fun.

And it didn't make for good copy.

TWENTY

THE INVISIBLE HAND that had chosen to afflict the Continental Illinois Bank on July 21 in more than one year took a pass on July 21 this time.

Dramatic symmetry called for the climax of the Continental affair to occur on July 21. If the bank had died that day, the event would have confirmed forever the views of a lot of people that sunspots, planetary positions, and the full moon hold the secrets to the market.

But July 21, 1984, was a Saturday. Nothing happened. No dirigible crashed through a window, no gigantic crane came crashing down to a street. There were no corporeal deaths this time, and no corporate deaths.

One small thing did happen on July 21 that was worthy of coverage in the Monday *Wall Street Journal*.

The Continental Bank publicly released a seventy-page, single-spaced report on its investigation of the Penn Square disaster two years before.

The purpose, stated in a memo signed by both Dave Taylor and Ed Bottum, was "to put behind us a most difficult period and to explain to employees, shareholders and customers how such a situation arose in the first place."

It was a hard-fought victory for the press. For eighteen months *The Chicago Sun-Times* and *The Wall Street Journal* had sought the release of the investigation, the explanation of the Penn Square enigma. Two Federal courts had ordered the release of the data as part of the official court record of the shareholder suits. The bank could either make the release this week or appeal to the U.S. Supreme Court.

But the seventy-page report didn't tell reporters, employees, share-holders, and customers much that they didn't already know.

It said there had been substantial evidence of negligence by lending officers John Lytle, John Redding and Gerald Bergman.

On loans Jack Redding refused to approve, "the money was already out the door." But he was aware of John Lytle's lending practices.

Gerry Bergman should have investigated the practices.

George Baker should have looked into the "red flag" reports that cropped up. But he was too far removed from the actual business to be called negligent.

Roger Anderson, John Perkins, and Don Miller were totally removed from the events that produced the Penn Square losses. The investigators had to stretch as far as they could to assert that Roger had received "fragments of information" over the course of time.

Faulty documentation was a big problem.

Faulty controls were a big problem.

Ernst & Whinney, the Bank's accounting firm, was sharply criticized.

The seventy-page report seemed hardly worth the eighteen-month wait. There were some colorful quotes by people who had been interviewed during the investigation. But Penn Square was as much of an enigma as always.

345

The *Journal* said that "lawyers familiar with the massive litigation against Continental and its executives filed in the wake of the Penn Square failure assert the report is a sanitized version of events designed to limit damage to the top officials. . . .

"Michael M. Conway, an attorney representing *The Wall Street Journal* and the *Sun-Times* . . . said he's asked U.S. District Judge John F. Grady . . . to identify other documents he relied on in making a ruling not to dismiss certain defendants in the case. The release of the documents will be sought."

George Baker, contacted by the *Journal* reporter in Chicago, said that the report was based on "many glaring errors and omissions."

The enigma was still there.

But the Penn Square case was buried for good. Time was about to cover it over, because bigger things were going to happen in Chicago during that week in July 1984.

TWENTY-ONE

O N THE MONDAY, JULY 23, that the newspapers carried the articles on the release of the Penn Square investigation, the board of directors of the Continental Bank held its regularly scheduled monthly meeting.

The agenda:

1. The second-quarter operating results of the Continental Bank. Public release of these figures was out of the question until the crisis was resolved.

2. The search for a new chief executive. The Taylor-Bottum team must be replaced.

3. The proposed deal with the Federal Deposit Insurance Corporation – the U.S. government – regarding their intervention in the affairs of the Continental Bank.

4. The continuing loss of deposits.

The loss of deposits. The run. That was what the Continental affair was about – the run.

With the May 17 deal, the formal involvement of the U.S. government, reporters stopped talking about the run and started watching for merger partners.

The entire month of June passed – the time of the First Chicago and Chemical and Citibank speculations; of the battle of Springfield, Illinois; of the Goldman, Sachs research; of the concept of George Baker or Bob Abboud or Fred Joseph as a new J.P. Morgan who would create solvency from chaos. But there was no important mention of the run.

If the market had put $40 billion in the Chicago bank when it was on its own, how much more would it put there with the backing of government officials?

The run was still going on. The more the government reassured, the more money left the Continental Bank.

While the Continental Bank had been the Continental Bank, it had commanded deposits and interbank placements of more than $40 billion. More than $8 billion of that was overnight money from the world's other great banks.

When the Reuters rumor hit the trading-room printers in May, young traders at some of the Japanese banks held back their overnight deposits. Someone they knew at the Continental Bank asked them to put the money back, and they did so.

Then there were the outside assurances, just to make sure. "This was an unusual enough case that I chose to violate the policy," Conover had said. "I decided to do something that was unprecedented. I issued this press release."

Every time the government pronounced, it assumed authority. Every time it assumed authority, the authority of the Continental Bank – a fiduciary – diminished.

It became less than the Continental Bank was supposed to be.

The day after the comptroller's public statement on Thursday, May 10, the deposit run had soared to $3.6 billion.

After the announcement on May 14 of the first bank package and the "tacit support of the Federal Reserve System," the run went over $6 billion.

347

The formal government package was announced on May 17.

The run really got going then. It became immense. It was beyond all prior conception. It wasn't being reported.

By the end of June the run had reached $12 billion.

It would be inane to call it the biggest bank run in history. The biggest run before this one had been the run on the Franklin National in 1974: $1.7 billion.

On July 17 *The Wall Street Journal* reported that the Continental had lost half its deposits; the run had exceeded $14 billion.

Two days later, the *Journal* ran a boxscore: $5 billion-plus from the Fed, $2 billion from the FDIC, $4.1 billion from the twenty-eight American banks in the safety net, more than $4 billion in additional funds from U.S. banks through foreign branch deposits, and $5 billion in deposit reduction because of asset sales.

It had been a $20 billion run.

However you counted it, it was beyond the concept of records.

Washington now had the ball.

At the time of the Continental Bank crisis of 1984, the Federal Deposit Insurance Corporation had reserves – cash of its own – of $16 billion. If it had been a real insurance company, its net assets would have just about covered the loss of this one bank.

The Continental crisis couldn't be blamed on the comptroller of the currency any more than it could be blamed on Reuters or on Robert Novak or on McKinsey or on The Sign of the Trader.

But it was hard to give the government credit.

> However the Continental affair ultimately is resolved (provided, of course, that it doesn't set off a chain of bank failures), it will be heralded as a triumph for the bank regulators, a heroic episode in which the Federal Reserve, the Federal Deposit Insurance Corporation, and the Comptroller of the Currency rushed into the breach and saved the banking system. In fact, the Continental saga reflects little credit on the regulators. They seem to have done the only thing they could in May, when they arranged a $7.5 billion loan package. But Continental's troubles have been obvious for nearly two years, and the situation might never have come so close to disaster had the regulators done their jobs properly earlier.
>
> By the time they finally acted, the Fed and the FDIC had to issue a blanket guarantee for Continental's entire $40 billion of liabilities to quash the panic.

A. F. Ehrbar wrote this in *Fortune* after the FDIC first stepped into the Continental affair on May 17. The FDIC put up $2 billion to go with the $5.5 billion from the U.S. banks. Their director, William Isaac, issued his own statement that everything was all right now.

The *Fortune* piece pointed out the irony: the first inspectors - the people who hadn't noticed the cow, the hay, or the kerosene lantern - would be acclaimed for pumping water on the blaze.

TWENTY-TWO

T HE TALK HAD BEEN OF OLD FRIENDSHIPS, of wealthy men, of customers who remembered the past, of the years of support by the great bank that had brought great wealth, of men who said, "I can let you have five hundred million. I can let you have a billion."

The talk had been of powerful financiers in Middle America who would bring capital to the Continental Bank because of a statesmanlike interest in Chicago and in the Midwest, because of their conviction that neither should have to lose the greatness of its financial industry.

But when the time arrived, nobody came around except a bunch of people trying to cash in on a distressed situation, to carry away what they could for as little as they could, and to junk the rest.

It was, as people said during the days of the McKinsey bank, a matter of business orientation.

The Bass organization at least made an offer. They did work at it. Through most of Thursday, July 12, the lawyers and accountants and financial people and owners of the Bass interests worked on their proposal. Telephone calls to FDIC offices in Washington told the regulators the proposal was on the way.

It wasn't easy. The Bass people were looking at the same figures that the First Chicago and Citibank and Chemical had looked at. Only by now – a month after the First had turned it down – the figures were a lot worse. Another $5 billion in good assets had been sold, half the deposits were gone, and the bank was, a banker said, "peeling itself back to the bad stuff."

"There was nothing left to buy," another banker said afterward.

"The FDIC found it would have to assume so much of the poor loans that they simply decided to assume all of them," still another banker said.

So when the Bass offer finally came in, late on the evening of July 12, hours before the Friday the thirteenth deadline, the FDIC turned it down.

That was the only offer.

The old bank was all alone now. Nobody had a billion for it. Nobody had a dollar.

It wasn't even doing its own negotiating. The Bass offer had come to Washington, not Chicago. The last phase took place in Washington. Dave Taylor and the closest members of the Continental officer corps were negotiating with the government, negotiating with themselves. There had been high drama before, but now the journalists found it hard to wring anything colorful out of the ending.

The ending was all lawyers and accountants and government officials poring over documents.

> At night the Continental negotiators usually huddled in Room 707 of the Madison Hotel, a suite occupied by Continental Chairman Taylor. Anywhere from 7 to 14 members of the Continental team gathered for hours in the room, ordering dinner from room service night after night. To make it easier for the harried hotel waiter, everyone ordered the same appetizer – the Dolly Madison salad – and the same dessert – raspberries – but different main courses. It became known as "the dinner with the hole in the middle."

That was all the *Journal* could wring out of it. One last human interest detail. Fourteen guys in a hotel room going over documents.

The next morning, Luis Ayala in New York, as well as hundreds of other Continental bank people in the Telex rooms of offices in thirty-odd countries on six continents, would go to the machines to see if there was anything on the wire.

TWENTY-THREE

*E*VEN TO THE LAST, some people tried to read the fortunes of
the bank in the stock market.

The stock had been hit hard by the May rumors. Just before the
Reuters "bankruptcy" story a Continental share had sold for fourteen
dollars; before May was over a share was selling for less than 7 dollars.

More Continental stock was unloaded on the New York Stock Exchange in May than any other stock. There were eight days when more
than a million shares were sold and four days when more than two million
shares changed hands.

But the losses after May hadn't been so serious. Some of the big shareholders were holding on to their Continental shares, figuring they had
survived the worst of the loss.

On July 17, when *The New York Times* carried the RESOLUTION
NEAR, SAYS CONTINENTAL headline, the stock rose half a point, to 5
1/8. It dropped to 4 3/8 the next day, when the financial press reported
the FDIC meeting in Washington and the government plan to take 80
percent of the bank.

A day later, 1,388,400 shares were sold – the highest volume since
May. The share price dropped a full dollar to 3 3/8.

On Tuesday, July 24, the stock went up 3/4 of a point, to 4 3/8,
on almost a million shares traded.

But on Wednesday, July 25, there was no more speculation among the managers of the major American stock portfolios. In the papers that morning appeared this comment: "Under the plan to be implemented by the Government, the value of the shares of the present holders of Continental could be worth as little as 1/1,000th of a cent apiece."

On that Wednesday, the day before the press conference that would formally close the Continental affair, 1,937,900 shares of the Continental Bank were sold on the New York Stock Exchange, for less and less. At the end of the day, the share was worth less than $3. It had dropped a full dollar fifty.

On July 26, the day the FDIC agreement was announced, there was a sharp new demand for shares of Continental Illinois on the New York Stock Exchange. Two million shares changed hands. The price rose 7/8 of a point. It closed at 3 3/4.

Somebody thought they were getting a bargain, but the market professionals were puzzled.

The consensus was that the buyers were the little people – Mom and Pop, the Rell Smalls of the world, coming back again with faith in the system, just as they had after the crash of 1929.

They thought it could be another Chrysler. It had the ingredients: an essential large American institution, an enormous problem, government aid. Chrysler, with Lee Iacocca, had shattered the pessimists. Everybody who had stuck with Chrysler had made money. This could be another Chrysler.

It wasn't going to be another Chrysler.

TWENTY-FOUR

T HE MOST APPEALING IMAGE OF A BANKER is still George Bailey, the small-town building-and-loan man played by James Stewart in *It's a Wonderful Life*. The only thing that kept Bedford Falls from becoming Pottersville was George Bailey.

Bailey has just married Donna Reed and is just about to leave Bedford Falls, carrying his two-thousand dollars in life savings for an around-the-world honeymoon. But that very day, the national bank crisis hits, and all the building-and-loan customers line up to take their money out.

The money isn't there, of course. Bailey tries to explain this to the people. The money is in Pete's house and Joe's house and so forth. That's the way a bank works. There's no need to panic. Let's have faith in each other.

But they panic. Not even James Stewart, talking to only some fifty people whom he has known since he was a kid, can persuade them to hold fast. It's every man for himself. The first man in line wants *all* his money.

Potter, in the meantime, has heard about Bailey's trouble and offers fifty cents on the dollar to the shareholders of the building and loan. Potter hasn't lent anyone money to buy a house. He's going to take over the town; he'll own these people. But they're panicked.

George Bailey solves it by paying people with his own money, the two-thousand dollars he was going to use to get out of that little town.

The building and loan makes it to the end of the day with two dollars left. Bailey will never leave Bedford Falls.

Frank Capra's greatest hero was a banker. James Stewart's favorite role was that of a banker.

"I think Taylor just didn't get it done," a bank analyst would say long after the Continental affair was over. "He failed to make his case. He didn't persuade the depositers."

"Persuade them of what? Once the rumors started, it was all over in a week."

"I don't know. If you get a bunch of people in a room, anything can happen. He just didn't make it happen."

"Bunch of people in a room? They were all in Japan, in Switzerland. They were ten thousand miles away."

It was a far cry from Bedford Falls, farther from Chicago, and farther still from 1945.

TWENTY-FIVE

D AVE TAYLOR'S LAST MEMO, on July 26, began this way.

To All Continental Staff:

This has been a tough one. But at last we can close a difficult chapter in the history of Continental and open an entirely new book. Today I am announcing the foundation for Continental's comeback, through an agreement reached with the FDIC. For many, it is not the hoped-for solution, but it is an opportunity for a fresh start.

Several months ago, I told you that all of us would see our dreams postponed or altered in some way. One of my own dreams was to see Continental through this difficult period. That dream must change.

Dave Taylor's last memo was accompanied by a fourteen-page press kit, including a chart that attempted to simplify the complex agreement with the U.S. government, the one that had taken hundreds of men and women thousands of hours to negotiate.

But everybody who had read *The New York Times* a week before knew the essential details. Bob Bennett's front-page story on July 27 could only reiterate them.

> The FDIC made formal and legal an investment of $1 billion in the Continental Bank, and became owner of 80 percent of its shares.
> The FDIC would pay an additional $3.5 billion to the Continental Bank as the purchase price for loans of doubtful collectability totalling $5.1 billion face value.
> The U.S. Government – the FDIC, Federal Reserve, and Comptroller of the Currency in joint agreement – guaranteed full protection of all depositors and general creditors of the Bank.
> The shareholders of the Continental Bank would retain a 20 percent interest in the new Bank.

On July 27, 1984, Ed Bottum made the front page of *The New York Times.* The days in Belgium had been gray, but no Belgian weather had been grayer than the emotional weather at that Chicago press conference, where he sat in a chair next to Dave Taylor.

U.S. WILL INVEST $4.5 BILLION IN RESCUE OF CHICAGO BANK, VOWING MORE IF NEEDED.

2 Officials Named

Continental Illinois Also Reports a $1.1 Billion Loss in the Quarter

At the top was a shot of two men laughing, the new leaders of the Continental Illinois Bank. They were John Swearingen, formerly the chairman of Standard Oil of Indiana, and William Ogden, once vice chairman at the Chase Manhattan Bank of New York.

In the middle was a photograph of the hero of the day, the chairman of the Federal Deposit Insurance Corporation, William Isaac, looking neither happy nor sad but simply wise.

Beneath were photographs of Dave and Ed, strained and somber, sitting to the side of things, watching events take hold.

ELEVEN

*Nightmares
Vanish,
Too*

TWENTY-SIX

T HE *NEW YORK TIMES* CARRIED SEVERAL LONG ARTICLES, and *The Wall Street Journal* led from a full column on page one to an entire page twelve, as long an article as the *Journal* printed on anything.

The Continental Bank's memorandum accompanying the press release again claimed that "this is not an FDIC takeover," but no objective reporter bought that.

THE FIRST NATIONALIZED BANK was the *Newsweek* headline. BETTING BILLIONS ON A BANK - THE FEDS COME TO THE RESCUE OF FAILING CONTINENTAL ILLINOIS was the headline in *Time*.

In *Fortune*, THE NATIONALIZATION OF CONTINENTAL ILLINOIS.

The Federal takeover of Continental Illinois Corp., until recently the nation's eighth-largest bank holding company, raises a host of disturbing questions. There is the matter of whether the bailed-out bank can sail on its own, of interest not just to the holding company's shareholders but also to the Federal Deposit Insurance Corporation, which has committed $4.5 billion - and said it would spend whatever it takes - to prop up the bank. But the most unsettling questions arise out of a single illusion-shattering aspect of the Continental episode: contrary to what most of us were taught in high school, we now have seen that the federal government, even when it pulled out nearly all the stops, couldn't stop a run on a major bank.

Conover, the comptroller, went beyond this. In a letter published in *The Wall Street Journal* he wrote,

> The issue is not whether large banks can be permitted to fail but how they are handled after they have failed. In the case of Continental, a payout of insured depositors would have had a severe detrimental impact on the domestic and international financial system and thus on the economy. This is why we put together the long-term assistance package. . . .
>
> For all intents and purposes, the Continental did fail. It is under new management. Its shareholders have lost 80% of the value of their stock; they stand to lose everything if the FDIC incurs losses on the loans it purchased from Continental that exceed the remaining shareholders' equity in the bank. Directors and former management face potential legal liability for their handling of Continental's affairs.

As the financial experts on the media arrived at their conclusions about the failed bankers, you found interesting divisions.

The Wall Street Journal pointed out the Continental's excessive concentration on oil lending, Roger Anderson's background in international banking, and John Perkins's background in money-market funding. It noted that

> Despite Continental's reputation for management expertise, its "corporate office" troika didn't have the best credentials to run the major domestic lending bank that Continental was becoming.

The New York Times praised the credentials of "the aggressive new team," which consisted of

> a businessman whose authoritatian presence cast him as a defender of the beleaguered oil industry in the 1970's, and a banker who commands the respect of the international financial community.

John Swearingen had run the Standard Oil Company of Indiana for twenty-three years. William Ogden had been chief financial officer when he resigned from Chase Manhattan in 1983, after spending most of his career in international banking.

So the old Continental management team, which lacked "credentials" because of its emphasis on the oil industry, international lending, and the funding side of banking, was replaced by a team of two men whose backgrounds were in the oil industry, international lending, and the funding side of banking.

The *Times* highlighted its assessment with quotes from leading bankers across the country:

"A master stroke."

"The rationale makes a hell of a lot of sense."

"These are two tough executives, and that's what Continental needs at this time."

"Tell John and Bill that we are delighted that Continental is healthy, that we wish them the best and that we'll see them on the football field."

This last was from Barry Sullivan, chairman of the First Chicago.

There were dozens of editorials and dozens of letters to the editors of business journals and financial pages. Out there in the unseen audience was a phantom committee, a CRED without portfolio but with methods and views as earnest and as thorough.

The Continental case proves the banking system is in chaos.

No. The rescue of the Continental proves the strength of the banking system.

The failure was caused by antiquated regulations – specifically the Illinois law against bank branches, which kept the Continental from normal deposit sources and forced the great bank to rely on foreign money. Therefore, further deregulation of the industry is necessary to prevent future failures.

No. The failure was caused by excessive deregulation. When the government ceased to watch over the banks, they forgot they were banks, forgot they were the trustees of other people's money.

The bank had a badly outmoded computer system, one that "couldn't give the time of day."

No. The computing machines worked well enough. It was the people using them who hadn't worked well enough.

The rescue shows the system works.

No. The rescue shows the system doesn't work. It is, John Kenneth Galbraith submitted, a high form of socialism, not "something that unduly softheaded governments do for – as they were called by George Bernard Shaw – the undeserving poor," and "the capitalization by the state of productive enterprises.

"But perish the thought that it be so denoted. Socialism it is, but socialism it must not be called."

Absent from the international commentary, from the long roll of opinions, were those of members of the Continental tribe itself. There were no long interviews in the losers' dressing room.

The collapse will haunt Mr. Taylor for a long time. He says a single thought runs repeatedly through his mind: In the final months, with Continental already teetering, "what the hell else could we have done that would have brought us to another end?" He draws on one of his ever-present cigarettes and adds, "I don't know what the hell else we could have done."

That, in *The Wall Street Journal,* was it for Dave Taylor. Otherwise reporters looked for proven authorities.

The New York Times assembled a forum of Hans Angermuller of Citibank, Thomas Lebreque of Chase, economist Alan Greenspan ("If a rumor is credible . . ."), and investment banker and former U.S. comptroller John Heimann. The forum identified the solutions as well as any forum could hope to: asset quality, loan diversity, deposit mix, geographic diversity, good management, information systems, higher capital, and credit and audit controls.

It was CRED again, reorganized and reempowered. Everything the forum pronounced was beyond challenge. A recitation of the litany, a rippling of the beads.

Except that it was after the fact.

The problem was that the Continental Bank – and the financial industry that had followed its every step – had thought it possessed all those qualities, with the exception of the geographic diversity that Illinois laws prohibited.

A writer for *The Wall Street Journal* had done a story during the July crisis headlined, LONG BEFORE THE "RUN" AT CONTINENTAL ILLINOIS, [THE] BANK HINTED OF ITS ILLS, which quoted an analyst saying that if someone had looked at page thirty-two, line ten, of the annual report of 1981, they could have seen the bank's "inherent weakness."

Where were you then, mister?

(Look back at those annual reports, at the press coverage, at the praise in every one of them. Not least of it was by *The Wall Street Journal* in 1981. Not even "the aggressive new team" had been so applauded.)

The same guys who had explained, position by position, why the Redskins would win the Super Bowl by nine and one-half points were now explaining – the same guys – why the Raiders had won and could not but have won by the score of thirty-eight to nine.

And it was okay. It is human. It is the only thing that sportswriters and financial analysts, the best of them, can do.

Most of the writers cited "poor management" in passing as a factor in the failure but then moved quickly on to the substantive reasons.

Only *The Wall Street Journal* – ANATOMY OF FAILURE: HOW BAD JUDGMENTS AND BIG EGOS DID IT IN – dwelled on the people involved.

Most of the articles, the editorials, the letters dealt less with the Continental Bank itself than with what the disaster meant to the industry.

FIX BANKING'S ROOF BEFORE THE HEAVY RAINS BEGIN. BANKS AREN'T FOR GAMBLING. RESCUE PLAN SIGNALS EXPERTS ON NEED TO CHANGE BANKING. AMERICAN "GO-GO BANKING" IN NEED OF BRAKES.

Some of it got pretty ugly. In Maxwell Newton's column in the New York *Post* you read this:

> "As Continental Illinois squirms in its death pangs like a hemorrhaging and untouchable leper, depositors around the world stare glassy-eyed at their friendly bankers and wonder who else is germinating the dread disease. The disease, however, has been germinating for a long time. The wonder is that depositors were so late in waking up to it."
>
> With these words, Peter L. Bernstein, the award-winning consulting economist, begins a report on "the origins of the crisis" in the world banking system.
>
> "The banking system in all countries today is rotten at its core," says Bernstein – "rough words but few would deny them."

(Do you remember Peter L. Bernstein? "These fellows . . . are actually involved in a much more exciting business than they might be willing to admit. They are, in fact, star players in the drama," Peter L. Bernstein had been quoted as saying in the Continental "Profiles" brochure of 1966.)

But the cruelest touch was done by the magazines that had published the "most-feared-bank" piece on the Continental in the fall of 1980. *Institutional Investor* named Roger Anderson its Banker of the Year.

> In years past, *Institutional Investor's* bankers of the year have been individuals who built their institutions into global powerhouses, whose accomplishments not only transformed their institutions but sometimes even the entire banking world around them. . . .
>
> But impact – be it in politics, the arts or finance – also has its darker side: Influential people can leave a distinctly negative impact on the world. . . . Every so often, a banker comes along who seems to sum up not the virtues of an era but the excesses, whose example does not offer a beacon for others to follow but a warning light.
>
> Such a banker was Roger Anderson.

Roger's picture was on the cover in full color, a larger picture than the one *Dun's Review* had printed, a larger picture than anyone had printed.

The "invisible hand" was reaching down again, that vague form that so many thousands of hours of faithful financial analysis had been unable to seize. Now you could understand why. It wasn't the market at all; it was the imp of the perverse.

363

When Penn Square failed . . . Anderson blamed "people problems" for the bank's woes – meaning, in the view of some observers, other people. He forced out his onetime heir apparent, lending chief George Baker, along with other top executives but vowed to hang on as chairman. . . .

The Continental debacle had fostered a new awareness among bankers that unchecked lending, the blind pursuit of asset growth and a laissez-faire organization is a recipe for disaster. For his indispensable contribution to that awareness, Roger Anderson is *Institutional Investor's* Banker of the Year.

TWENTY-SEVEN

D URING SEPTEMBER 1984, the second month after the end of the Continental affair, several events of interest happened.

In Chicago the shareholders of the Continental Bank were called together to vote on the government deal. In Oklahoma there was an acquittal. Also in Chicago there were indictments. On the North Shore there was a wedding.

And in Washington, the federal bank examiners were called to testify before the House Banking Committee.

Congressman Fernand St. Germain, who had spent so much time with John Lytle and John Perkins and George Baker two years before, was questioning C. Todd Conover about the government handling of the Continental crisis.

Not all the congressmen were happy with it.

C. Todd Conover was there for five hours, defending the rescue.

"We could have easily seen another hundred bank failures," he said. The bank was too big to let go. The government had done what it had to do.

But out of five hours of testimony, the point that made headlines was the severance pay for Roger Anderson.

It was bad timing. The bank was absorbed on July 26, and the shareholders were told they might lose all their money. Then came this public hearing a couple of months later, and the defenders of the people demanded justice.

The amount paid Anderson was $12,212 a month, a consulting fee, to be paid for two more years. About $146,000 a year. There were other payments: $269,792 as a pension supplement, $77,000 for shares forfeited on early retirement, and odd amounts as dues for club memberships.

Roger wasn't the only one. John Perkins and Don Miller got settlements, too.

Yes, it was true that an attorney for the comptroller had studied the severance during the summer and had argued against messing with it. For one thing, it had been settled before the crisis of May, when no one in the world had even conceived of such a disaster. For another, it was too small. Compared with the multimillion-dollar "golden parachutes" that the Bill Agees of the world had awarded themselves, it was almost embarrassing.

Ah, but that was real money. Twelve thousand dollars, you could go after.

The lost billions were harder to go after.

The individual bank examiners – the fire inspectors – were called before the House Banking Committee.

"It's not apparent," said Congressman St. Germain, the chairman of the committee, "that the Office of the Comptroller of the Currency ever did anything about the information it received concerning the bank's deteriorating condition."

Why had the government agency, the supervisor of banks, failed to diagnose the situation? Why had the examiners who spent May through August 1982 – the very period of the Penn Square collapse – given high ratings to the oil and gas lending officers of the bank and to some of the worst loans they had made?

Why hadn't the examiners been aware that the bank had bought several hundreds of millions of dollars' worth of loans from the Penn Square Bank?

"What went wrong?"

"What we did was totally appropriate to our guidelines," said an examiner.

They were there for hours, face to face, the congressmen and the bank regulators. Over and over again, the questions were asked: What went wrong? How could you have overlooked this?

"We followed proper agency procedures."

How could the examiners give high ratings to million-dollar loans that were declared total losses within weeks of the examination?

"Proper agency procedures were followed."

"On balance, we were reasonably satisfied with the bank's internal controls."

What about $1,056,000,000 in loans made to or bought from a small, failing Oklahoma bank?

"Proper agency procedures were followed."

It wasn't us. We did right. It was them – those procedures. That system.

"Maybe the comptroller's handbook needs to be revisited," said congressman St. Germain.

The examiners said they would be against changing their agency's system of examining banks.

Never apologize, never explain.

TWENTY-EIGHT

ON SEPTEMBER 26, two months to the day after the government action, the shareholders of the Continental Illinois were called to a special meeting in Chicago. It was held at the Art Institute, in the same auditorium where, five months before, the last of the old leaders of the bank had spoken of a great team of managers, employees, and shareholders. In April, most of the seats in the auditorium had been filled. Today, there were all taken, and people were standing in the aisles.

The new managers of the Continental Bank were asking the shareholders to approve the government deal.

But the deal was a little hard to understand.

Even with the printed materials and the lengthy questioning, most of the Continental shareholders couldn't really grasp it.

The deal left them with 20 percent of a bank they had once owned all of; it gave the other 80 percent to the government. If they didn't vote in favor, they might get nothing at all. It was better to have 20 percent than nothing. Besides, there were some kind of options in the "new" bank.

This deal was what all the lawyers and bankers and government officials had spent so many hundreds of thousands of hours working on in Washington in middle July.

What they had designed was this:

The old Continental Bank had 40 million shares.

The new Continental Bank would have 200 million shares.

The lawyers would create a new entity – Continental Illinois Holdings – whose assets would consist of a conditional holding of 40 million shares – 20 percent – of the new Continental Bank. The old bank shareholders would own this entity.

So, by virtue of owning a hundred percent of Continental Holdings, the old shareholders would own 20 percent of the Continental Bank.

They would also have rights to buy more shares of the next Continental Bank at fixed prices during fixed time periods.

The rest of the new bank would be owned by the government – the FDIC – through an option on 160 million shares, the other 80 percent.

For these shares, the FDIC paid $720 million. It also paid $280 million for preferred stock, which would pay a dividend.

It was a little complicated. Not everyone understood it. It had taken many hours to construct.

But it loooked as if the FDIC had paid a billion dollars for an 80 percent interest in an equity worth – according to the annual report – about $1.8 billion. After the $1.1 billion write-off in June, the book value of the old shares was still almost $800 million.

The total FDIC "package" was $4.5 billion. In addition to the billion dollars in bank capital, the government was lending the Continental Bank $3.5 billion.

This $3.5 billion was to buy problem loans from the bank. These were loans that weren't paying interest; but the bank had to pay interest on the money it had borrowed to make the loans, so they were a big drain – maybe $350 million a year – on the bank's income. The government gave the bank that money so the bank could get those loans off its books.

This was, in effect, a secured loan. For $3.5 billion the bank would give to the government notes – obligations signed by various private borrowers – in the face amount of $5.1 billion. $1.6 billion of these obligations already had been "written off" – accounted for as losses – by the bank: $600 million prior to the 1984 crisis and a billion afterward.

People studied the materials, the boxes, and the columns of figures, but they weren't easy to understand. However you looked at it, the issue seemed to boil down to 20 percent of something versus a hundred percent of nothing.

But there was another catch.

The $3.5 billion loan, besides being collateralized by the $5.1 billion in problem obligations, also was secured by the remaining equity of the old shareholders.

The catch was that if the government couldn't collect all $3.5 billion, what they didn't collect would be charged to the old shareholders.

And what this meant exactly was that if the government could collect only $2.7 billion out of that $3.5 billion, the entire remaining equity of the old shareholders would be wiped out.

It was so specified in the agreement.

If the losses exceeded $800 million, a share in the old Continental Bank would be worth one-one-thousandth of a penny.

The presentation by the new leaders, Swearingen and Ogden, was not unlike those of other shareholder meetings. It was a professional presentation, it dealt with operating questions, it dealt with the plans of the Bank.

"Our first task is to re-establish and strengthen our credibility in the marketplace," Ogden said.

"Our chief goal is to get back on our feet," Swearingen said.

It was unclear to the shareholders in this auditorium what the "our" of the "feet" was.

The shares held by those present might become valueless, the new chairman conceded; but if the rescue were not approved, their value could be wiped out immediately.

"What are our chances?" one man asked.

No one could say.

"What about the old farmer who was on your annual report cover a few years ago?" someone asked. "The one who bought his shares in 1929. Does he still have those shares?"

No one could say.

One man called for an adjournment of the meeting and a try at a new agreement with the FDIC.

"Where's your fiduciary responsibility?" he asked.

But he was voted down.

The Wall Street Journal headline read, BAILOUT CLEARED BY CONTINENTAL ILLINOIS HOLDERS – BANK EXPECTS TO BREAK EVEN IN 3RD QUARTER; RESCUE EFFORT BY FDIC IS COMPLETED

The *New York Times* headline: CONTINENTAL BANK SEES RECOVERY – HOLDERS BACK RESCUE BY U.S.; CUTBACKS DUE

USA Today had a reporter there that day. The viewpoint of that Middle American journal was different from that of the Manhattan-based newspapers. The *USA Today* headline read, CONTINENTAL SHAREHOLDERS GIVE AN ANGRY "YES"

The quotes were all from the audience.

"The directors of this bank are a bunch of knuckleheads if I ever saw them."

"You never lose $1 on $1 lent, that is, unless you're a blooming idiot."

"I'm very disillusioned to think that something like this could happen."

This was Vincent Ardito, who used to work in the auditing department. He had retired in 1972. He was seventy-one years old now.

"I expected to live well [in retirement]."

Some people didn't quite understand the arrangement, but it didn't make sense that the situation could be as bad as they said. The new leaders knew what they were doing; they would get the bank back on its feet.

Because if this situation wasn't salvaged, the twenty-two thousand dollars' worth of stock you had owned at the beginning of the year, the retirement nest egg that you had put in bank stock because it was the most conservative investment in America, was going to be worth one penny.

And there was no Federal Deposit Insurance Corporation insurance on a Federal Deposit Insurance Corporation takeover.

98.6 percent of the shares in the auditorium, representing 71.9 percent of all shares in the old Continental Bank, were voted in favor of the FDIC agreement.

TWENTY-NINE

THE SAME SEPTEMBER 27 newspaper issues that carried the story of the special shareholders' vote also carried an item, out of Oklahoma City, on the trial of William G. Patterson, formerly of the former Penn Square Bank.

Bill Patterson – he of the beer in the boot, the Mickey Mouse ears, the Wehrmacht helmet – was charged with twenty-five counts of violation of federal bank law. For two weeks a jury had heard prosecution witnesses describe the deeds of this brash Oklahoma kid who had sold $2 billion worth of snake oil to the biggest banks of New York, Chicago, Seattle, and Detroit.

The defense had only one witness, the defendant himself, and it took only one day.

He had only been doing what he was told to do, Patterson told the Oklahoma jurors. He had lost everything he had in the Penn Square bank. He was now mowing lawns to feed his family.

Every once in a while he would break into tears.

Bill Patterson was contrite now rather than colorful. He was no longer a kid.

An innocent victim, the defense attorney described him, used and abused by the much older, much richer ranking officers of his bank.

As seventy-one-year-old Vincent Ardito was listening to the verdict in Chicago and 98.6 percent of the Continental jury accepted the demise of their trust in the old bank, thirty-four-year-old Bill Patterson listened to the verdict in Oklahoma City.

He was acquitted on twenty-three of the twenty-five charges: not guilty on seventeen counts of misapplication of funds, four counts of wire fraud, two counts of false entries.

That left two counts of wire fraud to be decided. The jury acquitted Bill Patterson of those counts the next day.

The New York Times didn't send a reporter to Oklahoma City for the Patterson trial; it used the Associated Press coverage. But *The Wall Street Journal* had a man there. So the *Journal* had the good quotes from the Oklahomans.

"Any time you go to the third or fourth level down to prosecute someone, the jury is naturally going to say, 'How about the guys he worked for, what were they doing?' The government should have started at the top."

"It's kind of hard to swallow when you've got a thirty-four-year-old kid sitting there and here's a 50-year-old millionaire oilman saying this nice young boy made me do this."

"In Oklahoma, the government tried to sell an attempt to defraud banks in other cities for the benefit of Penn Square, and people in Oklahoma don't care about banks in Chicago. In Chicago, it will be easier to sell an attempt to defraud the home-town bank."

And so it was.

On the day Patterson was cleared by the Oklahoma jury of the last two charges, a federal grand jury in Chicago indicted John Lytle on sixteen counts of wire and bank fraud.

THIRTY

*I*N SEPTEMBER THERE WAS A WEDDING on the North Shore. Among some people on LaSalle Street, there was a keen curiosity to know who among the Continental Illinois officer corps had been invited and, more than that, who had attended.

Anne Elizabeth Baker was being married. George and Marianne were hosting the wedding.

"Did you go?" a Winnetka man, an executive of the Continental Bank, asked a Wilmette man, another executive, on Monday morning.

"Yes, of course. It was a spendid wedding. The bride was lovely."

"Who was there?"

There were quite a few. John Jones and Carrie were there. Al Miossi and Blanche. Hollis Rademacher. Phyllis Sherman made it, even though Roger was at home with a cold.

Years before, when Gerry and Pat Keeley were leaving Chicago, George hadn't gone to their good-bye party, but Marianne went. Marianne always went.

One of the women there repeated a remark heard often among corporate wives in the 1980s: "The only difference between men and boys is the size of their toys." There were nods but no laughs.

372

For more than thirty years some of these people had known each other, shared the commute to 231 South LaSalle Street, shared the winters, shared Chicago, shared Richard Daley, the Big Ten, Ravinia, and family visits. Business was business, but it wasn't altogether separate from life. If all politics was local politics, all society was local society.

It was a happy event, the wedding. There was an orchestra at the reception. George danced with Blanche Miossi.

"It's a shame what happened in the bank," George said.

"Yes, it is," Blanche said.

"We should all get together for dinner sometime," George said.

THIRTY-ONE

BEFORE THE END OF 1984, the board of directors of the Continental Bank – "the cream of Chicago business," as the press called them – were fired by the new owners.

Ten of them were told by the FDIC that they had to go.

Jim Bere, chairman of Borg-Warner, the most active member of the board and who had been rumored would be named chairman to end the crisis, was one of them.

Vern Loucks. Bill Johnson, the director most involved in the board's investigation of the Penn Square mess. Bob Malott.

The Rev. Raymond C. Baumbart, president of Loyola College.

Jewel Lafontant, the celebrated Chicago lawyer, the first woman and first black to be elected to the Continental board.

Marvin Mitchell. Paul Rizzo. Tom Roberts. Blaine Yarrington.

In any other context it would have been astounding. But the firing of "some of the nation's finest businessmen," as financial writers said, hardly surprised anyone. It wasn't a personal thing, after all. It was a class thing. They were all Chicago people, all long-time Continental board members. They were tainted by the association.

Afterward

AFTERWORD: THE LAST SHAREHOLDER

*I*N APRIL 1986 I went out to Chicago for the Continental Illinois annual meeting. I had bought a few of the new shares before I started writing this book.

The weather in Chicago was nice in late April, and it was good to see old friends. A number of us got together over at The Sign of the Trader, and I told everybody about the book project. One or two people said they would like to write a book; others said they felt they already had.

People still talked to each other every day about the events of 1984. The motto was "Let's put the past behind us," but it wasn't working. The past, as William Faulkner once pointed out, isn't dead; it isn't even past.

People continued to worry about what would happen next. "You don't know from one month to another," somebody said, "whether you're getting a service award or getting laid off."

There were new rumors of merger. A Japanese bank, possibly. A Canadian bank, more likely, because of the compatibility.

There was still much twisting in the wind.

But still there was no grasp of the people damage. A figure on the loss of officers had never been published, and when the question came up in conversation with Continental officers still there, the estimates were low. Twenty percent, said one. One-third, said another.

There was some surprise when I told them that more than half the officer corps had been lost. Of some two thousand in the directory of May 1982, the month before Penn Square, more than a thousand were gone now and others were leaving.

Some of the strongest of the corps had come through the disaster. Gene Croisant, the last of the Continental "Profiles" of 1966, still not fifty years old, was still there. Garry Scheuring, who had kept the respect of all factions in the Bank C period, was there. Mike Murray, the last of the Group H-N New York team, was still there.

And because it was a corporation, some of the weakest "survived" beside them. A man who had approved a $30 million loan to a Venezuelan development corporation without asking the officer, a loan that was lost the moment it was disbursed, was still there. The ranking officer known as Weathervane was still there.

There was no pattern, no spreadsheet. The human element, as Roger once said, does not show up in the balance sheet.

It didn't take long for the secretaries in the bank to size up both John Swearingen and William Ogden and to fill in most of the blanks necessary for the rumor mill.

Swearingen was okay, they said. He had a slow, sure, and encouraging style, stopped to say hello to people, rarely frowned, often smiled, and seemed not to worry about anything unless it was Ogden.

Ogden was seen as a nervous type, a chain smoker, wrestling with figures, impatient with people. At one of the international banking functions the staff rented him a gray stretch limousine, and he sent it away until they could find him a black one. That was all some people wanted to know about Ogden. People immediately liked Swearingen, so they were sensitive to all his good points – he got rid of the big bank limos and replaced them with mid-size Lee Iacocca sedans. Ogden made them uneasy, so they were sensitive to all his bad points. It was a standard reaction. This was a small town.

Mainly the talk was about the bathroom.

Just a couple of weeks before, the "Inc" column in *The Chicago Tribune* had carried a report of a rumor from inside the Continental Bank that one of John Swearingen's first acts of management of a bank that had lost all its shareholders' money was to order the construction of a private bathroom next to his office at a cost of several hundred thousand dollars.

But the *Tribune* retracted the report right away, in print. It wasn't true.

If only Reuters had been so responsible in May 1984.

It wasn't Swearingen's bathroom at all. It was Ogden's.

That same week, I read in the newspaper that William Isaac, the former head of the FDIC, was in town.

Isaac, now a private consultant on financial services, told *The Chicago Tribune* that the "funding revival has been almost miraculous." The *Tribune* headlined the interview, CONTINENTAL "DOCTOR" PLEASED BY RECOVERY.

"The return of morale at Continental has been very exciting to see," he said to the *Tribune*.

Reading through the 1985 annual report, it was as if all had returned to normal. It was a handsome publication, toned in reddish brown, with almost fifty pages of financial data, all of it verified by the corporation's new accountants, Price Waterhouse. It carried a full summary of pending legal proceedings against the bank, against some of its former officers, and against its former accountants, Ernst & Whinney.

In its first full year after the crisis and the government intervention –1985 – the Continental Illinois Corporation turned a profit of $151 million.

The special funding by the Federal Reserve System, which had reached $12 billion at one point, was ended. So, too, was the safety net of special funding by other U.S. banks. Before Christmas 1985 the new managers called a press conference to announce that the bank was fending for and funding itself.

The Continental Bank was still there. You could still stand at the corner of LaSalle and Adams and look south at a scene – the Rookery, the Continental, the Board of Trade, the Federal Reserve – that was unchanged since 1980. You could still stand in the middle of the Midwest and you could believe that everything was the same as it had always been. Your eyes would tell you it was so.

The cover omitted the traditional illustration of the building at 231 South LaSalle and its formidable columns and used instead several clipped photographs of employees at work: "The employees of Continental Illinois have been working hard to give customers excellent service."

Work was the theme of the bank's new advertising campaign. The tagline was "We work hard. We have to." Under the ad's illustration was the legend "To a Continental banker, this is a sweatsuit." The illustration was an empty three-piece business suit.

The home game was different now.

The First Chicago people, who had presumed to be the acquirers of the Continental Bank, who had been given free entry into its hallways, and whom the press had celebrated as the winner of the home game, announced one of the largest losses in banking history shortly after the Continental affair. It was larger than the original loss that the Continental had suffered during the Penn Square quarter of 1982. The First had been under special scrutiny by the U.S. government ever since.

They were still the largest two banks in Chicago – the First first, the Continental second – though it was harder now to stay in the top ten in the country.

There was still business, still banking.

But there wasn't a game anymore. Barry Sullivan couldn't talk about seeing John and Bill on the football field, except pathetically.

The game was rigged. The other team had scored a hundred touchdowns, but they were not being counted. Anybody could win if the score didn't count. The game was over.

You could sense this in the mood of the annual meeting.

The annual meeting of stockholders of the Continental Illinois Corporation was held on April 28, 1986. It was at the Art Institute again.

John Swearingen and William Ogden sat on the stage, along with Dick Brennan, the corporation counsel.

In the first two rows of the auditorium, facing the stage, the backs of their heads visible to the gathering, were the new directors of the bank and the senior managers. Dave Taylor's head was easy to spot. Ed Bottum's, of course, was very easy to spot.

John Swearingen chaired the meeting. He introduced Ogden. He introduced the board members, who stood one by one and turned to acknowledge the shareholders.

There was a curious tone to the event, a mood. Compared to the raucous shareholder meetings of the previous two years, when people had shouted and stood in the aisles because all the seats were taken, this one was almost silent. Perhaps that was the curiosity: it seemed not to be an event at all.

And there was a vague sense of oldness about it, of the past without nostalgia.

At a distance John Swearingen could have been Dave Kennedy. He looked like him. He had a deep voice, and the sound was true. There was little doubt why he had been selected to chair the frenzied corps of 1984. He was sixty-seven years old. He had already finished his career before he had come back to do this work. If he stayed five years, he would be past seventy. Not as old as Walter Cummings, and yet sufficiently old, sufficiently lasting.

The new directors he introduced were old, too. There were thirteen of them, and six were over sixty-five; another was almost sixty-five. The youngest was fifty-six.

Like Swearingen, all of them – Chicagoans – were the proof of time, were time's guarantee. All were figures from the great American business period, the true generals back to serve again.

And there was in the scene the impression of a reaching backward– consciously or unconsciously – for the formula, for that secret combination that we had once possessed, by work or grace, and that we had somehow put aside.

The mood of the event was muted, not at all celebratory of the new profits. The government had removed all the losses; the bank could not have but made profits. The event seemed artificial.

One man kept getting up and asking questions on behalf of a shareholder in New York. He read from one of the books on the Penn Square case. "Is McKinsey still being used?" "No, they're not." It was nuisance stuff. There are people who make a hobby of doing this. Inane stuff, but within the parliamentary rules. The man knew the moves, knew he could require answers. John Swearingen handled him deftly; he had handled dozens of these jokers. There was some humor in it. This was America, and there was still humor to be found in annual meetings.

But there was another man.

This was the 1980s, and America had a President who thought in terms of movie scripts and registered life in terms of anecdotes. This was doubtless the secret of his popularity because most Americans thought in terms of movie scripts and anecdotes.

There was another man, and he was out of a Frank Capra movie. He was dressed in a short black jacket, and he had been wearing a black cap when he entered. He was an older man, but his hair was still black, straight, and parted. He was burly; he had a Chicago face: ethnic. When he said his name, standing as he asked his questions, it could have been Rabin or Ruben or Ravik. He was a working man. He looked as if he felt uncomfortable there, as if it were a restaurant that was too expensive for him, one that he shouldn't have entered.

And in fact he was at the wrong meeting. He was one of the old shareholders. The shares he owned were now denominated as Continental Illinois Holding shares – the new "entity" that had been created in September 1984 as a resting place for the original investors. This was the CI *Corporation* annual meeting. The CI *Holding* meeting wouldn't be held for another several days.

Although ill at ease and uncomfortable to be speaking aloud in public, the man was determined to have his say. It was not easy for Swearingen to handle the questions, for it was not clear what the questions were.

The man was trying to ask about his shares, something about his rights, but he seemed unsure about what both the shares and the rights were.

He was still trying to find out what had happened to his money.

Swearingen handled the man's questions kindly. But they went on for a long time, each as vague as the one before, and at last Swearingen ended the exchange.

It was a vaguely embarrassing moment for all in the auditorium. Another questioner, a gadfly speaking for a New York investor, was not an embarrassment. He was hip, he was a part of the culture, and he knew what he was doing; there were some laughs.

The meeting went on. After Swearingen spoke, Ogden spoke. The bank's problems were far from over, the work was just beginning, and so forth.

After a while the man in the black jacket rose from his seat, walked up the angled aisle with his cap in his hand, and left the auditorium. He had a Chicago face. Age lines. Work lines. He had been up against it for a long time. He knew these fellows weren't the enemy, probably not. But they were the ones in charge.

INDEX